MASTERY
MATHEMATICS *for*
PRIMARY TEACHERS

Sara Miller McCune founded SAGE Publishing in 1965 to support the dissemination of usable knowledge and educate a global community. SAGE publishes more than 1000 journals and over 800 new books each year, spanning a wide range of subject areas. Our growing selection of library products includes archives, data, case studies and video. SAGE remains majority owned by our founder and after her lifetime will become owned by a charitable trust that secures the company's continued independence.

Los Angeles | London | New Delhi | Singapore | Washington DC | Melbourne

MASTERY MATHEMATICS *for* PRIMARY TEACHERS

ROBERT NEWELL

Los Angeles | London | New Delhi
Singapore | Washington DC | Melbourne

Los Angeles | London | New Delhi
Singapore | Washington DC | Melbourne

SAGE Publications Ltd
1 Oliver's Yard
55 City Road
London EC1Y 1SP

SAGE Publications Inc.
2455 Teller Road
Thousand Oaks, California 91320

SAGE Publications India Pvt Ltd
B 1/I 1 Mohan Cooperative Industrial Area
Mathura Road
New Delhi 110 044

SAGE Publications Asia-Pacific Pte Ltd
3 Church Street
#10-04 Samsung Hub
Singapore 049483

Editor: James Clark
Editorial assistant: Diana Alves
Production editor: Nicola Carrier
Copyeditor: Andy Baxter
Proofreader: Tom Bedford
Indexer: Silvia Benvenuto
Marketing manager: Dilhara Attygalle
Cover design: Naomi Robinson
Typeset by: C&M Digitals (P) Ltd, Chennai, India
Printed in the UK

CONTENTS

ABOUT THE AUTHOR

Robert Newell has worked at the Institute of Education (IOE) for 15 years; full time for the last six. He works with Primary PGCE (Postgraduate Certificate in Education) trainees and School Direct students; he has previously worked with Teach First participants. His career started as a primary school teacher, taking responsibility for maths in several schools before progressing to two deputy head posts and then a headteacher role.

Primary maths teaching, though, has been his biggest passion. He has worked as a numeracy consultant and also delivered a PGCE Maths programme to a London SCITT (School-Centred Initial Teacher Training centre) for three years. He is now part of a small maths team serving several hundred trainees at the IOE, now merged with UCL (University College London). He has two passions that underpin his work. One is ensuring that primary maths children are taught in a way that engages them and focuses on understanding. The other is the belief that, in the main, it is only anxiety that stops more trainees feeling comfortable about teaching maths. Part of his working role at the IOE is linked to supporting trainees with less-secure understanding and allowing them to see how much they can offer. Many realise that although anxiety has affected their self-perception about mathematical understanding, this process can be reversed.

His dissertation focused on the different ways trainee teachers can learn to use different levels of understanding effectively in their primary school maths teaching. Here, he commits to print a range of ideas and activities, refined over many years and linked to ensuring all primary teachers can teach for understanding. His first book, also published through SAGE, entitled *Big Ideas in Primary Mathematics* came out in 2017. It aimed to support trainees and teachers seeking to learn to teach for understanding.

ACKNOWLEDGEMENTS

This book has come about through contacts made over several years through my time at IOE UCL. A number of trainees put me in touch with teachers and schools who were happy to meet, talk, discuss, and be observed. In short, a 'community of practice' (Lave and Wenger, 1998) has underpinned the book. This is particularly true in Chapters 5, 6, 7 and 11.

I would like to thank Jack Corson at Byron Park, Conor Loughney at Torriano School, Ciara Sutton Fitzpatrick and Gemma Field at Wimbledon Park Primary, and Pinal Sheth at Elmhurst Primary. They formed the main input for discussion about teaching with mastery-trained teachers. In addition to this Sukwinder Shah and Farzana Ahmed also at Elmhurst Primary assisted my thinking. I want to acknowledge the input of Kim Clark in the chapter on Early Years (Chapter 11).

The time with Iona Mumby at Clapham Manor, David Cunnelly at Shoreditch Park Primary and Lucy Gallantine at St James Primary was invaluable. They shared practice and gave time to discuss issues, which was extremely instructive, related to Chapter 6. Other useful input came from Anna Willis, Ben McClellan, Lucas Motion and James Coleman.

I am supported and encouraged constantly by my family: Rachel, Tom and my wife, Carol.

CHAPTER 1:

THE CONTEXT FOR MATHEMATICS TEACHING

3=6

5+7=12

> What you will learn from this chapter:
>
> * The historical issues surrounding why teaching procedures have tended to be at the expense of teaching for deeper understanding
> * The strengths and weaknesses of primary maths teaching in the UK
> * What a mastery approach might bring to our teaching
> * The challenges and the possibilities that pursuing mastery teaching will face
> * Clarity about how teachers need to understand their mathematical knowledge to teach effectively and how we can best support them

BACKGROUND

As a lecturer in primary mathematics for the last ten years, I have seen a number of changes involving the National Curriculum and the extent to which teachers are told how and what to teach. The interactive whiteboard and the visualiser have changed the nature of class-led discussion significantly. The process of discussing maths has become more visual. At times this has been accompanied by an increase in the use of concrete resources. There have also been real attempts in some quarters to relate taught maths ideas to the real world.

Still there remain a number of truisms related to teaching and learning maths in the UK. It is often taught by very capable teachers, attempting complex pedagogical approaches with considerable success. Many, however, when it comes to teaching maths, are anxious and lack confidence. They seek to teach almost from a script, as it seems safer than attempting lessons that may invite contributions from children that they may feel ill-equipped to deal with. Only in a few cases is such a limiting approach the result of disinterest on the teacher's part.

SETTING AND TESTING

A lot of primary and secondary schools have employed a setting system for teaching maths, grouping by some form of measured attainment. It is not clear how much impact this has on different attainment groups. Indeed, in many cases, it may relate to the quality or range of confidence among the teaching staff. Other schools favour a mixed attainment approach, either random groupings or specific arrangements of children whose attainment is at different stages. The broad findings from research indicate that only the highest grouping is likely to benefit from a setting approach and that this isn't always guaranteed. Social constructivist learning theorists such as Vygotsky (1978), and more recent writers regarding effective development in attitudes towards learning maths such as Jo Boaler (2009), would be unlikely to be surprised by such outcomes.

PRIMARY TEACHER CONFIDENCE IN MATHS

The search for an effective learning pedagogy takes place against the backdrop of quite specific testing at ages seven and 11 where an interpretation of the curriculum content is evaluated. The mixed experience that many school children have means that in the later stages of Key Stage 2 there are often sustained, maybe belated, attempts to secure necessary strategies for solving problems that have not been developed successfully at earlier stages. Perhaps as many as half the teachers teaching maths in primary school would not list maths as a strength in their teaching. There is no shame here. It is, though, worthy of real attention as we seek a sound way forward; we need to increase confidence and achievement levels in maths among our school children.

My belief, similar to other writers on the pedagogy of primary maths teaching, is that it is a subtle skill that all teachers can excel in and yet a number have not yet learnt to. The fact that a sizeable minority of those who feared they would never teach maths effectively now do so, leads me to believe that this situation can and must change.

PEDAGOGY OF EFFECTIVE PRIMARY MATHS TEACHING

Alongside this, we have the conundrum about the performance of teachers who are also skilled in general primary teaching pedagogy and who have confidence and belief in their maths knowledge and ability to structure maths learning. What are their achievements and what is the impact of them? Well, many of the Shanghai teachers who have visited England to model their style of maths teaching have been in awe of our maths teachers who teach to add value to current levels of attainment across a wide range of achievement in our standard primary classes.

Our most confident primary maths teachers have, for many years, excelled at a number of things:

- They have modelled clearly in a way that has made lessons accessible to all children in classes with different learning needs and levels of attainment.
- They have allowed lessons to be accessed at different levels.
- They have managed independent learning whilst providing focused teaching to increase progress amongst an identified group of learners.

COMMITMENT TO INCLUSIVE TEACHING

In addition to this, they have enthused, guided and managed 'low threshold, high ceiling' tasks which allow a range of children to work at different speeds within common problems, tasks and investigations. Within this structure such teachers have created breakthrough moments that allow children to connect with more complex ideas and thinking within the class. Following on from the above point, they have and do show a belief in the potential of all children and allow many opportunities that might move learning forward.

These teaching skills and beliefs have been shown in sometimes challenging environments where some children are in fact resistant to learning.

CULTURAL ATTITUDE IN THE UK TOWARDS MATHS AND CONFIDENCE LEVELS

Such teaching skills also take place against the backdrop of home environments where maths is not a central part of life. Nor is confidence often there among parents who themselves may have suffered from a cycle of underachievement over several generations. In short, not enough engagement of all children has taken place to allow deeper, more-confident mathematical understanding to emerge. Not enough teachers have been able to plan and deliver lessons that allow most, if not all, children, to face and conquer questions and nuances around the maths being explored.

For example, younger children sometimes struggle to become secure around counting beyond ten, they confuse 30 and 13, likewise 14 and 40, even 12 and 20. Meeting this issue head on can assist development. Fourteen sounds as though the four should be written first but we write the ten first.

Multiplication is also a hard concept for young children to understand:

- 3 + 2 means we get three and two and put them together.
- 3 × 2 actually means we repeat two three times as in 2 + 2 + 2 or that we are finding three lots of two, easier for a young child to understand through known contexts such as shoes, socks or partners for lining up. It can also mean 3 (two times) as in 3 + 3.

HANDLING MIXED ATTAINMENT GROUPS SO THAT REAL VALUE ADDED IS ACHIEVED

Lessons with such emphasis are in fact quite common in our classrooms; identifying key points for learning and driving them home through reference to common experiences and real life, concrete situations. Yet, the class gets spread out so quickly in terms of achievement that understanding and learning maths throughout the school becomes an experience where confidence among children (and adults) is the domain of the minority.

CONTENT-LED CURRICULUM OR DEEPER MATHEMATICAL DISCUSSION?

In short, the field becomes too spread out too early among our children to allow a sound understanding to be the basis of all lessons being taught in Years 1 to 6 of primary school. Coupled with this, not all primary teachers who teach a range of subjects (as many as eight or more in a single week) have become confident enough to manage learning experiences in maths that prevent the gap between children in the class becoming too wide. The result of this is that the whole class delivery in mixed attainment lessons is not ensuring something equating to parity in value added. The stronger are surviving, the less strong are condemned to a slower rate of progress. The accompanying confidence levels among children and staff exacerbate this. Teachers who themselves learnt, as Richard Skemp (1978) articulated, 'rules without reasons' or 'instrumentally' are often ill equipped to delve underneath the surface to tackle, confront and lead further discussion that would make learning in maths more robust and ready for more rigorous challenges. Adult and child alike are inadvertently colluding to avoid deeper discussions that would be beneficial.

It is through the set of circumstances captured here that we have arrived at the following point. Some of our most promising young mathematicians really thrive. They achieve very highly. They do not all come from private sector schooling. Some achieve their full potential because enough state sector schooling has allowed them to thrive. They then continue the journey into higher education and beyond. The rest of the story is a variation on this, with students dropping out along the way and many passing GCSE but without a secure, deeper understanding and not seeking to expose themselves to the rigours of maths A level. Teaching to the tests at Key Stages 1–4 can sometimes limit the depth of understanding that takes place.

Thus the spread of achievement in maths across the nation needs close scrutiny. A basic qualification is often achieved but not deeper understanding. This process starts early and has to change. In our primary schools, the teachers whose knowledge is not yet secure enough to teach effectively for deeper understanding need support. Their pedagogical skills in general are often very sound.

SOUND PEDAGOGY NEEDS TO BECOME SOUND MATHS PEDAGOGY

It seems that the government response has been to look at the countries who are achieving more rigorous understanding across a wider range of children. Amongst other countries, the spotlight has fallen on China and Singapore. Serious consideration has been given to the style of teaching and learning that forms the basis of maths education in primary and secondary schools. Money has been invested in allowing groups of teachers and organisations from the UK to become familiar with the methods and approaches being used there. These are examined closely in subsequent chapters.

However, before analysing the style of teaching that has come to be known as maths mastery, I would like to consider a range of initiatives undertaken in England that are linked to the circumstances outlined above. They are part of the journey in primary maths teaching in England and they have had real impact.

The national interest in maths mastery is a worthy one. However, even if we implement it full on, with no adaptation, that system of teaching would still have to contend with the variables that have brought about the circumstances that exist in our schools and society regarding maths. We have already initiated some very interesting ideas and strategies in the last 40 years that have contributed heavily to some of the achievements that have been made in developing students' understanding in maths. Primary teachers in general have contributed to this, at least in part.

EXTENDED INSET, BEAM AND NRICH

The notion of developing teacher confidence and belief in the idea of teaching for understanding is not new. The debate has raged for 40 years or more as to how to make teacher maths knowledge in the primary age range more robust.

Extended INSET (in-service training) development in maths was a feature of most borough and educational authority provision. Through this approach, cautious teachers with traditional and formal knowledge became enthused with the ideas that lay behind mathematical concepts and how children could be supported in their learning in ways that were useful and interesting as well as relevant. The staggered nature of the course allowed for 'in school' development that was then built on when the course resumed.

The 'Be a Mathematician' (BEAM) publications bridged a gap in the 1980s between a formal, procedural style of teaching and a more open-ended pursuit of problem solving skills. It then supported the National Curriculum which included Attainment Target 1 (AT1) whereby children needed to apply knowledge as well as learn skills and memorise information. This helped to maintain an awareness of the importance of understanding maths itself rather than merely the procedures involved. BEAM publications were produced on a range of curricular-specific themes such as geometry, space, measure and number as well as child- or topic-centred themes such as 'wheels' or 'shops'. The emphasis was always on problem solving and investigation. The resources proved invaluable as a means of keeping 'mathematical thinking' and 'understanding' at the heart of the experiences that children needed to receive. This was at a time when content was sometimes dominating through a transmission of knowledge (Askew et al., 1997).

The NRICH organisation and website (https://nrich.maths.org) seems to me to be an extension of some of the work that BEAM championed for many years. Accessible swathes of mathematical ideas including many opportunities to problem solve, investigate and apply knowledge, support teachers very well. Accompanying solutions, comments and deviations provide food for thought as ways to continue and adjust ideas and problems. The discerning teacher may adjust tasks in the light of experience and knowledge of children's learning needs. The new iteration of an idea or investigation is submitted, thus widening and deepening the pedagogical and mathematical possibilities further. Finally, it is important to add that the interactive opportunities extend learning possibilities further in a way that is very different to earlier periods. The emphasis on 'low threshold, high ceiling' activities and investigations means that children can feed off ideas that others have, as the teacher scaffolds the learning experience and helps to empower children by assisting their ability to articulate their *reasoning*, a key requirement of anyone seeking to become a robust mathematician. More immediately relevant is that it is, commendably, a National Curriculum requirement.

However this approach does not achieve the goal that it is hoped that a mastery approach will achieve.

OFFICIAL MATHS TEACHING REQUIREMENTS IN PRIMARY SCHOOLS

The first iteration of the National Curriculum (in 1989) identified a body of mathematical knowledge to be taught and learnt for the primary age phase with national testing linked to this content. The attainment targets within the curriculum were mainly knowledge based, although Attainment Target 1 (AT1) was very much related to a child's ability to apply knowledge. Initially there was pleasing scope to evaluate understanding of their problem solving and investigative qualities. Time constraints and cost of evaluation meant that this was quickly streamlined to some application of knowledge through more formal standardised written tests. The sheer bulk of an entire document folder for each curriculum area was quite overwhelming. Thankfully, this was reduced in size quite quickly.

The introduction of the *National Numeracy Strategy* (DfEE, 1999) at the turn of the millennium was pleasing; a rare example of politicians, educationalists and maths-specific pedagogical specialists all coming together to produce quite explicit content, guidance and examples to underpin thorough approaches to teaching all maths but particularly number operations that really impacted on the thinking of teachers and therefore children.

Named approaches involving 'grid method' multiplication, 'division by chunking' and the use of the empty number line (ENL) became standard terms that schools managed to start sharing with parents, children and staff. In fact, a number of staff found the document eye-opening as it unpicked for them the logic behind methods they had hitherto learnt by rote without understanding and consequently taught accordingly. The guidance and examples section of this document is still being used in some quarters long after it has been superseded, firstly by the Primary Framework (in 2007) and then by the new National Curriculum in England (in 2014). There have been courses, videos and appointed maths advisors to assist with the implementation of what was essentially a real attempt to teach for understanding, albeit with a limited commitment to assisting teachers' confidence levels in delivering it.

A FOCUS ON SKILLS AND STRATEGIES

Schools often remained quite intent on getting specific strategies across to children alongside the ongoing and relentless pursuit of interpreting word problems. This may well have been linked to giving experience related to SATs-style questioning but often highlighted, to the discerning observer, children's lack of experience and maturity in understanding the underlying structure of maths questions and problems. This affected their ability to interpret the questions effectively.

PROMOTING PROBLEM SOLVING

A number of schools decided to ensure that a specific pedagogy developing problem solving techniques emerged. Thus a period of a week or more was safeguarded for this kind of work. Sometimes there was little more structure to the session than that. Other schools went much further, using staff meetings, CPD and even paired observation work, theory readings, Masters modules and school-based research to develop their practice. Some innovations had significant impact, others less so. It is hard to identify factors affecting outcomes. However, confident staff open to learning and reflection with good mentoring of new and less-confident members would be a fairly powerful model.

There are several schools in London (and elsewhere) confidently moving forward in maths with a mastery approach. In many, the blueprint is as follows. A headteacher committed to achievement in maths for all children and maths as a high priority subject across the school for all teachers, staff and children makes a pretty strong statement. We will hear of several throughout this book. Such a combination also makes such schools desirable to work in for teachers interested, and maybe confident, in the pedagogy of effective maths teaching.

The question remains how to ensure an equitable amount of progress in schools where less-favourable circumstances exist. The skill of problem solving is a teasing one, scaffolding without telling, developing resilience, valuing unproductive strategies, being curious about failure and success. It is all quite subtle and maybe requiring commitment or a leap of faith.

SPECIALIST MATHS TEACHERS IN PRIMARY SCHOOLS? OR SPREADING GOOD PRACTICE?

At my university, we have been part of two key initiatives to deepen the quality of pedagogy within the primary maths classroom. Firstly, the MaST qualification validated the recommendations of the Williams Report (2008). It validated the recommendation of the need for deeper knowledge expertise within all primary schools to spread and support good practice. Experienced teachers (5+ years) turned their general pedagogic knowledge into maths-specific knowledge to become such teachers within their own schools. Masters-level school-based research and discussion was a course prerequisite. The 2010 coalition government with Michael Gove as Secretary of State for Education withdrew funding for this, replacing it with our current PGCE maths specialism route. This includes a bursary to accompany the PGCE with a greater focus on the teaching of maths: 50% of teaching within school and a tailored M-level specialism module.

The difference between the two initiatives is that the MaST specialists were ready to have impact straight away and the PGCE specialists less so, as they needed to secure their own pedagogic knowledge and proficiency first. This had been a requirement of entry on the MaST route. Both were geared towards the same end: the spread of good practice and deepening understanding amongst children.

There are a number of teachers who have promising maths knowledge and confidence but still need to learn how to make this effective in the classroom. For me, such transition occurred during a Diploma in Maths Education at South Bank Polytechnic. Something triggers your mind and you realise that many children don't initially see how worthwhile maths can be. Beyond that, there is the rigour of understanding at a deeper level. Masters-level work in maths in education can provide theoretical underpinning for additional pedagogic wisdom, although direct links with the classroom become slightly more removed. Behind these initiatives lies a big idea. Effective teaching requires an interest and a belief that structuring learning as well as generating interest is key to creating a culture in the maths primary classroom. That means maths thinking and reasoning alongside fluency can develop easily and with confidence.

We have done many things in England to assist the process of teaching for understanding. The skill of ensuring rigour and depth across the class has been a huge challenge, as has consistency in teacher confidence and knowledge in maths to achieve this.

CAN EFFECTIVE SCHEMES HELP TO FILL IN THE GAPS?

Busy teachers looking for structure in a scheme or text are sometimes rewarded with exactly that by schools anxious not to leave less-confident teachers floundering. Does this work? Does this overcome the main argument that children's confidence and understanding at a deeper level can be developed securely through some less-confident and knowledge-able teachers following carefully crafted and scripted texts that act as lessons? Most people would say not. The teacher has to know the children, adjust, use discussion effectively in the moment and respond to lesson developments. So, no, not really. However, with men-toring, team planning, selected joint planning and growing clarity about the purpose of maths and what lies behind it, maybe this could work, as a springboard at least.

As we will see, the mastery approach (Shanghai or Singapore style) is quite specific. The structure in its pure form is precise with little real area for compromise. This will be analysed and raises questions as to whether we are seeking to implement it fully or not. Teaching style, preparation time, catch up and teacher knowledge are just four obvious focus areas for debate. However, the broad debate is a familiar one and the objectives of mastery are ones we have already been seeking to achieve. There hasn't been agreement how.

BOOKS THAT SUPPORT TEACHING FOR UNDERSTANDING

We have many significant maths pedagogy publications that are respected around the world in terms of coming close to capturing the essence of bringing maths teach-ing and learning to life. In addition to Richard Skemp's text from 1978, Tim Rowland's co-authored 2009 book identifies analysed features of effective maths teaching. Askew et al. (1997) distinguish between different forms of teaching in a seminal work. They argue that only through a 'connectionist' approach can any depth of understanding be achieved that allows what is being learnt to be used by children in new, unfamil-iar situations. Ryan and Williams (2007) also take the argument further with a series of named ways in which incorrect understanding can be classified and also addressed. This pedagogy, involving awareness of common and less-familiar ways of misunderstanding, has become rich territory for maths teaching analysts. It has also become a much more mainstream focus for classroom teaching and school practice: identifying common mis-conceptions as a prelude to tackling work in class.

Writers such as Haylock (2019) and Cotton (2016) across primary, and Sue Gifford (2005) particularly in early years, have sought to capture issues and effective teaching methods. Hansen (2014) and Newell (2017) have sought to bridge the gap that can leave less-secure trainees stranded or unsure how to teach for understanding.

Abroad, American writer Shulman in 1986 coined the now famous term Pedagogic Content Knowledge (PCK) that captured the combination of subject and teaching knowl-edge necessary to be effective in maths. Deborah Ball (Ball et al., 2004) too has done sound work analysing the strengths and limitations of trainee and teacher maths knowledge. All of these works show that for a number of years we have been knocking on the door of creating effective learning in primary maths classrooms. We are vulnerable though, we do not have consistency.

CONCLUSION

It is in this context that a focus now falls on mastery teaching in mathematics. We have to define it because the funding for its development has become quite significant. Momentum is building towards this being an approach that will underpin teaching of mathematics in our primary classrooms. The outline above is to contextualise what is sometimes seen as a radically different approach to maths teaching. Let us see whether or not it is.

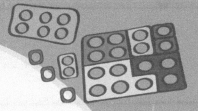

CHAPTER 2:

WHAT IS MASTERY TEACHING AT PRIMARY LEVEL?

What you will learn from this chapter:

- Some similarities and differences about Shanghai and Singapore teaching and learning in maths in comparison to the UK approach
- Awareness of some logistical issues and hurdles that will need to be addressed to manage and develop maths mastery in the UK
- Some clarity about what the essence of mastery is or could become
- An insight into how we can use what we have traditionally done well to ensure it has wider deeper impact

BACKGROUND INFORMATION

There has been a lot of discussion and questioning of what mastery teaching actually is, and what is expected from teachers and children.

This confusion is not due to a lack of awareness on the part of teachers in the UK. Maths leads in primary schools, in particular, have their fingers firmly on the pulse regarding curriculum content, developing understanding and managing staff needs. These needs relate to content and style of planning structures as well as the necessity of deepening teacher understanding. If anything, maths leads sometimes feel they have too many things to consider and develop simultaneously. Let me try to explain why.

In many ways, we are an extremely inclusive teaching society in the UK. Many teachers prioritise, very highly, the notion of equal access for all children with value added for as many as possible. However, we have to accept that we haven't managed to generate a level of understanding in maths among primary and secondary children that means, collectively, they have the skills to operate in the modern world as effectively as we need them to. Clearly some are outstanding. At the median point (50th percentile and below) this becomes worrying in terms of the level of actual understanding.

WHY THE GOVERNMENT HAS SOUGHT WHAT IT SEES AS A NEW APPROACH

A recent and rigorous research into cognitive psychology has shown, number knowledge and fluency in written calculation are not the antithesis of problem solving in mathematics. Rather, they are the royal road by which complex mathematical thinking is achieved.

Nick Gibb (2016), Minister of State for Schools

The Trends in International Maths and Science Studies (TIMSS) report, last published in 2015 and due again in 2019, places England away from the top positions. The Maths

Programme for International Student Assessment (PISA, 2012), referenced by Helen Drury in her foreword (2014) has us on a par with the USA, the Netherlands and some other European nations. We lie ahead of New Zealand, Australia and Germany. Yet we are significantly behind Korea, Singapore, China and Japan in terms of achievement. This is an international test designed to evaluate mathematical understanding in children across the industrialised world.

The performances of about 7,500 15-year-old students in each of the 72 countries on questions such as those recorded below places the United Kingdom in 26th place. Here are two PISA-style questions:

Question 1. Mount Fuji is only open to the public for climbing from 1 July to 27 August each year. About 200,000 people climb Mount Fuji during this time. On average, about how many people climb Mount Fuji each day?

A. 340   **B.** 710   **C.** 3,400   **D.** 7,100

Question 2. The Gotemba walking trail up Mount Fuji is about 9 km long. Walkers need to return from the 18 km walk by 8 pm. Toshi estimates that he can walk up the mountain at 1.5 km/h on average, and down at twice that speed. These speeds take into account meal breaks and rest times. Using Toshi's estimated speeds, what is the latest time he can begin his walk so that he can return by 8 pm?

The application of knowledge needed to answer these questions is not easily at the disposal of enough of our students. The journey towards such confidence and knowledge has to begin quite young and it has to be led with confidence by our primary and secondary teachers.

Some, or most, of the following things would, in my opinion, need to happen before success was likely for most children. They would need to:

- Be able to read the problem.
- Be able to represent the problem.
- Be clear what the problem is asking.
- Discuss a range of strategies and be able to identify which ones were and were not suitable for solving the task.
- Be able to listen to ideas from other children and evaluate the relevance of the comments.

The teacher perspective and performance would also be key. They would need to:

- Identify similar problems for children.
- Lead discussion to identify key features and information in the problems.

- Model representing such a problem pictorially, possibly in concrete form too, prior to this point.
- Lead discussion with children across a range of problems to establish what is similar and what is different about a number of problems like this.
- Evaluate the level to which understanding has taken place across the class.
- Ensure further scaffolding takes place for some children while others press on with what they are starting to feel confident with.
- Ensure that children are articulating clearly the key features of what is being clarified as a prelude to being able to discuss subsequent variations and changes.

Our teachers at primary level across the country have varied in both their confidence and belief in their ability and willingness to do some or all of these things. One approach to the second question is displayed in Figure 2.1. It depicts an understanding of mathematical structure that assists answering the question; it also assists solving variations to the problem. It does this through depicting the whole (the total journey) as well as the ascent and descent. These take place at different speeds. The two sections have an average speed.

1 hour	1 hour	1 hour	1 hour	1 hour	1 hour	1 hour	1 hour	1 hour
1.5 km	1.5 km	1.5 km	1.5 km	1.5 km	1.5 km	3 km	3 km	3 km
9 km ascending						9 km descending		
18 km								

Figure 2.1 Answer to Question 2

Developing such understanding requires the ability to unpick the key components of the problem and to represent them visually in a way that can be articulated and agreed. The journey to such proficiency would, of course, begin with less-complex problems.

In the past, there has been a tendency to replicate one kind of problem until it becomes a familiar problem, almost a rehearsed response. The subtleties involved in distinguishing between such problems are by no means impossible to achieve with a range of children. However the journey towards having the confidence, experience and flexibility to think through, adjust and solve such tasks requires more than rehearsing a particular kind of problem and then replicating it. The answers as to how we need to adapt our teaching to make learning more effective for a wider range of our children in maths are discussed throughout this book. For the moment, I want to consider the style of teaching being promoted in Singapore and China and the results that seem to have followed.

THE PUSH TO ACHIEVE MORE

Let us consider these goals from the Singapore education system in 2006:

- Problem solving curriculum.
- Emphasis on the development of intellectual competence such as the ability to visualise and heuristics (practical approach to problem solving).
- Emphasis on conceptual understanding.
- Systematic development of skills and concepts.
- Emphasis on the CPA (concrete, pictorial, abstract) approach.

Ministry of Education of Singapore (2006)

We can see that many of the goals from the Singapore education system are similar to teaching in the UK. Certainly there have been and are real attempts to promote problem solving as a feature of children's maths experience, and such an approach is often quite popular with our children. Writers such as Derek Haylock (2019), Rob Eastaway (2008), Robert Newell (2017) and NRICH resources all promote problem solving ideas and related pedagogy. This has been partially successful. So what hasn't it achieved? The answer, I feel, lies in some of the rigour and maybe in the consistency of approach needed to ensure successful implementation of goals such as those listed above. In addition to this, the CPA approach has been a common feature of maths in the primary classroom for many years. It has links with Jean Piaget (1936) regarding making sense of the real world, generating cognitive development and the opportunity to apply new learning, through experience, to new situations. Such a pedagogical belief also links to Vygotsky's ideas of children discussing work with their peers as well as the teacher, accessing what he termed their ZPD (zone of proximal development) (1978). This would involve children feeding off the ideas of those currently more knowledgeable and gradually learning to contribute effectively themselves. In addition to this, the concrete and pictorial representations make the learning able to be seen, discussed, and crucially a basis for moving away into a more abstract world. They act as a scaffold both to make learning meaningful and as a way to prepare for learning and discussion based on experience but not including concrete objects. Although used widely in England, concrete, visual resources have not been used consistently.

SUPPORTING TEACHERS AND BEGINNING TO CLARIFY EXPECTATION

The National Centre for Excellence in the Teaching of Maths (NCETM) has, for several years, been promoting significant resources, training and dialogue related to a mastery-style approach to teaching. They have been involved in funding trips to Shanghai as part of their training and development of teachers chosen to develop a mastery style of teaching and induct colleagues within and beyond their own school to develop likewise.

Their own documentation highlights some of the main features being promoted as a centrally funded resource for teacher development.

The main features identified include:

- Whole class interactive teaching.
- Early intervention to overcome failure to understand.
- Procedural and conceptual understanding are developed simultaneously.
- Deeper understanding is prioritised.
- Key knowledge is learnt and retained, for example number bonds and multiplication tables, to allow other discussion to be focused on more clearly.

This articulation is based on the NCETM document from June 2016 entitled *The Essence of Maths Teaching for Mastery*. There has been close involvement of the NCETM with both the government and the education system in Shanghai. Many teaching exchange programmes involving Shanghai teachers have taken place within the last few years.

WHY IS WHOLE CLASS TEACHING EMPHASISED?

The Ark Academy Education group, overseeing a large number of schools, committed themselves to mastery-style teaching a number of years ago, and were one of the pioneers in visiting Shanghai and Singapore. Helen Drury helped to found the Mathematics Mastery Scheme based on Ark Academy maths principles where she worked. The scheme was underpinned by her visits to Shanghai and belief in the teaching methods used there. Her book (2014) seeks to highlight a feature of class teaching in highly achieving countries as measured by PISA and TIMSS; that of whole class teaching. As well as championing the pursuit of depth of understanding she emphasises the need to provide 'achievement for all' (Drury, 2014: 20). This is a contentious but important pursuit. Ark claims that mastery is 'a highly effective approach to the teaching and learning of mathematics for all and could have particular benefits for pupils who tend to fall behind in the current system' (NAMA, 2015).

Are we saying that we haven't had the achievement of all children at the heart of our teaching to date? No, that cannot be said. Our capacity, in many cases to provide value added for children across wide-ranging attainment levels in class, has often been extremely commendable. The planning required to give children relevant work related to their current point of learning requires effort and commitment. At times some teachers have resorted to a 'one size fits all' approach. Drury (2014), along with a number of other analysts of higher achieving countries in primary maths, say the following; effectively, it is essential that the class does not become too spread out in terms of achievement levels and understanding. If this is not to mean curbing the development of confident children then it must be ensured that all children have a basic understanding that allows a full class discussion led by the teacher each day to move all children's learning forward. This key point is a crucial feature of the mastery approach.

Why then have we not managed to achieve this in our class and year profiles to date? How is this achieved in places such as Shanghai and Singapore? What would we need to do to make this a feature of what happens in England? As we shall see throughout the book, the answer relates to the belief that all children can progress well, with quality discussion with individuals, pairs, groups and classes; finally it has to involve the idea of re-teaching children who are insecure in their understanding. Thus, assessment of impact as we teach is key.

IS EARLY INTERVENTION A CONTRADICTION TO WHOLE CLASS TEACHING?

Our baseline testing in the foundation stage has always revealed vast discrepancies in what children can and cannot do on beginning school. This difference has remained and extended considerably and quickly. It is not necessarily the case that children with lower baseline profiles struggle throughout; some are younger, less mature and experienced, and can pick up quickly. However, statistics suggest that this is a real issue. Jo Boaler (2009) in her impassioned portrayal of the primary maths classroom in the UK and the US suggests that in fact our early 'attainment grouping', sometimes begun in reception, discriminates against children who haven't grasped early basic concepts quickly.

Moreover, their confidence has been eroded to such a degree that they feel they are unable to succeed and prosper in maths. Thus, we have ended up with a series of very capable teachers struggling to deliver a whole class message or lead an effective whole class discussion despite being very motivated to do so. Why? The answer is that the gap between the extremes in the class is so vast it is almost impossible to scaffold the discussion and work to be relevant to all children. This is one of the single issues related to mastery teaching that has to be dealt with if we are to succeed in achieving a modification to our teaching style in mathematics. It isn't the only significant issue or challenge but it is a real one.

HOW IS THIS GAP BRIDGED IN SINGAPORE AND SHANGHAI?

Although the emphasis is on genuine mixed ability groupings, Drury (2014) talks about a deeper smaller curriculum, drawing links with the idea of Askew et al. (1997) of a connectionist approach to teaching and learning in maths. She highlights the idea of children using full sentences to articulate their thinking and understanding. This approach is emphasised in nearly all of our schools tackling mastery teaching with vigour. Vygotsky's belief in the use of language to capture our cognitive understanding supports this focus. This idea is explored in depth throughout this book.

IS SETTING WRONG?

The answer to this question does depend on your point of view. Certainly it is true that there are several viewpoints to consider, these include the teachers, the parents, the school and different groups and subsets from the classes of children. This latter group, the children, is key and the answer has two features. The research to date (Ireson and Hallam, 2001; Boaler, 2013); indicates that by setting children for maths there is no gain for most children, some in fact regress. This tends to be groups of children in the lower sets, some of whom may slowly come to feel that they are not very good at maths, and therefore the effort and willingness to progress through such feelings weaken. There is seen to be a gain for children in the highest set(s). Not all but some of these show accelerated progress. A few fall away due to the pressure of sustained achievement by their peers.

Teaching in ability group sets for maths has been almost demanded by a number of parents. However, many of these parents also assume that their child will be placed in the top set. It may be that there is less enthusiasm for setting among parents whose children would be in the middle or lower sets. It is hard to factor in how the choice of teacher for such sets affects the outcome. There is both subject and content pedagogic knowledge to consider. Shulman (1986) coined the phrase Pedagogic Content Knowledge (PCK). This concept greatly expanded the definition of effective maths teaching, particularly in primary schools. It emphasised teaching, particularly maths, as a dynamic occurrence where a teacher needed to develop their subject knowledge to make it fit, both to know and use to teach. In addition, the teaching pedagogy was established as a key factor in engaging children through strategies and choices of how connections can be made from which understanding can grow. It is into this collection of issues that the analysis of the effect of setting needs to be placed.

When we are analysing how best to teach a range of children across a school, we have now the main ingredients to consider. Firstly, what is the impact of setting on groups of children? Secondly, what is the nature of the teaching population within the school that will deliver the maths teaching? Linked to this would be the idea of which teachers would teach which sets. Finally, the school needs to decide the most effective strategy to benefit the greatest number of children; presumably they would want to achieve this.

If the issue about effective whole class teaching is to be raised, then all of these issues are key. We need effective teaching of children whose mindset is such that they believe they can do well and understand effectively. If children are to be taught in mixed groups there will not be value added unless the initial delivery can have real impact on and benefit to all children. Many teachers have questioned how schools can manage to avoid this attainment gap which would preclude the validity of whole class teaching. In Chapter 9 we explore the organisational issues around a mastery style of teaching further.

My own view is linked to how serious the government is in achieving a rigorous set up for primary maths teaching. Time and financial issues are also accompanied by the need to support a very capable teaching population that is less secure about how to use mathematical knowledge and understanding to get to the heart of deeper mathematical understanding.

SHOULD MEMORISED KNOWLEDGE BE VALUED WITHIN AN APPROACH THAT EMPHASISES UNDERSTANDING?

This question is a logical one regarding Shanghai and Singapore styles of teaching maths. The belief in those countries is that there is a finite amount of active space in a child's mind when they tackle any new ideas including mathematical ones. Therefore, as the concepts become more challenging, involving application of previously studied or understood knowledge, then that knowledge needs to be secure. This, it is argued, reduces the cognitive overload and allows focus to be placed fully on the concepts in hand rather than needing to work really hard to deduce answers from calculations to solve, say, fractions or volume problems. The Singapore curriculum identifies certain subjects that are not covered until later points than in the UK. This list includes multiplication, division and fractions. Thus the emphasis is placed on having deep, full and secure understanding of addition and subtraction in the earlier years of schooling.

One standard response to this has been that young children in school would get bored with covering fewer themes in maths for longer at a younger age. The argument stands or falls by how the children spend this additional time. Although the current maths National Curriculum in England seems to favour content over style and understanding, implicitly at least, we will see in the subsequent chapters whether fewer themes explored more meticulously can be managed and whether or not resources and effective questioning can generate positive outcomes. Personally, my belief has always been that to cover anything thoroughly is a good idea. I do accept though that there has to be a plan about when all themes are going to be covered. There also has to be consideration given to one key idea: confident primary maths teachers will be better equipped to spend more time exploring learning around fewer key areas. Less-secure teachers will need assistance both in terms of content, subtlety, generating interest and, crucially, sustaining their own interest in what they are teaching.

HOW WILL PROCEDURAL AND CONCEPTUAL VARIATION DIFFER FROM WHAT WE CURRENTLY DO IN THE BULK OF OUR TEACHING AND LEARNING SITUATIONS IN MATHS?

This is an interesting question. The details relating to conceptual and procedural variation are covered elsewhere in the book in some depth, particularly Chapters 6 and 7 which look closely at maths teaching in London classrooms that pursue mastery. However, whether this is new ground in the UK is a key question.

A writer on the pedagogy of primary maths teaching such as Rob Eastaway would argue that at our best, we already possess plenty of what is required to motivate, engage and move children's understanding and willingness to progress forward. His workshop to a packed hall at Chobham Academy Maths Conference in July 2016 entitled, 'What can the Chinese learn from us?' was well received by both British and Chinese teachers. He highlighted our teaching strength among some teachers in using 'low threshold, high ceiling' tasks (as demonstrated on NRICH) as a basis for motivating and exploring learning potential with clear value added for all the class. Indeed the whole pedagogy of problem solving, pursuing ideas, learning and adapting unsuccessful strategies is part of this. We have shown we can achieve a lot here. Resources such as NRICH, BEAM (Be a Mathematician) and CAME (Cognitively Accelerated Maths Education) are used widely in schools and have become a base from which many teachers explore and extend children's thinking. Teachers from China, Singapore and Korea have acknowledged a certain amount of awe at the level of performance of a significant minority of our teachers who can teach and lead maths in this way. It is inspiring and has real impact on a number of children.

However, Eastaway and many others would, I believe, acknowledge that this alone is not having a sustained impact across a range of children. The rigour simply isn't there. The basic levels of understanding are not high enough among children beyond the strongest section of the class (maybe a third of children). The middle and lower third of the classes simply do not possess the confidence or understanding that allows them to feel positive about maths. To succeed beyond a functional level in maths you need some belief as well as a broad grasp of how things link together. I don't believe this exists in much more than half of the teachers. It isn't going to transfer easily to a majority of children without some kick starting. Therefore, although our best teachers and the best maths lessons in the UK are as good as anything anywhere, we need the vast majority of lessons taught to be good enough and part of a whole school, whole system approach to gaining depth of understanding.

MATHS HUBS

In conjunction with NCETM, maths hubs around the country are generating real thinking amongst maths leads and gradually amongst schools in general. There is real change in the offing. Is this new knowledge? Is it related to a pedagogy that we are unfamiliar with in the UK? In general it is not. However, the combination of initiatives and the tightness of structure being suggested does have to be strongly considered. I believe this is new territory for us.

Many maths leads in training institutions, as well as schools, question the need to implement so rigorously a system that reflects a culture and education system different to our own. I believe it does merit real consideration. If it is going to be implemented successfully it will require commitment at national level and within schools. It will need to involve enlightened Ofsted teams who are aware of the subtleties within the teaching strategies in England. It will need funding to ensure training at a deep level for teachers. Also a number of issues will need to be overcome, such as wide-ranging baseline assessments of younger children affecting their ability to access fully what a true whole class approach has to offer (see Chapter 9 for an interview with Sukwinder Samra, Head of the maths hub at Elmhurst Primary School).

HOW DOES A TEACHER ENSURE DEEPER UNDERSTANDING?

I have already mentioned the work of Shulman in starting to identify primary maths teaching as being much more than possession of knowledge. The trail of theorists identifying a prosperous and fertile approach to children learning maths is counterbalanced by the persistence of quite a dogmatic approach that models procedural learning, skills and techniques that get transmitted with honesty by teachers but without structure, and controlled emphasis on pre-planned micro targets for development. Furthermore it does not include effective questioning to allow new knowledge to be gained in a deep enough way. Assessment is used but isn't yet impacting enough on progress across a range of children. Teachers, many of whom have been ill-served themselves, feel overwhelmed by potentially dramatic changes to teaching maths, one of many subjects they are required to teach.

These teachers are worthy of deep support. Not through professional training off site but within school alongside colleagues, working together. This would fit models of learning identified by Vygotsky (1978) and involve expertise to call on, mentoring and peer support – the use of Vygotsky's concept of the 'more knowledgeable other' where teachers can simultaneously be mentored and mentor others.

Subsequent chapters focus on a number of initiatives that have to come to fruition for mastery style in the UK to have a big impact – in particular, staff development in understanding the structure of maths questions and therefore how teachers lead discussion on this. Schools will need to consider how to ensure planning allows development, progression and depth opportunities. Teachers respond well to clearly structured initiatives. This shouldn't be done on the cheap. It requires time, commitment and some rigour. Resources need to support teacher development. Maths leads in schools seem motivated and increasingly knowledgeable. Time and resourcing needs to be given to ensure that their impact isn't spread too thinly.

HOW DO WE PREPARE TEACHERS TO TEACH IN THIS WAY AND IS THERE ANY EVIDENCE THAT IT ACTUALLY MAKES ANY DIFFERENCE?

The Educational Endowment Fund published a report it had commissioned into the impact of mastery teaching on Year 1 children (Vignoles et al., 2015). The children had been taught by teachers who had been trained through the Ark Academy Training programme. It indicated some benefit to the children, not significant but worthy of consideration.

There had clearly been some funding implications to achieve this modest but noticeable improvement in maths performance – enough to merit further scrutiny. It is likely that the teachers involved had at least some confidence or willingness to participate. Most theorists about the pedagogy of maths teaching in primary schools, including myself, believe in the potential of the very vast majority of teachers. The road may be a long one in some cases. Some teachers were poorly served in their own schooling and are worthy of additional support. There is a large body of literature on ways to develop teacher confidence and support both in mastery teaching and effective maths teaching generally. Mentors, peer support, modelling, team teaching, lesson study and time. Not all of these are a given in a primary school but the journey is no different to any other. Where are we now? Where do we want to be? How can we bridge the gap?

CAN SCHEMES BE USED TO SUPPORT LESS-CONFIDENT TEACHERS?

This is a big issue for me. There is an analysis of schemes in Chapter 8. However, in short there are now some good resources, ideas and laid out structures in published, commercial form. Can they be the basis of primary maths teaching in isolation? The cost to fully fund, for example, 'Maths – No Problem!' is quite significant. In addition to teacher handbooks, the children's books and online resources involve quite a significant outlay. More confident schools feel they want teachers to be guided into their own created and crafted lessons rather than spoon fed. Other schools feel that time, confidence and transition of staff means that more guaranteed content may be more reliable in terms of providing some quality assurance.

In essence, can a good mastery-style lesson be virtually scripted for someone to teach? My instincts say no; certainly not as meaningfully and consistently as one would like. Yet, given the slightly vulnerable nature of teacher confidence in a significant minority of cases, these kinds of debates have to happen. Decisions need to be taken nationally and subsequently through hubs and schools themselves.

CONCLUSION

In deciding what maths mastery is, we might start with what it isn't. It isn't a teaching style that deals with a wide range of attainment across year groups as children move through primary school. It isn't choosing to set children to allow advanced progress among the higher attainers at the expense of the other children in the class. It also isn't maintaining an approach to teaching maths, highly commended around the world, providing value added for all children through 'low threshold, high ceiling' (McClure, 2013) activities, skilfully handled mathematically and pedagogically by teachers. Not in isolation anyway. Though commendable, some of these things are about a change in structure, focus and content to our maths teaching.

It is, or should become, an approach to teaching where key learning is emphasised quite specifically, small but important learning steps are identified, and the learning and understanding of them emphasised by teachers whose own pedagogic subject and content knowledge becomes more precise and reflective. This will require commitment at school, local and government level. It will require commitment from teachers; it should be supported by time, some funding and the commitment from central government to allow communities of reflective learners to develop.

Crossley and Watson (2009) question the merits of virtually borrowing policy from other countries. Jerrim and Vignoles pick up the argument. They cite two particular drawbacks:

> The first is causality. There are significant cultural, economic and historic differences between countries, meaning it is almost impossible to tell from studies like PISA what is leading to the differences observed. Consequently, there is very little evidence that East Asian teaching methods, however defined, are actually superior to those currently being used in England's (or other Western countries) schools. Second, even if some East Asian teaching methods are potentially more effective than the status quo, one simply does not know whether they can be successfully implemented within the English (or, indeed, other) educational systems.
>
> (Jerrim and Vignoles, 2016: 30)

Although current government thinking and some funding suggest that the East Asian teaching style is upheld, questions remain as to how it will transfer to the UK, whether its impact can be the same. Will it be round pegs in round holes or something different? Scepticism, often in the form of views similar to those shown in the quote above, will need to be listened to and issues addressed seriously. The effort and change required to produce an effective sustainable approach to teaching maths in primary schools is too great to take such doubts lightly.

CHAPTER 3:

KEY TERMS AND FEATURES OF MASTERY TEACHING

What you will learn from this chapter:

- An awareness of key specific terminology in mastery-style teaching and its meaning
- The relevance of the key terms to the wider process of teaching and learning in mathematics using such an approach
- An understanding of the distinction between mastery teaching and learning in a general sense and the more specific nature and features of maths mastery teaching as being developed in the UK

Terms covered and discussed: Fluency, reasoning, CPA (concrete, pictorial, abstract), manipulatives, part – part whole, bar modelling, stem sentences, connectionist ideas, identifying learning, variation, *dong nao jin*, multiple representation, abstraction, whole class teaching, intervention groups, teacher knowledge.

CHAPTER OUTLINE

The purpose of this chapter is both to act as a glossary of key terms that form the basis of mastery-style teaching and as an insight into the overall philosophy of what is being achieved with mastery approaches. Many schools have not sought or felt the need for such a strong focus on East-Asian-style approaches to teaching maths. However, this is a philosophy and approach to teaching that has come under scrutiny. The NCETM document related to mastery (2016) emphasises distinctive features of mastery-style teaching. It notes that 'the structure and connections within the mathematics are emphasised, so that pupils develop deep learning that can be sustained'. The list below is not aimed at identifying brand new ideas never previously considered. Many have been on our radar in the UK for a long time, we just haven't indicated them in such a precise way. The list is not designed to be selected from. All features listed should be present in mastery-style teaching. The degree to which this can and will have impact is discussed elsewhere in the book. The terms covered are not in alphabetical order; rather they are listed with regard to their connections with each other.

FLUENCY

I have chosen this term to be first because the Shanghai and Singapore approach is built on the idea that in order to succeed in mathematical thinking regarding harder, more complex areas of early maths such as fractions, algebra, ratio and, to a lesser extent, multiplication and division, children need to be fluent in recalling and using number, number bonds and tables. This includes number order, names, grouping, the repeated use of digits 1–9 and 0 as the placeholder, addition, subtraction and multiplication, division facts and inverse links. There is distinction between general mastery resources and resources produced for use in the UK. These clearly have to address national curricula and be fit for use to support their content. In Singapore and Shanghai, the curriculum content is different although some schemes being used in UK schools match aspects of the curricula. This is discussed in Chapter 10. In East Asia, those areas of maths deemed more complex are approached at a later point in primary school with more time spent on the fundamental key areas mentioned above in the earlier years. This is because the mastery approach holds that having basic knowledge and understanding at one's fingertips and the ability to articulate that knowledge easily is essential. This means that the cognitive load at any one point should not be too great for a child (Sweller, 1988). New ideas can only be taken on board if the demand in, for example, retrieving number bond or tables facts is not too great; thus the focus can be placed more clearly on the new concepts and their subtleties. Classroom discussion can be on the reason why and how a concept works, rather than on clarifying the answer. This is already a given. So fluency refers to both knowing key information and skills, understanding how it is achieved and being able to express this understanding in various ways including speech. For example, knowing $9 \times 3 = 27$ might include remembering this fact. It might also include articulating that it is linked to $10 \times 3 = 30$. It is one group of three less. It can also be shown as an array (Figure 3.1).

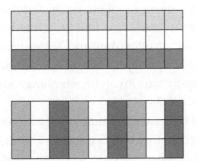

Figure 3.1 Two arrays visualising 9×3

It might also be accompanied by knowledge that 9×3 could also relate to different group sizes.

Three lots of nine ones could be linked to three lots of nine tens, or nine hundreds, even though the group sizes are different. Thus:

$9 \times 3 = 27$ (ones)
9×30 (three tens) $= 270$ (27 tens)

This is also knowledge that we have been keen to develop and emphasise in the UK for many years. I do feel that the difference is that ensuring the knowledge is both known and fully understood by the vast majority of children hasn't been compulsory, nor has it been easy to achieve with a content curriculum that is much wider in the earlier school years than one might expect to see in Shanghai, elsewhere in China or Singapore.

> Procedural fluency builds from an initial exploration and discussion of number concepts to using informal reasoning strategies and the properties of operations to develop general methods for solving problems. Effective teaching practices provide experiences that help students to connect procedures with the underlying concepts and provide students with opportunities to rehearse or practice strategies and to justify their procedures.
>
> (National Council of Teachers of Mathematics, 2014b)

Looking at this quote from the National Council of Teachers website in response to a question about the nature of fluency, it is clear that the purpose and nature of fluency are fundamental. Children need to be familiar with key facts. This will involve memorisation. The memorisation needs understanding in order to be more fluid and easily accessible. This involves focus, emphasis on key work and discussion that emphasises how the factual knowledge exists. In other words, the references to 'underlying concepts' and 'connecting procedures' contextualise how, as well as why, key knowledge needs to be known.

For example, why do the square numbers products follow a pattern that alternates between odd and even, when we also know that three quarters of all multiplication products are even? The discussion, exploration and subsequent clarification would, most likely, accentuate the fact that square numbers relate to combinations of odd × odd and even × even. They omit calculations involving combinations of odd and even numbers which always generate even products.

Thus, conclusions would be drawn that odd × odd as a combination gives us virtually half of all square numbers (the other half being even × even) but only one quarter of all multiplication products. This is because even × odd and odd × even multiplication facts do not figure in square number investigations.

The belief isn't just that this kind of reasoning deepens the way in which procedural fluency is known, it goes further: it helps to make the way knowledge is known better fit for efficient use. I would argue that in deepening the way this knowledge is known, we are also developing reasoning and working skills that go beyond the immediate task. There is a transferable quality to the way knowledge is known and can be used. This has implications for teachers' knowledge for teaching content knowledge. The following extract from the Cockcroft Report *Mathematics Counts* (1982) is referenced by NAMA (2015). More than 35 years ago, this report told us clearly what we are just beginning to accept today about what our teaching of maths should be achieving. Perhaps we need to consider why the findings were not able to be acted on significantly. Additionally, what makes us think that this time things will play out differently?

> We need to distinguish between 'fluent' performance and 'mechanical' performance. Fluent performance is based on understanding of the routine which is being carried out; mechanical performance is performance by rote in which the necessary understanding is not present. Although mechanical performance may be successful in the short term, any routine which is carried out in this way is much less likely either to be capable of use in other situations or to be retained in long term memory.
>
> (Cockcroft, 1982)

REASONING

A sizeable minority of our primary teachers have emphasised reasoning as a part of their pedagogy in maths for a long time. The commitment has been there for many. The rigour of how well children can reason consistently and whether all children are able to do this has not necessarily accompanied this. This is, I feel, partly because we haven't believed that a common understanding could necessarily be achieved by all children related to depth. We have had a belief in the absolute entitlement of all children to access the curriculum, maths included. Thus, more of a focus has been on similar concepts being covered at different levels; the higher up the primary school that you go the more spread out the attainment level is likely to be. Skill and commitment have been used to maintain positivity, children feeding off other children's ideas, avoiding labelling through setting and the use of peer support and promoting positive thinking (Vygotsky,1978; Dweck, 2007). Effective though this approach has been, the argument that might be put forward to extend learning more widely and deeply is this: unless specific key features of understanding are being achieved by all, then it becomes increasingly hard to manage a single-level delivery to all classes that effectively enlightens, consolidates learning and extends thinking in a way that is specifically measurable. Furthermore, it brings into focus the key idea that if a key concept is going to be accentuated, the teacher needs to have a *clear enough* idea of why this is a key idea.

I have deliberately emphasised the phrase 'clear enough' as I believe that it needs to be acceptable that confidence levels and knowledge levels among teachers will vary in primary schools where maths is one of many subjects taught. The alternative is to rely on more specialist teaching, but I don't think we're ready or willing to go down that route.

We do therefore need to ensure reasoning is an important, regular feature of our maths lessons. The use of language to express one's ideas is fundamental to the process; furthermore, children need time to record key ideas that are shared and ultimately accepted within the class.

Examples of reasoning that would emerge from using concrete and pictorial resources followed by discussion to clarify key learning include:

- Two odd numbers will make an even because the two odd ones make an even number.
- The bigger the denominator the smaller the value of the fraction if the numerator stays the same. For example $\frac{1}{3}$ $\frac{1}{4}$ $\frac{1}{5}$ or $\frac{2}{5}$ $\frac{2}{6}$ $\frac{2}{7}$
- The greater the divisor the smaller the quotient. So $10 \div 2$ will be greater than $10 \div 5$ or $10 \div 10$.
- Multiplication products can be arranged as arrays. This means there can be two ways to reference an array. Figure 3.2 shows both 2×5 and 5×2.

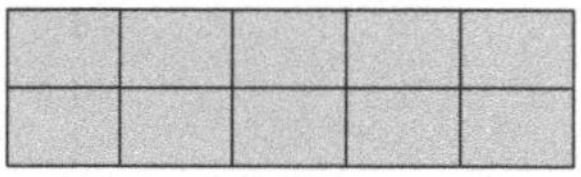

Figure 3.2 Array showing 2×5 and 5×2

For children to deduce or agree that these kinds of statement are true they need to have experienced the following things.

- Used resources to experience, understand and discuss ideas.
- Been guided towards key emphasis on certain features which are then discussed, tried out, adapted and finally agreed.

The skill of the teacher is to facilitate such development, which relates directly to the next glossary feature.

CONCRETE, PICTORIAL, ABSTRACT (CPA)

The commitment to concrete, pictorial, abstract (CPA) in mastery teaching is absolute, certainly in the primary age phase. The acknowledged roots of Singapore mastery lie in this approach. Professor Yeap Ban Har, speaking in 2013 and shown on the 'Maths – No Problem!' website (https://mathsnoproblem.com), acknowledges the clear roots to teaching come from the ideas of Jerome Bruner (1966) – specifically his three models of representation: enactive, symbolic and iconic – and Richard Skemp. Bruner emphasised the journey from the physical world to the abstract one and Skemp championed the idea of learning through relational understanding rather than non-negotiable rules that he termed 'instrumental learning' (1978). Effectively, the concrete, pictorial, abstract progression that Yeap Ban Har identifies is acknowledged as being very close to the progression identified by Bruner. Children learn through experiencing the real world, having it as a point of reference as the experiences are internalised. They are ready, in time, to be used without the concrete objects or experiences present.

The links between these theorists and others are clear: most of us wouldn't seek to question such a journey for children to understand fully. Piaget's cognitivist approach emphasised a child making sense of the real world and the curiosity that naturally followed. The idea of abstraction comes out of multiple experiences that are connected. Both Martin Hughes (1986) and Margaret Donaldson (1978) challenged some of Piaget's assumptions about what children couldn't do at a specific age. Hughes in particular demonstrated with his research about cubes in the box that when children are clear on the context and content of intended learning they can defy the time estimations that Piaget put on the ages that children can progress to reasoning without physical resources. A three-year-old boy is seen agreeing that three cubes have been placed inside a box; when he sees one of them removed he is able to conjecture that there are two left (Hughes, 1986).

Piecing all of these ideas together, it seems safe to say that we build on our experiences, we have more opportunities to deduce things from increasing the experiences that we have; one might argue that we have more to draw on, potentially at least. The same argument would apply to experiencing concepts through a variety of related experiences.

Different teachers might contest what makes such an approach as CPA new, or even worth mentioning; they might also say that such an approach to teaching maths with young children has to be a given. The Singapore and Shanghai models of teaching might claim they go further in as much as the physical and virtual resources are not to support a concept being discussed, a means of scaffolding the learning. They would say they actually form the learning itself. The range of different resources used form part of an organised journey towards abstraction. This is going further than we have gone to date in our education system in England. Certainly the consistency of approach is non-negotiable. The extensive use of concrete and pictorial experiences are the basis of the lessons and are seen as the only real means to allow children to obtain deeper more universal understanding that might be termed abstraction.

MANIPULATIVES

The discussion around manipulatives clearly links directly to the CPA approach. The belief is that the real world is the starting point for young children's discovery learning. In the UK, we would have little time for a philosophy that did not value this approach. We use many of our own resources to assist children as they connect the concrete world with more symbolic ways of representing value and meaning, pictures and symbols including number digits. The debate amongst teachers, within schools and among the school communities often involves the extent to which the use of manipulative resources develops understanding or prevents it going further.

There are still debates in the UK about when formal methods of recording and working out solutions should occur.

The general consensus, considering our teaching standards and, to an extent, our inspection procedures, is that the actual intended learning for children has to be made explicit. If a child is familiar with using the number line and is asked to carry out addition using it, we would be right in seeking clarification about what is the new learning expected. It might be to compare a concrete calculation using pencils with a represented calculation using the number line. It might be to start to scan with the eyes as a means of calculating with the number line. Or it could be to use Dienes or Cuisenaire to check or compare outcomes such as 7 + 5 and 10 + 2. Or to see that 8 + 5 is bigger than 6 + 6 and to discuss why. Either way there needs to be a rationale (see Figure 3.3).

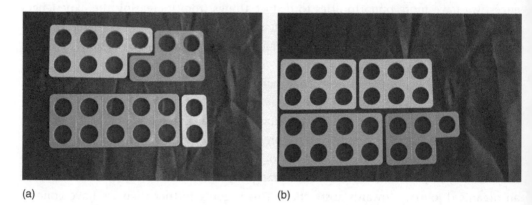

(a)   (b)

Figure 3.3(a) and (b)   Numicon pieces showing both odd and even patterns in addition to visual number properties

Discussion takes place around reasoning. Ten and two make the same total as six and six because one number has got bigger and the other smaller. The same has happened in Figure 3.3(a). However, the increase and decrease are not the same.

This is the kind of reasoning that underpins the complete commitment to CPA in East Asian mastery teaching. Familiarity with a range of manipulatives is key to exploring concepts using different, but connected, representations. It assists the journey towards children both knowing information and understanding why it is so. Is it a new concept for us? No. However, it may be a new idea that multiple representations of similar ideas are necessary to deepen understanding and explore connections. It is more an issue of commitment and consistency. The use of manipulatives is educationally sound. It has backing from a range of educational theorists and mathematical theorists.

In addition to the backing from Piaget and Bruner, the mathematical underpinning from using concrete and pictorial resources to allow for abstraction is supported by Rowland et al. (2009). In their reference to 'the knowledge quartet' (a four-stage framework developed by Rowland and his co-authors which acts as a tool for developing mathematical teaching) they cite the use of carefully prepared examples as a key way to deepen understanding. The specific choices made by a teacher, Rowland et al. believe, in framing and crafting examples in maths classes are key to ensuring children's participation and engagement, crucial if deeper understanding is sought.

STEM SENTENCES

The use of stem sentences is an interesting pedagogic issue. It brings into debate the question of how do we get children to internalise key information that may relate to understanding and also to deeper understanding?

If we take an issue such as learning tables, there has been an ongoing debate as to whether children should simply learn or memorise their tables or whether they should be able to deduce them because they learn how the number facts are derived. Although there has usually been a consensus that ideally we should have both (memory and understanding), the execution of this strategy has not been completely successful. We have not always achieved both swift recall of number facts and confidence in deducing forgotten or unsure knowledge.

The stem sentence approach as a strategy works as follows: the teacher will encourage children to repeat key phrases that are introduced during lessons. Often these are alluded to as the teaching unit progresses. In the NCETM videos from our mastery-trained teachers, Clare Christie models this quite clearly (NCETM Mastery Teaching Videos, 2016). At one point, she reflects on how she had tried to use a phrase that had emerged from a child's articulation that she then reflected on in terms of its ongoing relevance as the unit progressed. She seems to be internalising the idea that our natural inclination to be both inclusive and nurturing, although valid, has to be modified to take in this key aspect of maths teaching; new learning in mathematics needs to be very specific and built on incrementally through well-crafted lessons. The use of stem sentences underpins this approach.

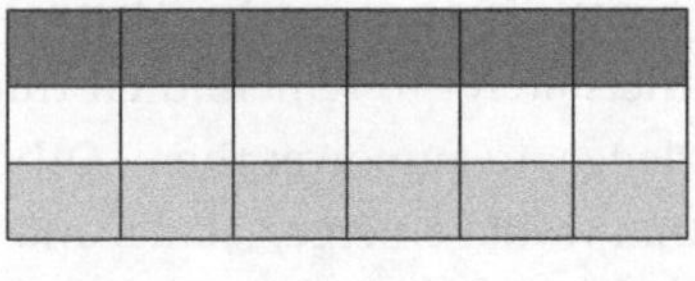

Figure 3.4 A 3 × 6 array

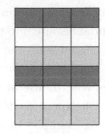

Figure 3.5 A 6 × 3 array

Figures 3.4 and 3.5 show 3 × 6 and 6 × 3 in arrays. The two calculations are interlinked. Mathematicians debate whether or not 3 × 6 means three groups of six or a group of three that is represented six times (3(× 6)). Either interpretation is represented clearly by the two arrays shown. These in turn generate the kind of stem sentences shown below that capture key points to be internalised by all children, partly through clear verbalisation. The verbalisation is one requisite feature of mastery-style teaching. It assists emphasis on key points of focus and activity that teachers oversee in children's learning: children need to attempt articulation themselves and be guided by teachers to say and repeat new learning that is established.

Stem sentences in multiplication:

- 'Our multiplication can also be shown as a repeat of addition.'
- 'The array shows our multiplication calculation in rows and columns.'
- 'The product of each array is the same if we total the rows or the columns separately.'
- 'Multiplying uses equal-sized groups.'
- 'When we multiply a number by a value higher than one the value increases in size ... unless the starting value is zero or below.'

We can see that the last statement might come about as a result of quite a lot of activity with concrete groupings of multiplication and pictorial representations. There might have been a variety of resources used to cover this theme. The discussion that led to this stem sentence might have come about as a result of a number of attempts to capture the idea. This might have had the teacher prompting and challenging children as the debate tried to establish correct thinking in amongst only partly correct thinking.

We can see that these soundbites can be related to key learning that children need to possess to work effectively in a given area of maths. There is a dilemma for us here, as for many of us our teaching instincts aren't to tell children things but to facilitate their discovery of mathematical knowledge; to empower them. Otherwise we fear it would be the instrumental understanding that would emerge, factual and limited. In the example mentioned earlier, Clare sought to use the child's comment as the stem sentence. However, it is often the context to these events that is key.

Many teachers using an effective mastery-style approach will ensure that the stem sentences emerge naturally out of work that is being discussed, looked at visually and that captures the key learning. The stem sentence is therefore vital. The process of all children repeating this stem would tie in with multisensory learning theory; doing, speaking, hearing would and could all play their part. The teacher is using a lot of dialogue, albeit with her- or himself at the centre, and taking the stem sentences within a lesson from that. Many teachers will plan stem sentences in advance, either in the lesson plan or in the plans for the week. Links can be made with the success criteria some teachers use to allow children to understand the important intended or actual learning. Rowland et al. (2009) highlight the relevance of contingency, the skill of using what children say, think, ask and articulate to shape lessons and increase engagement. Clare's attempt above fell in line with this. However, in the mastery approach if the intended ideas and key points are not coming from the children, then the teacher leads the way. The learning has to take place.

CHILDREN'S USE OF FULL SENTENCES

This links closely to the concept of stem sentences. If a stem sentence is being explored, then teachers will ensure this is regularly articulated by the children. For example, let us consider the multiplication 6 × 4 (Figure 3.6).

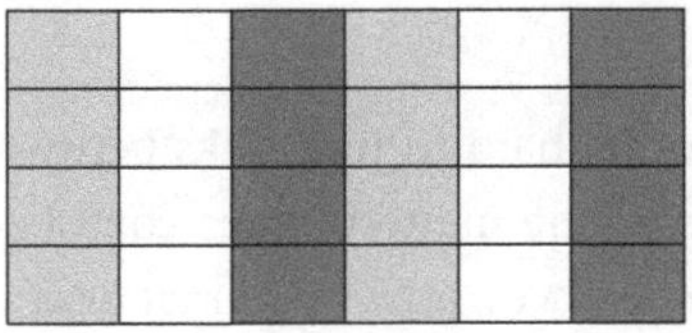

Figure 3.6 An array showing 6 × 4

A stem sentence related to this would be: 'When the group size (multiplicand) is ____ the multiplier is _____.'

The numbers here would be 4 and then 6, or 6 and then 4. If the child simply says the numbers, the teacher would insist on the child using the full sentence emerging from the stem so that the key learning point is emphasised and reiterated, for the child articulating, and subliminally for the rest of the class.

Mastery teaching in Singapore and China will emphasise key points that children will repeat either collectively or individually. The stem sentences act as success criteria, shaping children's awareness of the intended learning. Certainly, mastery teaching does seem to involve not only having a very clear idea of what you want the children to learn but also how you are going to get them to achieve it.

CONNECTIONIST APPROACH

This term relates to Mike Askew et al.'s (1997) work. In addition to this, Richard Skemp (1978) distinguished clearly the kind of learning that he felt assisted children's understanding, distinguishing between 'relational understanding' where learning built on and related to known and prior experiences. This was contrasted with 'instrumental understanding' which was seen as somewhat isolated knowledge acquisition involving memorisation and procedural learning. It often lacked children taking control of their learning and could come unstuck when application of knowledge was required, as it inevitably would be.

Maths mastery does not seem to relate directly to what Mike Askew et al. termed 'discovery learning' (1997). Discovery learning would emphasise learning experiences which may, or may not, lead to immediate understanding but would be based on what the child had worked out for themselves; thus it could be seen as being more significant for having emerged that way. In this model, mastery understanding has to be ensured within the lessons by applying the following principles:

- Learning is seen as separate from and having priority over teaching.
- Numeracy teaching is based on practical activities so that pupils discover and understand methods for themselves.
- Learning about mathematical concepts precedes the ability to apply these concepts.
- Mathematical ideas need to be introduced in discrete packages.
- Application is best approached through using practical equipment.

(Askew et al., 1997: 36)

If we look closely it would not be hard to find links between these teaching and learning features, but it would not satisfy the mastery ethos completely. Mastery is about practical resources. It is also, as Askew references, about children discovering things. The difference is that there is a time frame. The clock is ticking. The teacher is seeking to ensure that certain experiences and certain discussions actually lead to real understanding at that point, or quite soon afterwards. It does involve teachers specifying intended learning as well. Where it seems to link to discovery learning is that both approaches value the child having an understanding that they can articulate and that means something to them. As such, Askew's reference to the connectionist approach to understanding in the same article seems important.

> Teaching and learning are seen as complementary. Numeracy teaching is based on dialogue between teacher and pupils to explore understandings. Learning about mathematical concepts and the ability to apply these concepts are learned alongside each other. The connections between mathematical ideas need to be acknowledged in teaching. Application is best approached through challenges that need to be reasoned about.
>
> (Askew et al., 1997: 36)

The above paragraph links to the mastery goals identified through Yeap Ban Har, who oversees the Singapore-based 'Maths – No Problem!' approach and also the Shanghai-based 'Inspire Maths' approaches. There are distinct parallels. The only exception, I would argue, is the first statement.

Teaching and learning are indeed seen as complementary. However, the discoveries are not really negotiable. The teacher has identified them (either personally or through the textbook aims and content) and that is what the children will need to learn. The content, in that respect, is slightly prescribed. The teacher decides what will be learnt and when; the lesson doesn't deviate too much from that agenda. The argument in favour of an approach is as follows. The teacher will spend time organising relevant learning experiences and discussions in which the children are active participants. However, the outcome is almost always prescribed, therefore the lesson can't deviate too much. Spontaneity is not really an option. The rest of the mastery terminology covered in this chapter will support why this approach is needed. Can a basic and subsequently deeper level of understanding be achieved without such a specific approach? The answer, in my opinion, is that it would be hard. A teacher or a tutor working with one child can turn things around, responding to their interests and desires to follow a different route from the teacher's prescribed one. Achieving that with up to 30 children and being responsible for the answer is much harder. It would require outstanding pedagogic content knowledge and purpose to keep the ship on course.

IDENTIFYING LEARNING AND USING IT

Mastery-style teaching includes a commitment to making learning explicit and then ensuring that this becomes secure by allowing it to be used and applied. Helen Drury (2014) writing in connection with the Ark Maths Foundation, identified four relevant headings that are interconnected: practice, application, clarification and exploration (PACE). However, her reordered acronym of ECPA, although it doesn't trip off the tongue so easily, is wiser. Presumably, she reasons that the exploration precedes the clarification and that the practice and application follow that. I would agree. It would also add weight to the argument that the teacher is trying to engage children but be firmly in control of the content and direction of the lesson; that understanding is fundamental to this teaching method. Any deviations from such a belief would be exactly that. I have some concerns that we can implement such an approach fully, quickly or easily, but I can, and do, see why this approach has been considered. We want to be sure the vast majority of children learn and understand fundamental ideas in primary mathematics and beyond.

VARIATION

Structural awareness, or relational thinking in this context, involves explicit awareness of some 'range of permissible change' of some 'dimensions of possible variation'. These ranges of permissible change can be extended when other kinds of numbers and number-like objects are encountered. Variation, as Askew noted (2015), is different from variety which is often seen as a mixture occurring in a slightly random way. Variation is very different.

The notion of fluency came at the start of this chapter. The idea of variation in mastery can be linked to deeper subject and content knowledge on the part of the teacher. Good primary teaching in maths has relied on a teacher's ability to think around the curriculum that he or she has been asked to teach. *The National Numeracy Strategy* (DfEE, 1999) in maths went further than this. It identified many different strategies, often informal, that helped to ensure children actually knew what they were doing when it came to using formal column methods to solve the four operation problems. Even so, the effective teachers, who developed understanding, were the ones who were able to generate the kind of discussions that allowed children to make sense of both what they were doing and why. These two ideas underpin the variations of mastery, procedural and conceptual variation. For further discussion on this, the NCETM paper entitled *Five Big Ideas in Teaching for Mastery* (2017) identifies variation as being linked to both procedure and concept and the idea of connections.

PROCEDURAL AND CONCEPTUAL VARIATION

Procedural and conceptual variation should be built upon carefully connected and constructed sequences of experiences. Let us explore each type of variation in turn. Conceptual variation means varying the concept to deepen understanding. For example, see Figure 3.7.

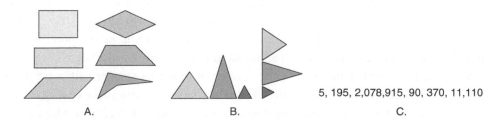

A.   B.   5, 195, 2,078,915, 90, 370, 11,110   C.

Figure 3.7 Quadrilaterals, triangles and multiples

The choice of examples to use affects greatly how robust the learning is. How much does it seek to keep challenging how the learner is thinking through what they are being asked to do? In Figure 3.7, the three examples used show variation within a concept.

Shape orientation, variations on shapes with a common name, and multiples of five. The exposure to variations within a concept feeds into the breadth of knowledge and experience children are then able to draw on when applying knowledge in new situations.

Can you make a quadrilateral with some right angles with one, two, three or four right angles? Four being the most there could be because there are only four angles in a quadrilateral. Can you make any of these? All of these?

These variations within and around a concept can deepen understanding through exposure to concepts in a wider sense. The idea that multiplying numbers doesn't necessarily make them bigger draws in values less than one, thus the conceptual understanding increases.

Similarly, with the triangles the conceptual variation comes by widening children's exposure to triangles with different orientation. Fundamental misconceptions with shapes at the primary level often involve overemphasis on a common, maybe regular shape rather than irregular shapes and shapes shown in a different orientation; these can allow discussion and understanding of a shape's properties and what distinguishes it from other shapes, even those in the same shape family. This approach is emphasised by Gu et al. (2004): 'The central idea of teaching with variation is to highlight the essential features of the concept through varying the non-essential features'. Thus, the shape's position is rotated to emphasise that this variation does not change the properties of the shape.

Procedural variation can be summed up in the following statement: 'In designing exercises, the teacher is advised to avoid mechanical repetition and to create an appropriate path for practising the thinking process with increasing creativity' (Gu et al. 2004; cited in Stripp, 2014).

This clear explanation of the philosophy behind mastery teaching gives us something tangible to discuss and to apply with rigour to our teaching. The progression of content within a lesson and between lessons should seek to take children on a journey towards deeper understanding, supported by meaningful discussion, activity and opportunities to think and reason mathematically.

Set A	Set B
225 − 180	110 − 90
527 − 145	112 − 92
112 − 92	109 − 89
227 − 182	225 − 180
110 − 90	227 − 182
109 − 89	527 − 145

Figure 3.8　Two sets of subtractions

Looking at the two lists of questions in Figure 3.8, we see that one is rather random and the other is created with progression to develop deeper understanding. The first two entries in set B, 110 – 90 and 112 – 92, have a connection. The minuends, 110 and 112, differ by two as do the subtrahends (90 and 92). Therefore the answer will be the same. The stem sentence linked to this might say:

- 'If I increase the minuend and the subtrahend by the same amount the answer (difference) will be the same.'

Each question allows either consolidation of the original idea or develops it a stage further. This approach is followed in a number of commercially produced schemes of work underpinned by East Asian mastery beliefs (see Chapter 10).

The progression in Figure 3.9 would take several lessons to teach, experimenting with multiple concrete resources and discussing, but would involve procedural variation to develop deeper understanding in a measured way.

Add 10		Add 10		Add 20		Add 30		Add 9		Add 11	
30		36		36		36		36		36	
70		76		76		76		76		76	
90		96		96		96		96		96	

Figure 3.9 Examples of procedural variation using addition

Dienes equipment, Numicon, 100 squares and number lines with Cuisenaire could all support this journey to deeper understanding (Figure 3.10) (see Chapter 4). The reason that the starting numbers only change from the first column (30, 70, 90) to the second (36, 76, 96) is that the variation thereafter, across the third to sixth columns, only relates to the addends changing, thus providing progression and depth of reasoning.

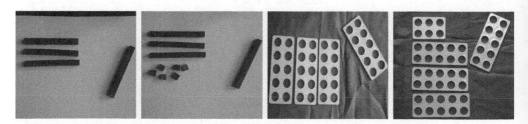

Figure 3.10 Multiple representations and variations from solely using tens, and the impact of adding ten to other numbers

Conceptual and procedural variations involve carefully connected and constructed sequences of experiences. They include comparisons that focus on similarity and difference and extend variation to include the different ways one can represent similar ideas through different resources. The aim of such an approach is to deepen understanding through the combination of these two things: connections (similarities) and differences (variations). The idea of variation gives great responsibility but also large opportunities for teachers to really think about progression and depth in understanding. John Mason et al. talk about understanding the structure of problems as a basis to seeing connections in maths. This is relevant to the debate about carefully chosen examples that allow connections to be made at a deeper level.

> Structural awareness, or relational thinking in this context, involves explicit awareness of some range-of-permissible-change of some dimensions-of-possible-variation. These ranges-of-permissible-change can be extended when other kinds of numbers and number-like objects are encountered.
>
> (Mason et al., 2009: 21)

Rowland et al. (2009) identify the selective use of examples and choices of questions as a key feature of effective primary maths teaching. Lee Shulman (1986) coined the phrase 'pedagogic content knowledge' (PCK) to refer to ways in which teachers need to know and use their maths knowledge.

As a teacher educator, I have noticed different profiles of trainee teacher with regard to subject knowledge. This includes knowledge about how to answer mathematical questions and problems. It also includes the ability and insight to seek ways to get ideas across to children. These are certainly very different qualities. Whereas we can all continue to move our subject knowledge forward, it is not the only quality required. The ability to use what we have to support the teaching process is the key. The mastery-related schemes of work now beginning to reach the market can be a very useful support to structuring work. If we use this to assist in developing our content knowledge we will prosper. Leading mathematical discussions and interpreting children's responses is something we need to track. The more we learn to do this independently, the better equipped we can become to be the lead learner in maths in the classroom.

DONG NAO JIN

> Shanghai teachers sometimes emphasise challenging questions by saying *dong nao jin*, meaning (I think!) *'Please use your head!'*
>
> (Stripp, 2015)

Teachers visiting China in the mastery training courses overseen by the NCETM in Shanghai refer to the mention by Chinese teachers of the *dong nao jin* question. The question that takes the thinking to the next level, the one where the variation comes at the right time to move thinking and learning to a new level. For example, in the concept of 'adding ten' explored above, the difference between counting in tens from zero as opposed to seven or 24 is a step up. We need to know that each will have one more in the tens column rather than simply saying numbers ending in a zero as ten actually does. The presence of 100s and 1,000s digits would increase the challenge again, as would the idea of having mixed numbers with decimals such as 38.4 or the effect of adding ten to a number where there are already nine tens in the number, such as 90, 94, 192, 1,095, 1,998 and 19.6. Thus, adding ten to 97 or subtracting ten from 104 or 104.3 is the 'I think' question that is a step up or a step on.

Children can be thrown by facing the *dong nao jin* question when they are unprepared or when it appears by accident (the teacher not having anticipated its arrival). In reality, there is always a way to remedy any learning situation. The alert and responsible teacher takes note of when difficulties are experienced by the children. They learn to anticipate them and thus can choose the *dong nao jin* questions deliberately as a pedagogic tool to move thinking on, rather than by accident. This is all part of developing pedagogic knowledge.

These choices and lesson set-ups all lead to opportunities for children to develop depth in their understanding. We can pull this together with examples of lessons exploring depth in learning opportunities.

MULTIPLE REPRESENTATION

As stated previously, it is a key feature of mastery teaching and learning that children experience use and discuss different but related representations of the same or similar concepts and calculations. This begins the journey towards abstraction where maths is understood by its permanency and isn't dependent upon real world and concrete relevance. The knowledge will be abstracted and applied to any situation.

Thus representations, for example, for the number 25, are explored through different resources such as Dienes, Numicon, number grids, number lines, 100 squares and Cuisenaire. One might argue that a conceptual variation here would involve deriving the total through different kinds of operation and calculation such as $\frac{1}{2}$ of 50, $\frac{1}{4}$ of 100, 0.5 × 50, $\sqrt{625}$, 5^2. A procedural variation might consider that the same amount would be, in fact, 50 in base five, 121 in base four, or 15 in base 20.

PART – PART WHOLE AND BAR MODELLING

A big feature of Singaporean maths teaching involves the representation of mathematical problems through the concept of different variables and their relationship to each other.

This has been shown to be a powerful teaching and learning model. The pictorial representations are both the result of deducing how to represent a problem and also the means to solving it. For example, consider the following problem: Kelly has £36 pocket money, half is saved and a third of the rest spent on sweets. How much does she have left?

The representations in Figure 3.11 can be made.

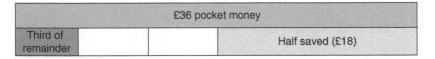

Figure 3.11 Representing Kelly's pocket money using a bar model

Here we can see the relationships outlined visually. If the half not saved has to be split into three equal parts, then there would have been six equal parts that would have been equivalent to the whole. Similarly, the amount spent on sweets is a third of a half of the original total.

Such a representation can be an end in itself or part of a discussion about establishing division of and by fractions using a pictorial bar model illustrating part – part whole. It can be both the means to establishing a solution and deepening the way one is able to understand, use and deduce information that can make understanding more robust.

ABSTRACTION

Abstraction in maths can be seen as a process by which we home in on the principle of a mathematical concept, removed from any real world, concrete, conception of it so that it is generalizable and applicable to a wide range of concepts. In order to achieve this a wide variety of related experience, analysis and deduction is necessary (Ferrari, 2003).

For example:

- Three tigers and another two tigers make five.
- Three sweets and two sweets make five sweets.
- Tillie is three years old. In two years' time she will be five years old.

The mathematical abstraction we take from this is that three and two more make five.

Given that reasoning, fluency, variation, coherence and structure constitute the NCETM key foci for mastery, the idea of abstraction is a large one. Unless we are able to pick out the structure together with similarities and differences, we are not moving towards increased efficiency in our thinking and depth in our understanding (Mason et al., 2009).

Thus, when adding ten, sooner or later we are faced with the idea that when we add ten in our counting system, the only digit that changes is the one in the tens column; for example Figure 3.12.

7	14	138	12.7	2,418
17	24	148	22.7	2,428

Figure 3.12 Examples of adding ten

As well as being a big learning idea that could be used as a stem sentence, this claim is slightly inaccurate. There are exceptions: if we add ten to the numbers in Figure 3.13 we will find the rule doesn't always apply.

	Add 10
93	103
196	206
1,290	1,300
−9	1
−5	5

Figure 3.13 Further examples of adding ten

Possible stem sentences here include:

- When we add ten to a number usually it is just the tens column which changes.
- If we have nine in our tens column and we add ten more, then one column may change.
- If we add ten to a negative number the tens value may decrease.
- If we add ten to a negative value between −9 and −1, the unit value will change to a positive value which complements the negative value in totalling ten, e.g. −1 becomes 9 and −2 becomes 8. The positive value and the negative value have a difference of ten that bridges the gap either side of zero.

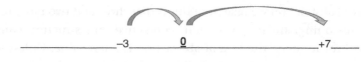

−3 plus 10 = 7

Figure 3.14 A number line showing three and seven total ten

The number line in Figure 3.14 illustrates this principle when adding ten to –3. The difference between –3 and 7 is still ten. The purpose of the example is to explain that abstraction is understanding as a result of thinking about a lot of carefully considered examples that would allow a deeper understanding of interrelated concepts to emerge. Planning for such progression in learning and understanding and bringing it about is the essence of mastery teaching.

WHOLE CLASS TEACHING

We should all be aware of what whole class teaching means and this is not something that only applies to mastery teaching. The relevance of it in this glossary of mastery-related terms relates to the idea that all children (at least 90%) should be taught the same content simultaneously. The issues related to this are many, including rates of learning, teacher knowledge and peer supported development, and are covered extensively throughout the book.

It is worth looking at the NCETM website for further discussion about this. Charlie Stripp (2014) highlights the issue about managing whole class teaching but not moving children on until they are secure in their understanding. The obvious notion that children become secure at different points in time creates the necessity for whole class teaching with caveats to allow reinforcement for some alongside developing depth of understanding in others.

ASSESSMENT

This is a key part of the teaching for mastery process; used both to adjust within and after the lesson. It links to the idea above about whole class or group and individual support.

INTERVENTION GROUPS

The dilemma of targeted intervention over a shorter or longer period is covered in Chapter 8 about different models being used in our schools.

DIFFERENTIATION

This will be covered in most chapters, particularly amid the ongoing debate about whether the whole class is taught together or not. Given that mastery maths teaching is designed to be about whole class teaching there is much discussion throughout the book about differentiation by re-teaching to secure understanding alongside opportunities to learn in greater depth. Sometimes these things happen simultaneously in the classroom.

TEACHER (CONTENT) KNOWLEDGE

This term is significant because the style of teaching needed to develop good, robust understanding requires the ability to compose planning that gradually secures both fluency of recall and in making connections. It requires the skill to adjust teaching and learning focus to provide variation that allows learning and understanding to go deeper. It also requires the cunning to evaluate which areas are developing more securely and which are not. Alongside this are distinctions about which children have developed secure understanding and how to allow different speeds of learning around a given theme when there are variations within the class. Some of these qualities may be supported by colleagues and texts through planning and discussion. The other features would need to be the focus of school development and individual development.

CONCLUSION

The glossary of terms explored in this chapter is a basis for defining mastery features and explaining their relevance to the overall process. Teaching maths is not a new concept in this country. Therefore, the definitions have also attempted to reference where there may be variations to our recent style of teaching in the UK. The concepts discussed here are exemplified through discussion and examples from observation and planning elsewhere in the book. The structuring and order of the definitions relates to how teaching and learning in maths take place within a mastery teaching framework. Namely, fluency is secured and used as a basis for discussion and activity to secure deeper understanding that applies the factual understanding that has been both memorised and understood.

REFLECTION POINTS

Read through different specific features listed here. Compare what is different about them to teaching you may have experienced at school or during observation.

- One way to evaluate the reason for each feature is to consider what would happen if it did not exist. For example, take stem sentences. Without these the likely things children would take from each lesson would be looser. There may not be learning common to most children. It is possible this would leave more room for individual connections by children that weren't common to many other children but that wouldn't assist the ethos of mastery-style class teaching.

- Read trainee teacher knowledge books such as Haylock (2019). Try to think of stem sentences that might be relevant to the big ideas he is highlighting through images and discussion related to the primary curriculum in maths.
- In addition to this the Rowland et al. book (2009) explores the pedagogic issues about how effective teaching is about four main ideas. Written a decade ago it ties in well with the key mastery features listed in this book.

CHAPTER 4:

MANIPULATIVES: THEIR PURPOSE AND USE IN A MASTERY APPROACH TO TEACHING

What you will learn from this chapter:

- An awareness of manipulative resources commonly used in primary teaching and their potential uses
- An understanding of how using manipulatives can allow learning to take place
- Clarity about how different manipulatives have relevance in different ways across the primary curriculum
- An insight into how using manipulatives supports deeper understanding of fundamental maths

CONCRETE, PICTORIAL, ABSTRACT

Young children need to use concrete resources. It supports their first experiences of the world, things that they touch as well as things that they see, to try to scaffold how our counting system works. Our natural world has many resources in it that children use and understand. In addition we have developed many resources to support other aspects of maths. This is a natural exposition of child development, valuing the initial impact and relevance of the real world. As many of you are already aware, if you ask a very young child what one and two makes they might just as well say 'who cares?' or, more politely, maybe, 'one and two what?'. The NCETM document (2017) *Five Big Ideas in Teaching for Mastery* relates to mastery style in the UK. The references to fluency, variation and reasoning have all been featured in our teaching methods for a long time. The mastery initiatives force us to consider more closely their place in our primary maths teaching pedagogy. The other identified area of 'representing mathematical thinking and ideas' gets to the heart of the idea that the beauty of maths is visual as well as abstract. Read many of the quotes from Professor Marcus du Sautoy about mathematics and they are likely to be discussing how effective mathematical thinking is in understanding and appreciating the world we live in.

It might be possible to discuss whether abstract thinking is possible without experiencing a variety of visual representations to identify and use patterns to capture mathematical thinking. However, most successful primary practitioners would argue that you ignore the concrete and visual forms of experience at your peril when working with children in the primary age phase. Professor Yeap Ban Har, consultant behind the Singapore textbook series, 'Maths – No Problem!' aligns the mastery approach within the textbooks to the theorists Piaget, Dienes, Vygotsky, Skemp and Bruner. In essence, he is saying that the exploration to process new ideas, implicit in Piaget's work, needs to be amalgamated with other learning theories, such as the collaborative interactions valued by Vygotsky, as well as the concrete, pictorial and abstract progression in learning promoted by Bruner.

The structuring of mastery texts keeps the work of these theorists at the heart of progression within its content.

Our own teaching methods for some time have been underpinned by the use of visual and concrete resources to aid understanding. The mastery approach quite explicitly seeks to use visual maths resources throughout the primary age phase to facilitate deeper discussion and understanding of fundamental maths as well as to develop broad, basic understanding. There have been occasions in our own pedagogy where the philosophy has been that 'you can use concrete and visual supports if you need to' rather than as a belief in how to develop understanding. With a mastery approach, it is non-negotiable. It is, in many ways, the essence of teaching and learning: through a range of linked visual and concrete experiences, a deeper understanding emerges in a carefully planned way. Perhaps this is worthy of consideration.

Resources that have been used to support learning now need to be utilised for longer throughout the primary age phase as a basis for deeper understanding and for a more secure process of abstraction to begin.

RESOURCES TO SUPPORT LEARNING

Sometimes when children use a concrete or visual resource they learn to achieve success but cannot achieve the success without it. They can become dependent on it. The varied and multi-faceted way that mastery expects resources to be used is meant to allow a deeper, connected understanding to be achieved. Let us examine some standard manipulatives that have been devised within the last few decades to support understanding in our modern base-ten world in both concrete and visual form (Figure 4.1). We will take them one by one and clarify their potential use: some manipulatives can be used to generate both fundamental and deeper understanding across the whole primary curriculum.

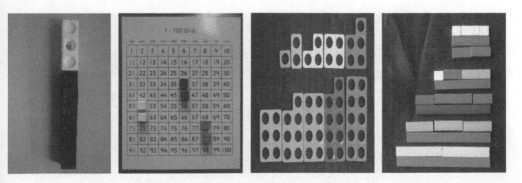

Figure 4.1 Multilink, 100 square, Numicon pieces, Cuisenaire

UNIFIX AND MULTILINK CUBES

The multi-coloured nature of this resource makes it appealing to young children. The variety of colours allows children to use them freely or to use the individual colours to help develop specific understanding. Very young children often have favourite colours which will motivate them to count groups, separate, share and regroup. Unifix cubes allow single towers (vertical) or blocks (horizontal). They can also allow distinctive ways of grouping and separating to be used and understood, including difference, subtraction and addition. On the string, the beads are grouped in tens, in alternating colours. This makes construction and interpretation of two-digit numbers more straightforward. The numbers are easy to recognise by counting in tens and then ones.

The impact of adding or subtracting ten is harder to evaluate (e.g. 23, 33, 43) unless the numbers are multiples of ten.

TENS FRAMES

This resource (Figure 4.2) is extremely useful for building up understanding of efficient methods of identifying numbers as well as conservation of number.

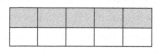

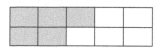

Figure 4.2 Tens frames

The tens frames allow patterns and proofs to be discussed, for example, 'I know five is half of ten' and 'The one on the second row goes with the top row with one missing'.

NUMICON

These are groundbreaking pieces of different coloured plastic and are often used in conjunction with baseboards for pieces to fit onto and tessellating cylinders to fit into the holes. As well as being a step on from one-dimensional linear resources such as Cuisenaire, there is the colour association, orange for one, light blue for two, through to dark blue for ten. It also allows extensive exploration regarding conservation of number and of area. The tens piece also allows construction and quick identification of two-digit numbers.

NUMICON WALL

See Figures 4.1 and 4.7 for examples of a fraction wall and a Cuisenaire wall.

CUISENAIRE

Cuisenaire rods have been around for a while. They were popularised by Caleb Gattegno, a maths writer in the 1950s, after their creation by Georges Cuisenaire, a Belgian primary school teacher. Cuisenaire is a single-dimension version of Numicon, and the number and colour connections allow relationships to be explored both explicitly by number and subliminally by size.

For example, the four and three pieces equate to the seven piece. Also, three of one piece valued at two equate to the piece valued as six. This allows exploration related to all four operations. It allows exploration of inverse in addition and subtraction; it also works with multiplication and division. In addition to this it has learning potential for both fractions and algebra.

HUNDRED (100) SQUARE

This resource has real value although opinion is divided about when most children are able to access it to enhance their understanding. Effectively, this is a number line that has been segmented into sections of ten numbers. Thus the final column has the multiples of ten and each column possesses only numbers with the same final digit, therefore it has become a useful resource linked to developing knowledge of patterns in place value. Many think it is unsuited for use with early years children, who are unlikely to have begun grouping in tens or partitioning to digit numbers. In addition to this, there is often confusion about using it as a counting tool for single digit or linear addition.

NUMBER LINE

This is now an absolutely standard visual resource in any early learning classroom. Large wall versions and table top personalised resources both serve their purpose. The claims in the 1970s and 1980s from sceptics suggested that the use of the number line to assist early counting was a form of cheating: giving children the answer. The argument missed the point that the focus when these were and are being used is about the process of counting. One-to-one matching was assisted by not having to strain too much to recall the actual count. The use of the number line itself can be scaffolded away once the process of counting is secure. Independent work away from the number line carries on anyway with younger children: songs, rhymes, chants, simple everyday problems from classroom life such as register details, fruit problems, lining up and date identification.

In essence, the number line serves two purposes: clarification about the correct sequence of numbers for counting and order, as well as a means to develop skills of counting on (or back) from one number to another.

EMPTY NUMBER LINE

This is not a myth from a Hans Christian Andersen story, 'the line that wasn't there'. The line is there, except there are no numbers on it. It provides the basis for children to choose which numbers to record. This happens generally when they segment a calculation to work it out in stages, as in the example shown (Figure 4.3).

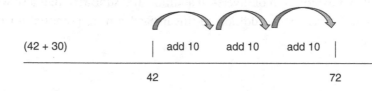

Figure 4.3   Empty number line showing the calculation 42 + 30

Children have difficulty planning the use of empty space, initially anyway. A period of time is spent modelling its use and scaffolding more straightforward tasks in preparation for them using this as an effective way of scaffolding their own thinking. The calculations on the empty number line itself serve as a preparation for mental calculation that ultimately would be done in the head, but based on efficient thinking that the use of the empty number line helped to bring about.

DIENES, PLACE VALUE CARDS AND COUNTERS

Named after the Hungarian Mathematician Zoltan Dienes (1916–2014 and pronounced Dinesh), the wooden blocks (although they are now plastic) serve as literal, concrete groupings showing our column values in base ten. It is clearly illustrated that ten units (ones) equate to a ten, that ten × the ten rod equates to a hundred, and that ten hundreds make a thousand. Originally the thousand block was solid wood and actually did replicate the wooden layers that represent a hundred. Now it requires a small leap of faith as the plastic thousand block is hollow, not solid.

Place value cards have been used to help children develop a visual understanding of the value of each digit in multi-digit numbers. The columns in the cards assist grouping and provide a means for exchanging. For example ten ones are exchanged for a ten in a calculation such as 38 + 25, or eight and five would sum to make 13, and ten of the 13 would be exchanged leaving a ten and three (13).

The literal nature of the visual relationships is felt to transfer well to mastery-style teaching where concrete 'and then' representations allow children and teachers to explore relationships more deeply because there is a shared experience; not simply one involving numbers shown only with symbols. Thus the focus can be on the number properties and their interconnections.

The counters, on the other hand, have come into use more recently as a later representation of the digit values. They tend to be used once it is felt that the children have accepted how these connections work. The counters are all the same size and the different group values are denoted by colour and a numerical value on the counter: These include powers of ten including part wholes, $\frac{1}{1000}$ $\frac{1}{100}$ $\frac{1}{10}$ 1, 10, 100 and 1,000.

MANIPULATIVES AND EQUIPMENT

It seems worthwhile at this point to try to distinguish equipment that it is necessary to use and is referred to as manipulatives. The use of the word 'manipulative' here is to define resources that assist understanding by the process of us interacting with them. It is as if in actually understanding how to manipulate such equipment one has to develop an awareness of connected knowledge. Efficient use of tens frames assists mental calculation ultimately even though the resource is very visual. The use of the number line in early number work assists understanding of effective counting. This process of using manipulatives compares with simply mastering or understanding how something works, for example angle measurers, trundle wheels or clocks.

Thus the following items would only be 'manipulatives' if developing an understanding of them led, also, to developing other related knowledge.

PLACE VALUE CARDS

Place value cards (Figure 4.4) emphasise the value of the digit within a number. This is part of an ongoing development as we get children to understand how to record efficiently and correctly within our base grouping of ten. The idea here is that we have separate digits for numbers from 1 to 9 as well as 0, our place holder. The use of the place holder legitimises the different value of similar digits in different positions, e.g. 19, 190 or 109.

Figure 4.4 Place value cards

Used in conjunction with Dienes and other informal methods of grouping in tens, such as straws, pens, etc., there is an intended gain in understanding. It is hoped that children will understand that by overlaying the values 100 + 30 + 4 as 134, the emphasis on the value of each digit will become clearer (Figure 4.5).

Whole numbers				Part wholes	
1,000s	100s	10s	1s	$\frac{1}{10}$	$\frac{1}{100}$
1	3	4	0		
	1	3	4	0	
		1	3	4	
			1	3	4

Figure 4.5 Place value chart emphasising the value of each digit.

PROGRAMMED CALCULATOR

Not always used in schools as much as it should be, the programmed calculator is an outstanding teaching tool and manipulative. Let us use three examples to illustrate this:

- 24 ÷ __ = 3 and 24 ÷ __ = 48. Even armed with a calculator, these calculations still require mathematical understanding or deduction to work out. It is still necessary to understand inverse operations to avoid trying to solve the problems by trial and error.
- Programming the calculator to multiply by ten, for example, allows patterns and rules with understanding to be clarified (Figure 4.6).
- 10 × × = 0 will programme most calculators to multiply by ten. Inserting a number and pressing = will ensure that number is multiplied by ten.

Starting number	7	14	2.7	1.05
×10	70	140	27	10.5
×100	700	1,400	270	105
×1,000	7,000	14,000	2,700	1,050

Figure 4.6   Using patterns to understand place value knowledge

In order to programme using a different operation, say subtract, use the subtraction signs instead of the multiplication ones. Similarly, to use a different number than ten, adjust the number accordingly. It works for the vast majority of calculators.

- Programmed calculators provide data and the opportunity to make connections in safe ways.
- Children in pairs or alone will happily try things out in a way they may not volunteer to do otherwise.
  - **Count in 21s:** 21, 42, 63, 84, 105, 126, 147, 168, 189, 210 (21 + + = 0).
  - **Count in fifths:** 0.2, 0.4, 0.6, 0.8, 1.0, 1.2, 1.4, 1.6, 1.8, 2.0 (0.2 + + = 0).
  - **Count back in quarters:** 5, 4.75, 4.5, 4.25, 4.0, 3.75, 3.5, 3.25, 3.0 (0.25 – – = 0).

FRACTION WALL

As we can see in Figure 4.7, the fraction wall is a very rich resource. It assists the exploration of some key learning intentions across the curriculum. The difficulties children often have are around several specific ideas. A fraction is a representation of a part whole as we see here. Then we have the idea of different denominations. Counterintuitively, the smaller the denominations the more of them it is possible to make. The fewer the number of denominations then the larger or greater each denomination will be.

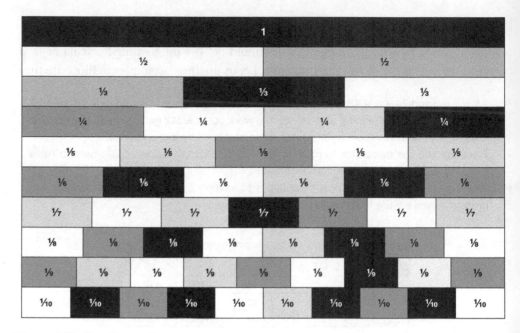

Figure 4.7 Fraction wall

In addition to these key points, we see that we can have equal-sized fractions with different denominators (often called equivalent fractions). Further still, we have the idea that similar fractions may not equate to the same amount, it will depend on the size of the whole (Figure 4.8).

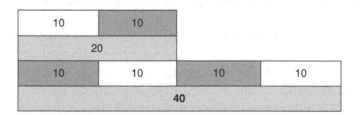

Figure 4.8 Further example of a fraction wall showing the value of ten as a fraction is dependent on the size of the whole

From this representation we can see that ¼ of 40 is ten and that ½ of 20 is ten. They are similar amounts but not similar fractions. Let us consider further examples of this:

- ¼ of 20 would be five.
- ¼ of 40 is ten.

The fractions are the same but the amounts are different.

Around the use of resources such as this, children progress from identifying fractions (in Year 1) to identifying equivalent fractions where the denominator is likely to be different (in Year 2). They are likely to start with halves and quarters where paper-folding activities lend themselves to this kind of realisation. The fraction wall assists again with the progression towards understanding that fractions with the same denomination can be added together $\frac{3}{7} + \frac{2}{7} = \frac{5}{7}$ (Year 3). We can see this from the fraction wall.

KNOWLEDGE IN THE RESOURCE, OR IN THE CHILD?

Clearly we want the knowledge to be in the child and not simply use the resource to solve the problem. Therefore the discussion around the resource would be key, as is the use of other resources and experiences to help the child become secure about learning in a way that allows the learnt knowledge to be applied in new circumstances and situations.

For us as teachers, this involves an understanding of how to scaffold learning, an awareness of ways children are likely to misunderstand common errors and misconceptions, as well as ears and eyes to identify less-common ones. For example, one reaction from children is to assume that when we add, we add everything. So why doesn't $\frac{3}{7} + \frac{2}{7}$ sum to total $\frac{5}{14}$? There is some logic in this misconception. Behind the misconception lies the idea that adding similar-sized wholes (such as sevenths) together will result in more of the same-sized whole. That particular idea would need to be visited in a number of different ways in Year 3:

Day 1: Clarifying and revisiting known information about identifying fractions, denominations, equal-sized parts and identifying in accurate representations where this isn't so.

Day 2: Introduction to the fraction wall. Identifying which fractions are bigger or equivalent, e.g. $\frac{2}{7}$ or $\frac{1}{4}$, with related stem sentences (see Chapter 5 on small-step progression):

- 'The *greater* the number of denominations the *smaller* the value of each one.'
- 'The *smaller* the number of denominations the *greater* the value of each one.'

Day 3: Using Cuisenaire as the basis for similar experiences involving say wholes, tenths and fifths.

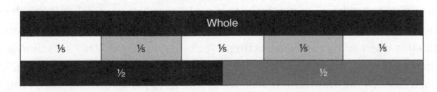

Figure 4.9 Wholes, fifths and halves

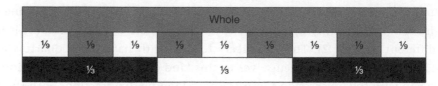

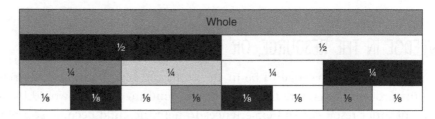

Figure 4.10 Wholes, thirds and ninths

Figure 4.11 Wholes, halves, quarters and eighths

Different choices would lend themselves to exposure of different teaching and learning points. For example, Figure 4.11 works well to explore equivalence, whereas Figures 4.10 and 4.11 or 4.9 might give greater opportunity to discuss and clarify 'greater than' and 'less than' in the context of fractions. One half, for example, is greater than two-fifths but smaller than three-fifths. The reinforcement of similar-sized parts being involved for each fraction would be emphasised.

The visual and concrete representation and comparison of each fraction becomes possible through this model. It is also starting to prepare the way for a later foray into comparing fractions with different denominators through the use of a common denominator. This will come later and will need some abstract thinking as well as visual representation. We are growing the pathways towards goals like this.

> **Days 4 and 5:** This might be the key moment of this Year 3 sequence of lessons. The children could actually be involved in adding and subtracting fractions with similar denominators.

This can be done through cutting up paper versions of the fraction wall and children can then add fractions with similar denominations. Although this may seem straightforward, there are many potential misconceptions that are hopefully being worked through by this process. Children are often tempted to think something happens to both numerator and denominator when adding and subtracting. We don't emphasise that $3 + 2$ could actually be written as $\frac{3}{1} + \frac{2}{1}$ (three pieces that are whole and two pieces that are whole). Maybe this would ease the transition and maybe we should have these conversations. Either way, they need, and benefit from, physical interaction with this big concept, this key stem sentence: 'It is only the numerator that changes when fractions with the same denominator are added'. Experiences with other similar contexts would also be beneficial, for example, pizza pieces, cake or eggs in a box.

It can help to repeat this with different-shaped wholes if possible to deepen children's experience and exposure to a range of representations. Let us look at fractions of the following rectangles as an example (Figure 4.12).

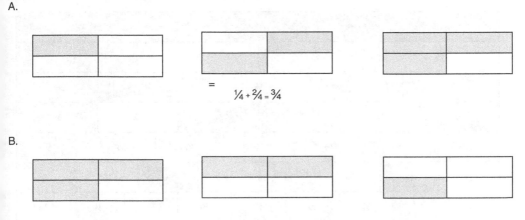

Figure 4.12 Examples that visit the concept of addition and subtraction through using fractions with the same denominator

This has been the *dong nao jin* moment: the planned variation that moves the learning forward, possibly to a new level, a new idea to build on the others. Possible stem sentences might include:

- 'Our *numerator* changes but the *denominator* stays the same when we *add* fractions with the same denominator.'
- 'Our *numerator* changes but the *denominator* stays the same when we *subtract* fractions with the same denominator.'

Progression from this point would, at some point at least, naturally lead to discovering what would happen if the value of the numerator exceeds the denominator. Given that there is a whole number when the numerator and denominator are the same there are discoveries to be had here. Again, Cuisenaire, fraction walls (Figure 4.13) and other part whole manipulatives, including bar models, will assist. Possible stem sentences include:

- 'We make a *whole number* when the numerator and denominator are the same.'
- 'If the numerator is higher than the denominator we have an amount that is greater than one.'
- 'If the numerator is a multiple of the denominator we have made a whole number.'

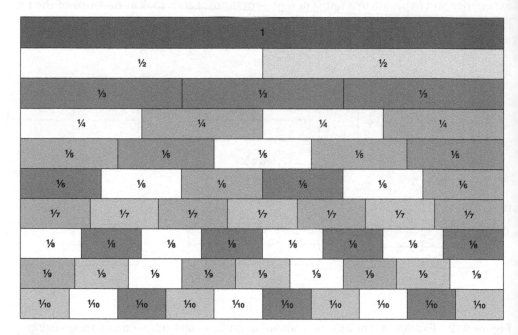

Figure 4.13 An example of a fraction wall

These stem sentences are showing the way to greater depth. Being able to explain why would also demonstrate depth of understanding. A child might say that they know that a numerator that was a multiple of the denominator was a whole number (because the denominator represents how many parts make one whole, therefore every repeating group of the denominator makes another whole). The need to understand fractions as equivalent decimals presents us with the challenge of understanding fractions related to base ten. Part wholes in our base refer to tenths, hundredths, thousandths and smaller amounts still. Each column value is ten times smaller as we move to the right, ten times bigger when we move to the left. Thus 3.5 means three ones and five tenths of a whole one. Ten tenths make a whole one and therefore five tenths make a half. Cuisenaire and Numicon can assist us in understanding five as half of ten. However, possibly Dienes blocks and bead strings more naturally lend themselves to grouping in tens.

KEY TEACHING POINT

Dienes equipment naturally lends itself to grouping in tenths but there can be confusion about using a ten stick as say, a chocolate bar. Therefore, five small cubes would then make half a bar. It requires a leap of faith. Previously, the ten Dienes rod meant ten. Now it is standing as 'one whole' (bar). If this can be overcome, the manipulative can be extremely instructive. Similarly, the 100 square can act as a good representative of a whole with a hundred parts, allowing representations with two decimal places. Thousand blocks provide a third model of a whole allowing the smaller-sized blocks to be used as tenths of a whole, hundredths of a whole and thousandths of a whole.

Entering the very late stages of primary education, children are now needing to be able to understand the impact of dividing part wholes by whole numbers and dividing whole numbers by part wholes. It is in the second of these that the grouping concept, related to division, becomes so important.

For example, $2 \div \frac{1}{3} = 6$ makes sense if we build on what has gone before and keep using the stem sentences, such as 'The *bigger* the denominator the *smaller* its' value. The two italicised words are interchangeable.

A series of experiences needs to make it clear to children that the more pieces a whole is cut into, the smaller the value of each piece will be. Thus each part of a whole cut into four pieces (¼) will have a value greater than a piece of a similar sized whole cut into seven pieces ($\frac{1}{7}$).

In addition to this, when dividing by part wholes, the grouping concept is our friend (Haylock, 2019). The calculation $6 \div \frac{1}{2}$ makes little sense if interpreted as six wholes shared among half a person. As a grouping idea it is much more straightforward: six wholes divided into groups of a half in each would give us two halves for each whole used. Therefore the impact of dividing by ½ equates to doubling the original number. Possible stem sentences for this could be:

- 'Dividing by a part whole increases the quotient.'
- 'Dividing by an amount greater than a whole decreases the quotient.'

Or another stem sentence, put another way:

- 'The smaller the group size, the more groups that can be made.'

FRACTIONS LINK WITH DIVISION AND MULTIPLES

Figure 4.14 assists discussion and experience that helps these connections to be known and understood. For example, 6 is a quarter of 24 because it goes into 24 exactly four

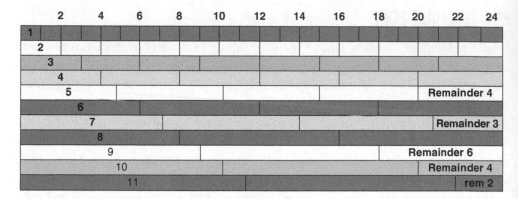

Figure 4.14 The wall of multiples shows the factors and remainders as well as how the changing divisor affects the pattern

times. Five does not divide into 24 exactly and so there is a remainder. The visual input is important as the basis for thinking, talking and understanding.

BAR MODEL

Covered in some detail in Chapter 7 about mastery teaching, the concept of the bar model is a manipulative that is part of trying to establish clear understanding with regard to structure. As we shall see, it can involve physical (or pictorial) manipulation of pieces that are relative in size to each other and to the whole.

BALANCE SCALES

These are a valid manipulative. Number balances provide clarity about balanced equations. They challenge the myth that can form in children's minds that the equals sign is merely something that goes before a single answer, e.g. 6 + 4 = 10 (as in six and four makes ten). The number ten is also equal to 6 + 4. Balanced equations help develop wider understanding of numbers or operations involving several numbers and operations either side of the equals sign. In addition to this, they support the understanding that as long as the same operation is applied to both sides of the operation then the answer or outcome will remain the same.

MANIPULATIVES OR NOT?

Angle measurers might be a means to understanding the measurement of turn. However, I would probably argue that a child needs to understand angle as a measurement of turn in order to use an angle measurer effectively. Rulers and trundle wheels would probably fall into the same category. Once the need for standardised measures (rather than informal measurements like handspans) has been understood, the stage is set to explore more closely different units of measure.

Working with clocks might be seen as a manipulative. With analogue clocks we see the impact of cogs and a working mechanism that uses logic as well as different speeds and connections – likewise the digital clock but in a different way.

Polydrons might be argued to be manipulatives as by using them deeper understanding can be achieved, for example, how shapes tessellate as single repeating shapes or as combinations, in two dimensions or in three. It can also be argued that dice, pegs and peg boards could provide similar possibilities for developing understanding if used appropriately to do so.

MASTERY TEACHING WITH MANIPULATIVES

Moyer and Jones (2004) are among a number of writers who have carried out research or drawn attention to the fact that teachers who specify or choose manipulatives to support children's learning help to increase children's understanding. Indeed, the purpose of mastery teaching in maths is to work through the concrete, pictorial world of manipulatives to develop several of the following qualities:

- Experience related to the real world and the mathematical rules that have been devised to make sense of it.
- Understanding of mathematical connections within our number system that create efficiency in use. Familiarity with truths that can be applied to make sense of unknown tasks and challenges that lie ahead. (Much of the use in our working world now involves application of prior mathematical knowledge in situations where previous experience needs to be drawn on and adapted.)

LINKS BETWEEN THE TAUGHT CURRICULUM IN MATHS AND THE USE OF MANIPULATIVES

Table 4.1 shows the possible links between the use of manipulatives and the curriculum in maths.

CONCLUSION

We see that manipulatives are an essential part of how the primary maths teacher supports children's learning in a mastery approach. The discussions and reasoning relating to the maths being studied have to come through the use of resources. The knowledge is

Table 4.1 Links between the taught curriculum in maths and the use of manipulatives (adapted from DfE, 2013)

Year	Area of mathematics	Specific objectives (selected)	Manipulatives and their possible use
1	Number	Count to and across 100, forwards and backwards, beginning with 0 or 1, or from any given number	Number lines, hundred square, programmed calculator, bead strings, Dienes and other groupings of ten such as straws, packets of pens
		Count, read and write numbers to 100 in numerals; count in multiples of twos, fives and tens	Number lines, splat square (online), place value cards, tens frame
		Identify and represent numbers using objects and pictorial representations including the number line, and use the language of: equal to, more than, less than (fewer), most, least	Numicon, real objects in groups of ten such as straws, pens, sweet packs, number line
		Solve one-step problems that involve addition and subtraction, using concrete objects and pictorial representations, and missing number problems such as 7 = __ – 9	Numicon, Cuisenaire, Unifix or Multilink, bar model, balance scale, tens frame
		Solve one-step problems involving multiplication and division, calculating the answer using concrete objects, pictorial representations and arrays with the support of the teacher	Unifix, Cuisenaire (with a number line), Numicon, modelled bar model
		Recognise, find and name a half as one of two equal parts of an object, shape or quantity	Cuisenaire, Numicon, 2D and 3D shapes, Dienes, regular and irregular designs, classroom and outside school resources
		Recognise, find and name a quarter as one of four equal parts of an object, shape or quantity	As above. Objects that are made up of four such as apple packets, tennis balls in a box, chocolate, cake, pizza
2	Number	Recognise the place value of each digit in a two-digit number (10s, 1s)	Splat square, 100 square, number line, patterns
		Add and subtract numbers using concrete objects, pictorial representations, and mentally, including: a two-digit number and 1s a two-digit number and 10s two two-digit numbers	Dienes, place value cards, Numicon, 100 square

Year	Area of mathematics	Specific objectives (selected)	Manipulatives and their possible use
		Show that addition of two numbers can be done in any order (commutative) and subtraction of one number from another cannot	Dienes, Numicon, bar model, number line (counting on and counting back)
		Recognise and use the inverse relationship between addition and subtraction and use this to check calculations and solve missing number problems	Bar model, empty number line, 100 square, Dienes, Numicon
		Show that multiplication of two numbers can be done in any order (commutative) and division of one number by another cannot	Arrays, pegboards, squared paper, Cuisenaire
		Write simple fractions, for example $\frac{1}{2}$ of 6 = 3 and recognise the equivalence of $\frac{2}{4}$ and $\frac{1}{2}$	Cuisenaire (strong), Unifix, Numicon, number line (with Cuisenaire), fraction wall, folded paper
3	Number	Compare and order numbers up to 1,000	Dienes (to establish addition of individual powers of ten), place value charts, place value cards for partitioning
		Identify, represent and estimate numbers using different representations	Dienes, Numicon, place value counters
		Estimate the answer to a calculation and use inverse operations to check answers	Empty number line, 100 square, bar model
		Recognise and show, using diagrams, equivalent fractions with small denominators	Fraction wall, bar model, Cuisenaire
		Add and subtract fractions with the same denominator within one whole (for example, $\frac{5}{7} + \frac{1}{7} = \frac{6}{7}$)	Fraction wall, bar model, Cuisenaire
4	Number	Find 1,000 more or less than a given number	Place value counters, Dienes, programmed calculator
		Round any number to the nearest 10, 100 or 1,000	Number line, empty number line, 100 square to identify nearer to 10 or 100
		Count backwards through 0 to include negative numbers	Number line (vertical and horizontal), programmed calculator
		Recognise and write decimal equivalents to $\frac{3}{4}$	Fraction wall, Cuisenaire, Unifix, empty number lines used for part wholes, decimal wall

(Continued)

Table 4.1 (Continued)

Year	Area of mathematics	Specific objectives (selected)	Manipulatives and their possible use
		Compare numbers with the same number of decimal places up to two decimal places	Part wholes, Dienes (with 100 block as the whole), place value cards and columns
5	Number	Count forwards or backwards in steps of powers of ten for any given number up to 1,000,000	Number line (either side of zero)
		Interpret negative numbers in context, count forwards and backwards with positive and negative whole numbers, including through zero	Number line (either side of zero)
		Solve addition and subtraction multi-step problems in contexts, deciding which operations and methods to use and why	Bar modelling (see Chapter 7)
		Know and use the vocabulary of prime numbers, prime factors and composite (non-prime) numbers	Numicon to establish factors for numbers up to 30, splat square
		Establish whether a number up to 100 is prime and recall prime numbers up to 19	Drawing on what needs to become known information – tables, etc.
		Solve problems involving addition, subtraction, multiplication and division and a combination of these, including understanding the meaning of the equals sign	Balance scales, Numicon, e.g. seven groups of five compared to 35, or 34, or 36
		Read and write decimal numbers as fractions (for example, $0.71 = \frac{71}{100}$)	Base ten Dienes
6	Number	Identify common factors, common multiples and prime numbers	100 square, number line jumps, calculator, Numicon (for smaller numbers up to 30, for example)
		Solve addition and subtraction multi-step problems in contexts, deciding which operations and methods to use and why	Bar modelling representations
		Use common factors to simplify fractions; use common multiples to express fractions in the same denomination	Fraction wall, wall of multiples
		Divide proper fractions by whole numbers (for example, $\frac{1}{3} \div 2 = 6$)	Paper wholes, part wholes repeated with different shapes. Part wholes are cut into pieces, multiplication wall

Year	Area of mathematics	Specific objectives (selected)	Manipulatives and their possible use
		Associate a fraction with division and calculate decimal fraction equivalents (for example, 0.375) for a simple fraction (for example, $\frac{3}{8}$)	Fraction wall, multiplication wall, decimal wall
		Recall and use equivalences between simple fractions, decimals and percentages, including in different contexts	
		Solve problems involving the calculation of percentages (for example, of measures, and such as 15% of 360) and the use of percentages for comparison	

held within the resources themselves: objects devised to represent key ideas within both our counting system and the way we know the mathematical world of part wholes, relationships and understanding of space and angle.

The skill is to use these as the basis of discussion, ideas and tasks that are varied bit by bit to build on what has already been learnt. A common approach in mastery teaching, using variation to deepen understanding, is as follows. A concept or idea can be varied through extended use of one resource, or, as is more common, an idea, having been introduced through the use of one manipulative, is explored through the use of another. This exposure to similar ideas explored through different manipulatives scores in many ways: it allows further experience of the same concept, the variation allowing the concept to be understood anew or through a different experience. It also starts or extends along the road towards abstraction. Piaget was not alone in thinking that young children develop by interacting actively and curiously with their real world. Mastery, maybe, differs from our recent commitment to effective maths teaching in one way. It doesn't seek to galvanise children and create momentum whereby children's excitement and passion become overwhelming. The ethos of it is quite rational. Key concepts are covered through multiple but connected experiences to achieve deeper levels of understanding. The learning is precise; it should be explicit. Mathematical concepts cannot be understood by children without sufficient experience of them in many different forms. This helps to show the permanence of mathematical knowledge that is present in many different but connected ways. The skilful teacher (we can all become suitably skilful, believe me), learns to deepen this understanding through these resource variations. These are discussed elsewhere in the book.

So, the very core idea of variation theory is that discernment is a necessary condition of learning: what aspects we attend to or discern are of decisive significance for how we understand or experience the object of learning.

In order for children's knowledge to be truly fit for purpose, to allow them to tackle independent mathematical problems confidently, they need to have explored areas of maths in many different, considered ways that allow experience and understanding to be adapted as 'to discern and focus on aspects (or dimensions of variation), the learner must have experienced variation in those aspects' (Kullberg et al., 2017: 560).

CHAPTER 5:

PLANNING FOR SMALL-STEP PROGRESSION

What you will learn from this chapter:

- An understanding about progression in primary maths
- How to transfer yearly objectives into manageable teaching concepts
- How to develop your own pedagogic teaching knowledge in maths

BIG THEMES THAT AFFECT PLANNING

It should become clear as you read this book that maths mastery teaching does not require a complete overhaul in content or strategy from what currently exists in our schools. However, there are several key areas that have to be addressed or we will not progress.

We already have teaching and learning which produces some benefit to most children and a lot to a few. We need to extend this to allow most children to make good progress in their mathematical understanding. In order to do this we must ensure that the following ideas are at the heart of our teaching:

- We need to provide learning experiences where children are active and engaged.
- We have to ensure that key ideas are understood by virtually all children.
- The teacher has to be able to move children's thinking on so that we distinguish between basic-level and deeper understanding.
- The children need to be able to retain what they learn, gradually building on known and secure knowledge.
- Known information needs to be able to be retrieved efficiently, being put to use to underpin harder concepts as they progress.

Linked to this, one important thing to understand is that the content of the maths curriculum needs to be taught so that new learning builds on the old learning. This content needs to be transferred into lessons and sequences that draw out many of the ideas listed above.

SMALL-STEP PROGRESSION BASED ON EVALUATION

One idea emerging through more-confident primary maths teachers seeking to implement mastery principles is that planning needs to involve small-step progression and ensure that the learning that emerges is secure. Crucially, the children need to be able to articulate what they are learning and engage in discussion to clarify this and find out how to progress further.

In this chapter, we will take an in-depth look at how this process can be made relevant to all of us as we plan and teach, by using an extended example of teaching fractions. We will also explore aspects of small-step progression in geometry and measuring time.

FRACTIONS

Ciara and Gemma at Wimbledon Park Primary were faced with a Year 5 class that, in the main, were struggling with this question:

$$\tfrac{3}{5} + \underline{\hphantom{xx}} = \tfrac{9}{10}$$

This is a mastery issue. If you look through the National Curriculum content for this topic, you see in Year 6 the following objective: 'Add and subtract fractions with different denominators and mixed numbers, using the concept of equivalent fractions'.

Leaving aside that this is a Year 6 objective for a moment, the two teachers were keen to evaluate from a viewpoint of children's journeys and understanding what they believed the children should know if they were to have a chance of tackling the question effectively.

They devised a list of pre-steps that they felt children would need to be familiar with to complete the given question:

1. To understand that a fraction is part of a number, e.g. ½ is one divided into two equal pieces.
2. To understand that ¾ is ¼ and ¼.
3. To find equivalent fractions by multiplying the numerator and denominator by the same number (times tables needed here).
4. To simplify fractions by dividing the numerator and denominator by the same number.
5. To add fractions with the same denominator, e.g. ¾ + ¼.
6. To subtract fractions with the same denominator, e.g. ¾ – ¼.
7. To add fractions with the same denominator when the total comes to one or more.
8. To add or subtract fractions with the same denominator and simplify the answer.
9. To recognise a common denominator.
10. To find equivalent fractions with common denominators.
11. To add and subtract fractions with different denominators by using a common denominator.
12. To be able to manipulate equations involving adding and subtracting fractions.

On talking further with Ciara and Gemma, it became clear that they also understood that children needed to understand two other fundamental things about working with fractions: that a fraction relates to part wholes and that the wholes can relate to numerical amounts of many different sizes and to physical real world concepts and objects. Crucially, when comparing two different fractional amounts it would be necessary to examine both the size of each fraction and also the size of each whole. For example, ¾ of a small total such as 20 would be worth the same as ¼ of 60, even though ¾ is a bigger fraction than ¼ when related to the same-sized whole.

Unless children are taught such ideas in a broadly sequential way, they will not develop understanding that is fit for use; that is to say they will not develop understanding that could allow them to develop mastery. They will be learning procedures (Skemp, 1978) that fail to prepare them for subsequent complexities.

What is important is that Ciara and Gemma were aware of more than simply what they wanted the children to be able to do. They were evaluating what was required of the children to be able to achieve a goal that would allow them to use what they had learnt and understood. In this case, a number of children had missed pre-steps from earlier stages of the learning process and this was factored into the work undertaken.

An accompanying issue that they had to engage with was the discrepancy between those who had more secure understanding and those who didn't. Their responsibility as teachers was to each of their classes. They had to trust that they could cover aspects of this work that would be necessary to allow progress whilst at the same time making work relevant to those whose knowledge was already fairly secure.

In terms of planning to teach this topic, we might add that near the start of this work children should develop an understanding of a fraction as a part whole, whether this relates to an object, a shape or a numerical amount. For example, a half is a part whole (Figure 5.1).

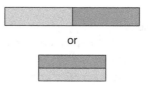

Figure 5.1 Two demonstrations of half as a part whole

Alternatively, the whole can actually relate to the number 12; therefore the fractional amounts would total 12, this being the whole (Figure 5.2).

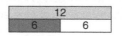

Figure 5.2 Halves of a part whole related to the number 12

In devising their list of pre-steps, Ciara and Gemma had thought through quite a range of concepts to ensure children would have the confidence to be able to add fractions with a different denominator.

$\frac{3}{5} + \underline{} = \frac{9}{10}$

They reasoned children needed to know fractions with a numerator above one would need to be understood as repeated addition. The denominator would provide the group size being repeated.

For example, $\frac{3}{4} = \frac{1}{4} + \frac{1}{4} + \frac{1}{4}$ (Figure (5.3)).

Figure 5.3 Exemplification of $\frac{3}{4}$

$\frac{1}{4}$ means one out of four equal parts (Figure 5.4).

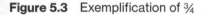

Figure 5.4 Exemplification of $\frac{1}{4}$

$\frac{3}{4}$ means three equal parts out of four or $\frac{1}{4} + \frac{1}{4} + \frac{1}{4}$.

They also reasoned that the children would need to have experience of expressing a fractional amount using different denominators (Figure 5.5).

For example, $\frac{1}{2} = \frac{2}{4} = \frac{4}{8}$

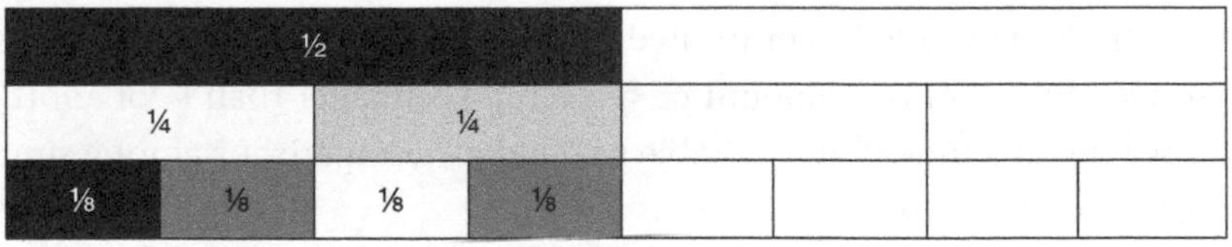

Figure 5.5 Examples of different denominators

These concepts should be explored through other resources; for example, Cuisenaire, Multilink, folded strips (which could be designed as shown in Figure 5.5 with one, two and three folds to reveal the above equivalent group sizes). In Upper Key Stage 2 classes, in the future it is to be hoped that children will have these kinds of experiences and discussion around resources and knowledge with the resources to hand. Indeed, in many of our younger classes this is happening. The absence of consistent use of concrete and pictorial support to inform teaching and learning, to date, means that currently we can find gaps in both experiences and understanding that Gemma and Ciara were seeking to both support and compensate for. Here, we know that in earlier years children would not have been able to have worked through understanding about, say, part wholes, through guided experiences involving Numicon, Cuisenaire, Multilink, and real-world examples such as eggs, apples or pens. These experiences are certainly happening at this school now with younger children. The ninth point on the list proved more problematic for the two teachers than they had initially planned for: 'To recognise a common denominator'.

The teachers' response to this was to spend longer covering this concept than antici-pated. Where had the difficulty arisen from? It is likely that children had not sufficiently mastered thinking around the meaning of the denominator. A focus on mastery style, stem sentences through activities, discussion and reasoning will allow the children to become more secure in their understanding. In future years similar aged children should have already had supportive experiences linked to this by this point.

POSSIBLE STEM SENTENCES

- 'The denominator indicates how many parts make up the whole.'
- 'The numerator tells us how many of these part whole amounts are in the fractions. Thus ¾ is gradually understood as an amount where the group size is one quarter (¼) of a whole and there are three of them in this amount.'
- 'The greater the denominator the smaller the group sizes (when comparing similar-sized wholes), for example ¼ of a whole will be smaller than ⅓ of a whole because there are more parts. Therefore each part must be smaller. The same amount of space had to be partitioned into more groups and so each one was smaller.'

This would not apply when different-sized wholes are considered. Therefore, the teacher is aware that children need to be confronted with examples that take their understanding further. The idea that ½ of one amount or space can be smaller than ¼ of another needs to be discussed but at a time that is suitable to build on comparisons among similar-sized wholes (Figure 5.6(a) and (b)).

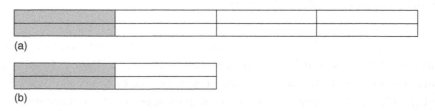

(a)

(b)

Figure 5.6(a) and (b) Showing the same quantity (amount) but a different part whole (fraction)

In Figure 5.6, the shaded areas appear to be the same size and yet one is half of the whole amount and the other is a quarter. This kind of discussion is key to understanding common denominators but would naturally fall after children have secured the ability to compare fractions of the same whole with the same denominator and then different denominators.

Ciara and Gemma also had other decisions to make that drew on their pedagogic content knowledge (Shulman, 1986; Rowland et al., 2009). This included deciding whether or not to tackle work involving mixed numbers, where the numerator is greater than the denominator and could be expressed as a mixed number. An example of this might be:

$7/4 = 1¾$

or

$9/8 = 1⅛$

Should this idea be tackled prior to reaching the point they were aiming at, or could it wait?

Ciara and Gemma had many dilemmas which they needed to resolve. They would also need to adapt their approach along the way as they identified further areas in which the children had not yet become secure. Questions they would need to answer as they taught included:

- What did the children know?
- What did they not yet know and needed to know?
- What prior learning would be needed to reach the goal?
- What resources, experiences and discussions supported learning and understanding?
- How long would be needed to develop the understanding needed?
- Were all children going to get to the required point and how would the teachers deal with this if the answer was no?
- How could an achievement for all children be squared with the different pace of learning within the class?

WHY MIGHT CHILDREN STRUGGLE TO IDENTIFY COMMON DENOMINATORS?

A common denominator can be defined as 'an integer exactly divisible by each denominator of a group of fractions' (Collins Primary Dictionaries, n.d.). For example 6, 15 and 21 are each divisible exactly by three. Three is the lowest common denominator of these integers.

If children struggled to identify common denominators, an active, engaged approach to teaching this issue can be to use a fraction wall as a visual resource (Figure 5.7).

From this fraction wall, we can see multiple links between twelfths, sixths, fourths (or quarters), thirds and halves. Decisions are taken by the teacher about what to put in and what to leave out.

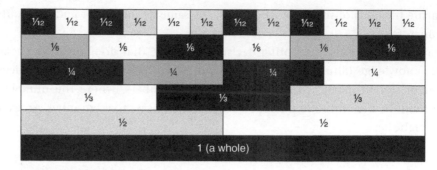

Figure 5.7 Fraction wall as a visual resource

The number 12 is rich in links. It has many factors for a comparatively small number. For example, it has more than ten would have. Just as the reciprocals to these fractions will become the factors of 12, Figure 5.8 represents the ways in which the part wholes are connected.

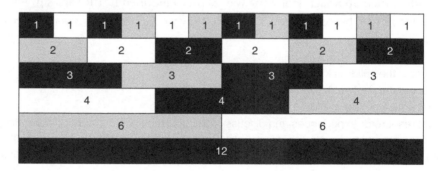

Figure 5.8 Links in the number 12

From such representations, much work and many stem sentences can emerge, including:

- 'The larger the group size the smaller the number of groups.' (This stem draws attention to the fact that six only fits into 12 twice, as it is quite a large group size. Two fits into 12 six times as it is a much smaller group size.)
- 'Equivalent fractions are the same part of the whole but the group sizes are different.'
- This stem is illustrated clearly by the fraction wall in Figure 5.7.

Using the fractions wall, children can play games to score points using stem cloze procedures:

- 'I can see that ___ covers the same amount of the whole as _____. They are <u>equivalent</u> fractions. They have a different <u>denominator</u>.'
- 'I can see that ¾ covers the same part of the whole as $\frac{9}{12}$.'
- 'I can see that ⅓ covers the same amount of the whole as $\frac{2}{6}$.'

All the stems would be articulated, initially by one child, then by everyone. Why everyone? The thinking is that articulation clarifies the meaning to oneself and acts as a scaffold for others. Saying and repeating puts the new language, terminology and vocabulary in context and also acts as a scaffold as to its meaning. In order to verbally complete the stems we have to internalise their meaning.

HOW WOULD THE FOCUS OF THE LESSON BE VARIED?

This example has used 12 equal parts making a whole and drawn the connection between the factors of 12.

Six lots of two make 12, so:

- Two is $\frac{1}{6}$ of 12
- Four is $\frac{2}{6}$ of 12
- Six is $\frac{3}{6}$ of 12
- Eight is $\frac{4}{6}$ of 12
- Ten is $\frac{5}{6}$ of 12
- Twelve is $\frac{6}{6}$ of 12

MOVING THE THINKING ON

Changing the highest denomination from twelfths (as shown here) to tenths, eighths or twentieths would provide the opportunity for the same idea to be explored through different numbers with different connections. This would amount to procedural variation. The concept is the same but the variation is to make the understanding relevant to multiple examples and have a greater chance of gaining transferable knowledge. This compares to the traditional approach in the UK, in some but not all classes, of learning the technique for a procedure with no real transferable use.

The fraction wall can also be used to clarify which fractions are not equivalent and which has the greater value:

- $\frac{3}{4}$ *is not equivalent* to $\frac{2}{3}$ because it takes up a *greater part* of the whole; $\frac{3}{4}$ has a *greater* value than $\frac{2}{3}$.
- $\frac{1}{6}$ *is not equivalent* to $\frac{1}{4}$ because it takes up a *smaller part* of the whole; $\frac{1}{6}$ has a *smaller* value than $\frac{1}{4}$.

Stem sentences relating to this include:

- 'The *greater* the denominator the *smaller* the value.' (The more equal parts a whole is cut into then the smaller each part becomes.)

- 'The *smaller* the denominator the *greater* the value.' (The fewer parts a whole is split into then the larger each part is.)

The meaning is as important as the stem sentence. These examples show, partly, the reason why children often find learning easier in known contexts that are based on experience and are visual.

WHY IS THIS DISCUSSION RELEVANT TO MASTERY?

All of these examples carry real relevance to mastery teaching. They are relevant in several ways:

- They identify specific steps in learning.
- They utilise the model of CPA (concrete, pictorial, abstract). The concrete resources are used to provide real opportunity to experience concepts and relationships directly that lead to seeing connections and ideas that can be reasoned, articulated and clarified.
- The teacher uses variation to allow greater understanding of initial ideas and paves the way for understanding at a deeper level.
- The work uses reference to real life and the teacher tries to break down the experiences to allow him/her to introduce the children to key new ideas.

NEW IDEAS FOR THIS TASK

There are a number of ways that using fraction walls could be developed further. Two particular themes need to be explored when the teacher feels that the children are ready.

- One involves a key point about the model of the fraction wall. The two walls (see Figures 5.8 and 5.9) were subdivided in a particular way with 12 equal parts making the whole. Why weren't they split into seven or five parts?

  This is because some smaller numbers (factors) do not divide exactly into larger ones as in the factors of the '12' wall.

- The second reason is that the fraction wall can be split into fifths and sevenths, but these don't have any equivalences to the other denominations (see Figure 5.9).

  For example, ⅕ is equivalent to tenths, twentieths and other multiples of five and ten. Similarly, ⅐ is equivalent to denominations with multiples of sevenths, fourteenths and twenty-eighths.

- Pedagogical choices are based on knowledge of interconnections and structuring learning. This is both to clarify and understand, but also, crucially, to challenge with thinking that goes deeper as best as the teacher is able to do. This is why we should always strive to know what we know to an ever deepening level. This will give us more choice.

The possible ways to induct children to understanding what is happening might be to choose numbers where it can be seen that five and seven are primes and therefore don't

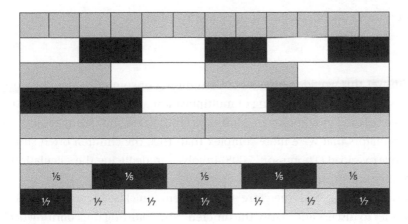

Figure 5.9 Fraction wall including fifths and sevenths

subdivide exactly (they have no factors). We would need to choose fraction walls that give multiples of these numbers to spot any equivalences (for example, tenths and fifteenths to go with fifths; fourteenths, twenty-eighths for sevenths).

This work would pave the way for an exploration of factors of particular numbers. Sevenths and fifths do not subdivide exactly into twelfths because seven and five are not factors of 12. One, two, three, four and six do divide into 12 and therefore halves, thirds, quarters and sixths do have equivalent fractions that use the denominator 12. Thus a fraction wall broken into 15 equal parts with a denominator of 15 won't have equivalent fractions where the denominator is an even number. This is because even numbers don't divide exactly into an odd number.

THINGS TO DO AND TRY

Here are some examples of things you could do and try:

- Try to make a fraction wall with eight, ten or 20 or even 21 denominations to show equivalent fractions.
- See what happens when you use a prime number such as 11 as the denominator on the fraction wall. There should be no equivalent fractions with a smaller denominator. Are you able to put into words why?

There will be no equivalent fractions with smaller denominators (such as halves, thirds or quarters) because none of these numbers divide into 11.

We would make equivalent fractions by changing the denominator into multiples of 11 such as 22, 33 or 66, etc.

Let us return to the original question being investigated:

$\frac{3}{5} + \underline{} = \frac{9}{10}$

To fully answer this would require an understanding of common denominators, equivalent fractions and an understanding of multiplication as repeated addition with fractions using the common denominator. In addition to this, Ciara and Gemma found when they had denominators that were more complex than this, the children often struggled with the cognitive overload (Thompson, 2008) involved in deducing the calculation as well as understanding the process.

$\frac{3}{5}$ converts to $\frac{6}{10}$ and therefore the problem quickly becomes $\frac{6}{10} + \underline{} = \frac{9}{10}$. Opportunities to discuss and clarify the difference by counting on, counting back and bar modelling would deepen understanding; the pictorial representation is still likely to be key for many and should be encouraged.

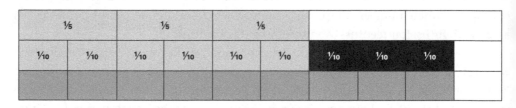

Figure 5.10 Showing $\frac{3}{5}$ as equivalent to $\frac{6}{10}$ and this can be compared to $\frac{9}{10}$ to deduce the answer

Many children in Upper Key Stage 2, for reasons alluded to already, are not yet secure in their tables. Thus a problem such as $\frac{2}{3} + \underline{} = \frac{5}{7}$ is likely to place heavier weight on the concentration needed to calculate rather than focusing on the process or procedure. Changing thirds and sevenths to a denominator of 21 is a longer journey. In time, greater exposure to both the understanding behind patterns in multiplication coupled with the rigour of internalising the facts themselves should ensure secure knowledge for most children, although we're not there yet.

Ciara and Gemma identified additional tables work for some children as a prerequisite to children undertaking this work. A number required additional classes. These are the kind of steps our teachers excel in, in terms of identifying understanding, gaps, and barriers to understanding. This is what Gemma and Ciara are emphasising to us. The knowledge needed has to be secure otherwise the cognitive challenge will be too great.

This is a principal reason why the Shanghai and Singapore curricula have a heavy focus on fundamental understanding (Ma, 1999), so that number operations are completely understood and basic knowledge is immediately to hand so that the focus can be on the new maths concepts being explored, not on retrieving factual knowledge that should be to hand. This will take time for maths teachers in the UK.

DOES SMALL-STEP PROGRESSION WORK WITH ALL AREAS OF MATHS?

I think we know the answer to this. Yes, it does. Ciara and Gemma are not just applying this approach because they are being mastery trained. They are utilising knowledge they already know and believe; progress is made by knowing what you are trying to achieve and deciding what is needed to be understood to achieve that goal. Let us look at two different mathematical concepts.

BEING ABLE TO MEASURE AN ANGLE TO THE NEAREST DEGREE

Let us leave to one side (for a moment) the crucial question of why children need to know this. This is crucial because it affects engagement and context can act as a catalyst to seeing the target.

What skills and knowledge might be required to achieve this goal? Well, I would want children to be familiar with what an angle actually is. This is by no means a given and a number of children in Key Stage 2 are unable to explain this. The progression discussed below is part of the way towards matching up what is currently required in our curriculum with what might also be needed but isn't yet indicated. It also uses awareness of stem sentences to emphasise that the specific understanding and articulation of key (stem) sentences is a crucial part of the teaching of mastery needed to allow deeper understanding to emerge: not the repetition of the sentences but using this as one means to securing an understanding of what the stems mean.

KNOWING THAT AN ANGLE IS IN FACT A MEASUREMENT RELATED TO THE SIZE OF A TURN

Constructivist learning theory as outlined by Piaget, Vygotsky, Bruner and others suggests strongly that this understanding should come from children's physical experiences and discussion with peers; jumping through different sized turns, in context, off benches or to follow routes and markings on the ground.

KNOWING THAT SOME TURNS, JUMPS, CORNERS OR ANGLES ARE BIGGER THAN OTHERS

In addition to using the angle measurers correctly, children can experience ways of comparing different angle sizes (Figure 5.11). Jumping through different angles on the ground grows this pathway well and generates obvious discussion points.

Figure 5.11   Examples of different angles

It is much easier for children to relate to the physical experience of jumping through turns than trying to abstract the knowledge from what they see. Cutting out such angles and overlaying one confirms which jump, turn or angle is bigger (see the chapters on Geometry and Measurement in Newell, 2017).

IDENTIFYING ANGLES BIGGER THAN, SMALLER THAN AND EQUAL TO A RIGHT ANGLE

In addition to the traditional right angle template that is often used, children need discussion about and experience of confronting such turns in different orientations (Figure 5.12).

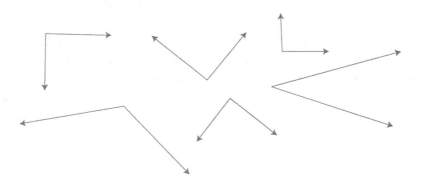

Figure 5.12   Further examples of different angles

Is it a right angle? Isn't it? How can we find out? How can we spot these variations? Which ones are smaller, bigger? How many make a whole turn? How can we find out? This is crucial for me. Children need to be exposed to ideas, discussion and experiences that emphasise different starting points away from north, indeed away from any of the standard four compass points (Figure 5.13).

Children need to be familiar with relevant vocabulary. This would include right angle, acute, obtuse, degrees, protractor or angle measurer. They need to be familiar with key knowledge: 90° in a right angle, 360° in a whole turn. In addition to this they need to be developing a feel for estimating angle. This is likely to need discussion; for example, in

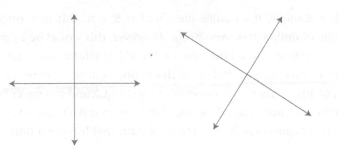

Figure 5.13 Developing greater understanding about angles in different orientations.

the form of shared whiteboard calculations as well as physical experience of measuring. The discussion would be based on how predictions were being made. It would emphasise reasoning. Examples of how such discussion could develop include:

- 'I know it is about 120° because I can see it is more than a right angle but not that much more.'
- 'Yes. I can see that it is about a third of the whole turn. About three of those angles would fit into a whole turn.' (Some teachers will encourage children to use angles made out of card to estimate how many repetitions will complete a whole turn. This will lead to the stem sentence that identifies the more times an angle fits into a whole turn then the smaller the size of each repetition.)

At this point children are clearly ready to use the angle measurer. They now bring both experience and some understanding of what the angle measurer is trying to achieve; namely, to describe the size of a turn around a fixed point.

Asking them to predict the size of an angle as either a right angle, an acute angle or an obtuse angle prior to measuring assists them as they interpret two sets of numbers on the angle measurer. Placing the angle measurer precisely over the angle requires skilful scaffolding by the teacher. The main idea is that we need to have 0° on one edge of the angle and read around the numbers to identify the size of the angle or turn. This is far easier to achieve once the purpose of the task is understood. Careful attention will be paid by the teacher to assisting children's understanding that the angle will be the same if the angle measurer is used to measure in an anti-clockwise or clockwise direction.

IS IT IMPORTANT TO MEASURE TO THE NEAREST ANGLE?

Unless there is a purpose, children don't really have the need to make a measurement as accurate as possible. Some teachers increase the challenge by saying there is a correct answer. I would emphasise that accuracy is crucial and try to ensure tasks undertaken reflect this. For example, if an angle measured is 5° out, this may only mean a difference of a couple of millimetres over 20 cm. However, this would be a cm in every metre, a metre in every 100 m and a kilometre in every 100 kilometres. Thus a plane journey of several hours could, in fact, end up in the wrong country. The necessary accuracy for measurement of any sort is always dependent on the task and can never be totally precise. Is the need to be on time an absolute necessity? Often it isn't, but when seeing the start of something that begins exactly or catching a train that leaves on time, in these circumstances real accuracy is important.

Using key knowledge about total angles in a triangle or quadrilateral can ensure greater accuracy. The sum of the interior angles in a trapezium total 360° *because it is a quadrilateral* (Figure 5.14). Behind this statement are links, established knowledge and the world of proofs and proving. All polygons with the same number of sides have totals of their angles that are exactly the same.

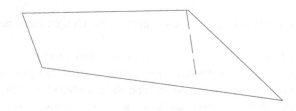

Figure 5.14 Trapezium

ESTIMATE, MEASURE, CHECK

The teacher has the chance to develop deeper understanding. There have already been hints of mastery as children actually become able to articulate what angle is, measuring and identifying which angles are bigger by reasoning; for example, a statement such as the following would demonstrate good conceptual understanding: 'I believe it is an obtuse angle because I can see where the right angle template goes and it is bigger than that'.

Identifying reflex angles which are greater than 180°: these are harder to recognise as internal angles on a shape (Figure 5.15).

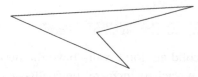

Figure 5.15 Internal angles on a shape

Understanding simple proofs such as 'the angles on a triangle total half a turn' and that 'the angles of a quadrilateral total 360°' is relevant at this age; however, it is only of use in primary teaching if the understanding is developed through discussion related to both concrete and visual representations. For example, I would want children to explore and understand that as each angle is adjusted in a named polygon the adjacent angles are affected correspondingly, so that the overall sum of the angles within the polygon stays the same (Figure 5.16).

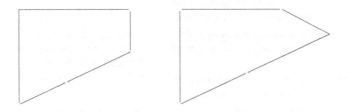

Figure 5.16 How angle increases are compensated for within a given polygon

If we now look at curriculum content relating to angles we can see that the sense of progression needed to measure an angle discussed above accurately maps fairly well onto the curriculum content, particularly when we consider the curriculum statements alongside the non-statutory guidance (Table 5.1).

Table 5.1 Curriculum statements on geometry (DfE, 2013)

Year	Curriculum	Non-statutory guidance
1	Describe position, direction and movement, including whole, half, quarter and three-quarter turns	Pupils make whole, half, quarter and three-quarter turns in both directions and connect turning clockwise with movement on a clock face
2	Order and arrange combinations of mathematical objects in patterns and sequences.	Pupils should work with patterns of shapes, including those in different orientations.
	Use mathematical vocabulary to describe position, direction and movement, including movement in a straight line and distinguishing between rotation as a turn and in terms of right angles for quarter, half and three-quarter turns (clockwise and anti-clockwise)	Pupils use the concept and language of angles to describe 'turn' by applying rotations, including in practical contexts (for example, pupils themselves moving in turns, giving instructions to other pupils to do so, and programming robots using instructions given in right angles)

(Continued)

Table 5.1 (Continued)

Year	Curriculum	Non-statutory guidance
3	Recognise angles as a property of shape or a description of a turn. Identify right angles, recognise that two right angles make a half-turn, three make three-quarters of a turn and four a complete turn; identify whether angles are greater than or less than a right angle. Identify horizontal and vertical lines and pairs of perpendicular and parallel lines	Pupils should be able to describe the properties of 2D and 3D shapes using accurate language, including lengths of lines and acute and obtuse for angles greater or lesser than a right angle
4	Identify acute and obtuse angles and compare and order angles up to two right angles by size. Identify lines of symmetry in 2D shapes presented in different orientations	Pupils compare and order angles in preparation for using a protractor and compare lengths and angles to decide if a polygon is regular or irregular
5	Identify 3D shapes, including cubes and other cuboids, from 2D representations. Know angles are measured in degrees: estimate and compare acute, obtuse and reflex angles. Draw given angles, and measure them in degrees (°). Identify: angles at a point and one whole turn (total 360°); angles at a point on a straight line and half a turn (total 180°); other multiples of 90°. Use the properties of rectangles to deduce related facts and find missing lengths and angles. Distinguish between regular and irregular polygons based on reasoning about equal sides and angles	Pupils become accurate in drawing lines with a ruler to the nearest millimetre, and measuring with a protractor. They use conventional markings for parallel lines and right angles. Pupils use angle sum facts and other properties to make deductions about missing angles and relate these to missing number problems
6	Recognise angles where they meet at a point, are on a straight line, or are vertically opposite, and find missing angles	These relationships might be expressed algebraically, for example $d = 2 \times r$; $a = 180 - (b + c)$

TELLING THE TIME

Let us now move onto a different area of measurement: telling the time. Whereas the example about angles showed a similar progression between the National Curriculum outline and my attempt to break down the concept of measuring accurately in degrees, I am not so sure the concept of telling the time works as well. There are some big ideas that appear to have been missed. Table 5.2 gives relevant statements from the National Curriculum in England programme of study.

Table 5.2 Curriculum statements on measuring (DfE, 2013)

Year	Guidance	Non-statutory guidance
1	Time (for example, quicker, slower, earlier, later). Time (hours, minutes, seconds). Tell the time to the hour and half past the hour and draw the hands on a clock face to show these times	Pupils use the language of time, including telling the time through the day, first using o'clock and then half past
2	Compare and sequence intervals of time. Tell and write the time to five minutes, including quarter past/to the hour and draw the hands on a clock face to show these times. Know the number of minutes in an hour and the number of hours in a day	Pupils become fluent in telling the time on analogue clocks and recording it

In Year 2, the idea of comparing intervals of time for length seems sound. However, prior to this I believe other things need to be happening. Here is a list of conceptual ideas relating to time and the order in which they need to be understood; you may find that one or two of these are open to debate:

- Children understand that a measurement of how long something takes would be useful and make life fairer.
- There are many ways to achieve this including water or sand clocks, based on how long it takes these substances to pass at a steady rate. Sand clocks are used with young children because the visual repeated nature of the experience gives an insight into what can be achieved within that period. This can relate to informal or formal units of measure.
- Clocks measure time in hours, minutes and seconds that make up a day.
- The large numbers on the analogue clocks tell us how many hours have passed.
- The hour numbers and hands are very logical. If the hour hand is between the three and four then it has gone past 3 o'clock and not yet reached 4 o'clock. The further past the three it has gone the nearer to 4 o'clock it is.
- The longer, minute hand tells how much of the next hour has gone by. It measures how many of the 60 minutes of each hour have passed.

         (See Newell, 2017, for expanded discussion of these points.)

Further ideas that build on these would include:

- If we only had one hand we would still be able to see roughly how much of the next hour had passed.
- The two hands travel at different speeds but get measured on just the one clock.

- The minute hand travels all the way around the clock to register an hour in the time it takes the hour hand to move through one of the hours on the clock face.
- Our clock is telling us how many hours and minutes have passed.

These statements can also act as stem sentences that could underpin our lessons.

ACTIVITIES

Activities that would allow us to have discussions that would help develop both basic understanding and begin to develop mastery understanding include:

- Building up lots of understanding about what can happen in ten seconds, 30 seconds, a minute, ten minutes, 30 minutes, an hour.
- Sequencing events in order of when they take place.
- Seeing the day as a number line with a series of events. At the end of the day a new one begins. Making the link to the clock face.
- Looking at the cog clock to see how fast each hand travels. The hour hand travels from one number to the next in the time the minute hand goes the whole way around.
- An hour is actually minutes.
- An hour takes the minute hand all the way round to where it started, wherever that may be.
- We tell the time by describing how many hours and minutes have gone by.

In this extract from the NCETM Mastery guidance for Year 2, Mike Askew and the team distinguish between basic and deeper understanding.

Which of these clock faces (Figure 5.17) shows a time between 5 o'clock and 7 o'clock?

Figure 5.17 Clocks representing different times

This gives a range of times showing o'clock, half past and quarter past times some of which are between 5 o'clock and 7 o'clock and some aren't. For example, the deeper understanding is clarified through children responding to a claim (see below).

Jack says, 'There isn't any point in having a minute hand on a clock because I can still tell the time without it' (see Figure 5.18).

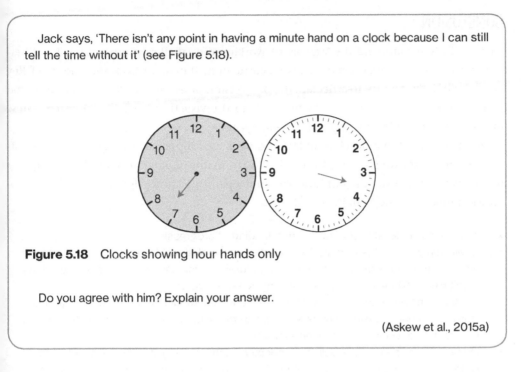

Figure 5.18 Clocks showing hour hands only

Do you agree with him? Explain your answer.

(Askew et al., 2015a)

The evidence of mastery is reached through the understanding that needs to be present to respond to the claim.

- Stem sentence: 'We can tell approximately what time it is by seeing how far between the two whole hours the hour hand has travelled.'
- Stem sentence: 'The purpose of the minute hand is to indicate more precisely how much of the new hour has elapsed.'

The same is true of the second hand when related to the minutes that have passed.

- Stem sentence: 'Measuring anything is about being as precise as we need to be for the purpose in hand.' We can never really achieve exact precision.

The 21:02 train from Euston to Birmingham will not leave at precisely 21:02. It will be a second or so out at least. If it does leave on time, it will be according to a clock or time system that has been calculated by machines made by humans; accurate to a degree, maybe a significant degree.

In the above clock faces (Figure 5.18) it is clear that the times are about half past seven and just after three o'clock even though the minute hands are missing (see also Newell, 2017, Chapter 6 'Time').

CONCLUSION

I would fully recommend the strategy of working out small-step progression for different areas of primary mathematics. Take a curriculum statement from the middle of Key Stage 2. Sit down and try to articulate the progression of learning and understanding that would allow you to feel secure teaching this to the year that has been allocated. These experiences should ideally begin in the early years.

Teaching for a deeper level of understanding is well supported by experience of assisting children in making sense of the curriculum in maths in previous years. It also requires us to have an understanding of how we can deepen this knowledge. The small-step progression model should help in several ways.

- It will help you develop your own understanding of progression.
- It will help you see the progression identified in the National Curriculum. Chunks of the curriculum for England lend themselves naturally to mastery. In other areas, the links aren't clear and the deeper understanding is more obscure.
- It will also help you match up what you feel children should know and understand and learn as a means to evaluating progression in the schemes of work now on the market that seek to develop mastery understanding.
- Many mastery-trained specialists in primary maths coming through now believe that schemes should be used in a committed way; however, they can only get you so close to meaningful discussion and activity that creates a cognitive shift. This means that the sooner you can understand the progression within a scheme the better you will be able to adapt the conversations you have with the children.

You can and should match up what you have outlined, just as Ciara and Gemma did with fractions, and I explored for angles and time.

It is a significant step towards developing content knowledge. Once you start to become clear about what children need to understand – as opposed to know – you start to think about setting up learning situations that will or can lead to children taking ownership of their own learning.

Clarification and practice gradually give way to reasoning, explanation and application of knowledge. We explore this further in subsequent chapters. I believe that accredited schemes of work will be underpinned by small-step progression. In Chapter 8 we explore this issue more closely.

ACTIVITIES RELATED TO THIS CHAPTER

- Create alternative fraction walls, using the template as shown in this chapter.
- Identify objectives from Key Stages 1 or 2 to consider pre-steps and prior understanding needed to teach, learn, understand and apply knowledge related to this idea.

- Compare this progression as well as that identified in the National Curriculum 2014 with the progression identified in any maths schemes being used in schools you go into.
- Look at school-year distinctions between basic understanding, mastery and deeper mastery outlined on the NCETM website under the heading 'Teaching for Mastery: Questions, tasks and activities to support assessment' (www.ncetm.org.uk/resources/46689).

Read the works of these writers:

- Rowland, T., Turner, F., Thwaites, A. and Huckstep, P. (2009) *Developing Primary Mathematics Teaching: Reflecting on Practice with the Knowledge Quartet*. London: SAGE.
- Gudmundsdottir, S. and Shulman, L. (1987) 'Pedagogical content knowledge in social studies', *Scandinavian Journal of Educational Research*, 31(2): 59–70.
- Yeap Ban Har (2011) *Teaching to Mastery Mathematics Bar Modeling: A Problem-solving Tool*. Singapore: Marshall Cavendish.

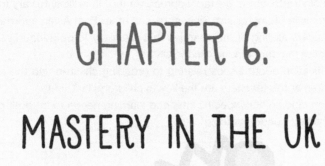

CHAPTER 6:

MASTERY IN THE UK

What you will learn from this chapter:

- The realisation that children's starting points are key to a mastery approach
- An awareness of how good pedagogy in the UK needs to be matched to specific requirements for a mastery approach
- An insight into why a mastery approach in the UK is likely to vary from the models and contexts in Shanghai and Singapore, and other East Asian approaches
- An understanding of the changes that are likely to be needed as we move towards effective mastery teaching in the UK
- Clarification about issues relating to grouping children and the extent to which the children or the teachers are the key to children's learning
- Understanding how specific intended learning needs to be both precise and related to children's understanding

This chapter is important as it is a real opportunity to identify what we will need to achieve in the UK that will be different from what has been done before. Life is a journey and having embarked on this one some things will disappear permanently.

The first key point is that traditionally our whole class teaching has accepted that children learn at different speeds and that our teaching needs to reflect this, as discussed in Chapter 1. From now on, we will no longer be able to accept this. We will need to have the vast majority of children ready to take in, fully, each new idea being put forward in the daily maths lesson which builds on what has gone before. This is indeed different to what has happened in the past, even in the classrooms of the most effective primary maths teachers.

WHY WILL THIS CHANGE BE IRREVERSIBLE?

I believe whole class teaching as a basis for children learning maths has to stay, at least, as the basic working model in primary schools. There are two reasons for this. One is that if the goal is to achieve a greater level of confidence in the lower two thirds of the class we have to learn to teach so that the vast majority of children learn from the initial teaching that takes place (this has been termed as 'wave 1 whole class teaching').

Secondly, it can be argued that most teachers who favour setted maths work for primary children do so for reasons related to convenience of teaching, often for those who are less secure in their content and subject knowledge. Although this is understandable, it is not in the best interests of the children. Thus, development of confidence of teachers is a prerequisite for ensuring effective whole class teaching and learning in primary maths.

Countries such as China, Singapore, Japan and Korea all ensure children, whose early understanding and progress is not secure, receive support in the early years to make sure they are ready to access whole class learning. Essentially, this involves daily additional input. However, in some cases where misconceptions remain in the longer term, targeted support in a small group may be considered. Therefore, I believe, if we ever loosen our commitment to mastery teaching (that we seem to be progressing with currently), some teaching features will remain. First, as stated, is the idea that children need to be made ready to access whole class teaching and that this position is maintained through whatever means is necessary. Second is the idea that we need to make learning explicit in our maths teaching.

LEARNING ETHOS

At my university, we have had a view that children hold the key to their own learning journey. The teacher is obviously crucial in empowering the children as they start to take ownership of what effective learning is and how they can take control of this through self-awareness, metacognition and what would be termed as a 'social constructivist' approach to this learning happening in the classroom. Constructivism can be defined as 'the philosophical and scientific position that knowledge arises through a process of active construction' (Mascolo and Fischer, 2005: 49). Writers such as Vygotsky (1978) and Bruner (1960) emphasised the collaborations between learner and learner as well as teacher and learner as the means to constructing understanding.

Thus, although teachers should, ideally, have a strong grasp of and pedagogy related to the learning in hand, they then use the knowledge discerningly to allow children to make connections themselves that are thought to impact at a deeper metacognitive level (Shulman, 1986; Rowland et al., 2009).

The philosophy of mastery teaching is rather different to this. Having spent a lot of time considering the pedagogy of maths teaching in the primary classroom and a socially constructivist view of learning through our university pedagogy with trainee teachers, I feel this is a big area. It is what Piaget might term a chance to accommodate rather than assimilate a new idea (Piaget, 1952). Festinger's term 'cognitive dissonance' might also apply (1962). Why?

The key question is how do we ensure children learn specific things but with only a guided, general approach to facilitating learning? The answer is that I am not sure that we can, easily at least. I feel we need to emphasise learning more closely, ensuring that learnt knowledge is both understood and then applied. This links to Chapter 5 on small-step progression.

MATHS AS A PROGRESSIVE, HIERARCHICAL, LEARNING EXPERIENCE

Security of understanding is key to development in maths. Although it is possible to understand problems mathematically without being able to calculate them, generally one needs knowledge that is understood and learnt in order to prosper.

Let us look at this example:

> In finding how many apples would be needed by 30 children eating four a day for a week, some children might be able to identify that 120 would be the daily requirement and that multiplying by seven would achieve the answer. They might not be able to calculate the answer. However, in the main knowledge of both is required.

Thus, clarity of intended learning is key. The word that stays with me from watching a range of teaching in primary maths is being 'explicit' about learning. We sometimes struggle to make learning explicit in our maths teaching. Reasons for this might include:

- We don't wish to make learning too obvious and that children will be stronger for the journey through personal discovery.
- We struggle to facilitate understanding by other means than telling children what to do. Although important, this is almost a polar opposite to the first statement.
- Our personal position regarding mastery of fundamental maths means that we struggle to emphasise the salient points that would empower children in their understanding.
- Linked to the previous point, we personally might need further work to be secure in understanding progression regarding learning in primary maths. Again, this can lead to feeling comfortable in making key learning explicit.
- We may not realise just how much reinforcement is needed to ensure that key understanding is securely understood. This point is related to the distinction between emerging understanding in children and full understanding that is fit for use in application of knowledge and in understanding further learning that builds on the initial learning.

Building on the above points, I believe our primary teachers are extremely sound in their pedagogy and versatility, although their confidence in mathematical pedagogy and knowledge is less consistent. These are issues that we need to address because our teachers are worthy of support and our children are worthy of the benefits that this would bring. This theme is explored further in Chapter 8.

CASE STUDY 1: LUCY

Lucy is a newly qualified primary school teacher. Focusing on place value of digits, grouping and regrouping, she sought to deepen children's understanding. The children in Year 4 were using Dienes equipment to assist their thinking. The broad purpose of the lesson was, firstly, that children could use Dienes base ten equipment (see Chapter 4 on manipulatives) to assist them in clarifying how to represent the totals given using the next column value. For example, 1,153 + 1,959 were laid out as in Figure 6.1 with the digits of each number represented with the pictorial version of the place value (Dienes) blocks. The columns were then worked through, grouping initially in tens and then hundreds and thousands.

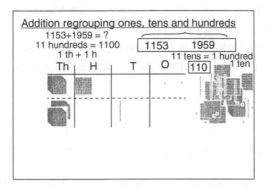

Figure 6.1   Whiteboard modelling of regrouping in addition of larger numbers using Dienes

The lesson is sound; the Dienes apparatus supports the key teaching point. However, ultimately, the key concept of grouping in tens around different columns is quite a vast one. Lucy articulated that she had covered work on changing ones into tens and tens into hundreds separately, whereas this lesson was mixing up the groupings. That seems logical and worthwhile.

There are also key stem sentences that would make learning more explicit, including:

- 'If we have more than nine of one group size we need to make a new group'. This takes into account ten ones being equivalent to a ten, ten tens to a hundred and so on.
- 'When we record numbers we can only use one digit in each column.' This relates to the idea that digits can be used in different columns to represent different amounts. Let us look at the example of 9:

  91: The value of the 9 is 90
  129: The value of the 9 is 9
  1907: The value of the 9 is 900

- 'For every ten ones we have we can make a ten.'

This is then extended to all columns in as much as ten tens make a hundred, ten hundreds make a thousand (Table 6.1). Crucially the system also applies to smaller amounts and so ten tenths make a whole, ten hundredths make a tenth.

Table 6.1 The column visual as a support to Lucy's use of the Dienes equipment

Th	H	T	O	$\frac{1}{10}$	$\frac{1}{100}$	$\frac{1}{1,000}$
1,000	100	10	1	0.1	0.01	0.001

Numicon would or could have been a prelude to this process. Counting in money using place value amounts might work too. For example, 1p, 10p, 100p (£1), 1,000p (£10) could also work. However, these are pedagogic choices for the teacher, dependent on the situation and main lesson focus. They would be true to one of the four main mastery themes of multiple representations to secure and develop understanding.

Lucy then takes the lesson on through discussion emphasising that she wishes the children to use re-grouping.

a. 4,217   b. 2,457   c. 6,417   d. 7,235   e. 5,207

\+ 3,195   \+ 5,231   \+ 4,258   \+ 5,665   \+ 4,661

The task is for children to regroup where necessary to solve the addition problems. Some will use Dienes to support their work and others will simply work in columns.

In talking with Lucy beforehand, she is receptive to the idea of asking children to identify in pairs whether they can see which ones will need regrouping and which ones will not. Children are encouraged to try to put into words something that will explain their thinking. Sometimes this needs a scaffold to make the learning explicit. The stem sentence 'I need to regroup when …' could be used in this case.

Lucy draws out children's thinking and they are able to establish that they need to regroup when the total in a given column reaches ten. I believe this will need emphasising and revisiting to secure this understanding. I also believe that the intended learning might have begun with smaller numbers.

This is a deep conversation that Lucy has carried out successfully. Some children will be within their comfort zone, others on the edge of it. Thus a similar task, around maybe just tens and ones, could have reduced the cognitive load (Wiliam, 2017). It is a professional but important choice.

65   48   63   55

\+ 34   \+ 42   \+ 35   \+ 67

Which one(s) here will involve regrouping?

I discussed afterwards with Lucy whether such a reduction would have been beneficial and she felt that this was so. Alternatively, there was another option. She had a good grasp, it seemed, of the children's current capabilities. There might have been the option to let those who were secure enough at the original task to progress, whilst an identified group went through the task linked to tens and ones. This could have been made even more explicit by modelling and discussing the strategies with Dienes blocks on the whiteboard if necessary.

Where is the depth here? Well, the metacognition relating to the stems mentioned provides depth:

'I will need to regroup when the total in a group reaches ten.'

Lucy was good enough to allow me to make an intervention when the children had articulated this stem. I asked them whether they could see a problem where they would need to regroup but the total in the column hadn't yet reached ten.

Let us look at an example mentioned previously:

	Th	H	T	O
	7	2	3	5
+	5	6	6	5
1	2,	9	0	0
		1	1	1

We can see that the tens column currently totals nine but will become ten once the regrouping from the 'ones' column has taken place.

At this point there was a buzz around the room as children began to ponder and theorise about this. This too relates to depth. The later articulation in the lesson of when and why this happens is evidence of depth of understanding. An example of a stem sentence that could be used here is: 'You can regroup when the digits total nine (or even eight) if the previous column has also regrouped'.

In addition to this, children could be invited to create their own problems involving no regrouping, regrouping in one column only, regrouping in two or more columns and regrouping involving columns that initially totalled only nine. It is, of course, possible to regroup when the total in a column initially is less than nine if we are adding several numbers.

	H	T	O
	1	7	3
+	2	9	4
+	5	5	2

This would require a new stem sentence, for example: 'Regrouping can occur when a column initially totals eight or less but would require summing more than just two numbers'. This is now ringing bells as mastery-style teaching and learning. Lucy is a capable and receptive teacher. She had the confidence and mindset to welcome me into her lesson, to teach in front of my curious eye and the willingness to adapt her teaching mid-lesson. She could both question and listen to adjust and move her practice further. Partly, this links to trust. In most schools, trust exists amongst staff even if it doesn't always exist fully regarding relationships with senior managers. The answer lies within. We can and should support each other's development through shared experiences and discussion. Here, I believe, Lucy and I both made connections and moved our practice forward.

WHY MASTERY IN THE UK?

This is a key point for me. We cannot implement mastery teaching fully yet, as valued by East Asian countries. We are not yet ready to do so. However, we could begin to follow the road that might ultimately allow us to get to that point. Currently there are some big differences between the way our maths teaching works, the context in which it exists and the people delivering it. These differences include:

- Teaching background of teachers: In Shanghai, virtually all teachers teaching maths at primary level have a Masters in maths teaching. That means they are experienced in research into maths content and issues within maths at quite a significant level. They will have carried out research within primary maths and be part of quite extensive teaching and learning communities. This will also include a lot of time spent in lesson study. Within this structure, the teachers take turns to teach lessons that are open to the public, well attended and discussed by a range of people. There is much discussion about rationale for decisions and choices within the lesson taught and seen.
- Teachers in mastery schools in Shanghai teach three 35 minute lessons a day in the main. They have time to prepare subsequent lessons. They may carry out intervention groups where children are not secure in the areas that were covered during the day.
- The vast majority of parents are well informed about maths. They seek and receive detailed feedback about their children's progress. Any difficulties the child may be having are discussed almost immediately. Maths has a very high profile in the family and in society, not just for a few people.
- Maths is therefore often taught by teachers for whom that is their most confident and competent area of understanding and who have trained at length to reach that point.
- Additional interventions take place to ensure children are in a position to access whole class teaching on a daily basis. A significant contribution to this access comes through early and extensive intervention in a child's school life so that heavily differentiated or set maths teaching is neither sought nor needed. Most Chinese children feel that they will study and understand maths to a significant level and it will play quite a big part in their lives.

In addition to this, there is a repeating structure where there will always be a significant number of teachers willing and able to take both their subject and teaching knowledge to a deep level alongside their understanding of child development.

In the UK, all of those features exist but to a much smaller degree. The area where I feel that we are well-equipped is in the general pedagogy of teaching. We have many teachers who are smart at teaching a range of subjects to a good enough standard; some of them very well. The three teachers focused on here are no exception. They are all excellent primary practitioners; maths was not necessarily the reason that they trained to teach.

CASE STUDY 2: IONA MUMBY, CLAPHAM MANOR PRIMARY SCHOOL

Iona is newly installed as the Assistant Head at the school. She teaches for a sizeable part of the week still and co-plans with her year partner in Year 6.

Iona articulates that the range of understanding and the confidence levels within the class are extremely diverse. Confident articulation with key knowledge at the fingertips is contrasted with difficulty in seeing and making connections. Furthermore, reasoning that is forthcoming is not always accompanied by fluency regarding key knowledge. This places a heavy cognitive load on the children grappling with a Year 6 curriculum. So how does Iona view and tackle this situation?

She and her year partner will meet to discuss issues that have come to their attention regarding fluency and understanding. This is a weekly stopping off point to debrief on last week's teaching and to highlight issues that have emerged for sections of the class that affected progress in some way: misconceptions and weaknesses. On one of the weeks I was there, the issue of inverse operations was under the spotlight.

A. $\_ + 12 = 20$

B. $35 + 3c = 62$

C. $52 - \_ = 51.09$

D. $\frac{1}{4} \times \_ = 16$

E. $8t + 2.8 = 10$

F. $\_ - 9.7 = 23$

G. $\_ \div 3 = 32$

H. $\_ + 5.5 = 15$

In addition to this, children needed to tackle a problem.

RE-ARRANGING CALCULATION EQUATIONS TO SOLVE UNKNOWN PROBLEMS

Let us take a look at this example:

$$4n + 5 = 21$$

First we have to start by asking what does this sum mean? How should we represent it? Do we draw it (a pictorial representation)? We could also use a real life maths story to represent it in order to answer the example above. The class needed to solve this using multiple representations, if possible.

Iona and her year partner had identified these two features: using and understanding inverse operations as well as solving algebraic problems through knowledge of inverse operations.

QUESTION E - SCOTT

We will now have a look at question E:

$8t + 2.8 = 10$

Scott was struggling to apply inverse to represent it as $10 - 2.8 = 8t$. He was able to achieve this with prompting from Iona but then was unclear on what to do next. With another prompt (me), he could see what the calculation equation was actually saying.

Table 6.2 Representation of the calculation $10 - 2.8 = 8t$

10								
8t								2.8
t	t	t	t	t	t	t	t	2.8
7.2								2.8

We constructed this together with me scaffolding.

Scott had connected knowledge. He was supported by visual representations and this made his reasoning more coherent, more quickly. His tables knowledge was slow but he possessed this knowledge at least in emerging form. He tried to calculate 7.2 divided by 8 and eventually settled on 9 and was able to make the connection that 8×0.9 would equal 7.2.

Let us now look at another example:

Dani is going to buy beans (79p) and bread (75p). If she gives £2, how much change will she receive?

She added successfully but struggled with the concept of change. Again, the bar model could have supported this.

Table 6.3 Example of a bar model to solve the problem

Beans	Bread	?
79p	75p	?
Money given **£2.00 or 200p**		
Total cost of beans and Bread **154p**		Change

Children also had to interpret and solve the following questions. They were allowed to use resources that time had been spent inducting them into using, such as empty number lines, column addition and subtraction, including with decimals.

BASIC SKILLS: CALCULATING WITH WHOLE NUMBERS AND DECIMALS

HOT: Use inverse to check calculation.

Peer coaching/pupils as teachers.

1. 9 – 0.75
2. Subtract 0.3 from 7
3. What is taken away from 5 to leave 0.15?
4. 10 – 0.19
5. 11 – 5.45
6. Subtract 0.01 from 2
7. Take away 0.34 from 5
8. 7 take away 0.08
9. Subtract 0.202 from 9
10. What number needs to be added to 0.91 to make 5?

Confidence level 7+ peer coach someone with a lower confidence level than you.
   Use yesterday's learning to determine whether you coach/be coached.
   Use visual tools – counting strings, number lines and explanations – and record models, notes and examples in your book for future reference.
   Time limit: 15 minutes.

In this Year 6 class, these questions were right on the money. The field was spread out. Some children were confident, some had only emerging confidence and others were struggling.

PEER MENTORING

The peer mentoring that followed was an attempt for higher-attaining children to support lesser-attaining and less-confident children. The mentors ranged in confidence too. Iona, rightly it seems, articulated that a default for a number of children is to reach for formal methods that have only been partly understood rather than think whether other mental methods and maths instincts could provide support. Thus, there were some really enlightened attempts at scaffolding by some children (peer mentors) and yet the skill of teaching for understanding is not a straightforward one for adults – a valid task and revealing to the teacher of understanding and flawed thinking.

Calculations such as 9 – 0.75 proved problematic to some children. Iona wanted to assist them to become better at regulating when to use formal methods. She also wanted children to know that when formal methods are being used, children need to have strategies for using them appropriately and know when they haven't been successful. It would have supported children who became confused by which number was the subtrahend.

Let us look at two strategies used to make the calculation:

(9 – 3 = 6) (minuend – subtrahend = difference)

a. 0.75–

 9

b. 9.00 –

 0.75

Strategy 'a' is tried and is inaccurate. Strategy 'b' is correct but impractical with decomposition across two columns needed to commence with.

Familiarity with fractional equivalents could have supported explanations. It is noticeable what Iona is seeking to do to help children regulate between written (formal) and mental (informal) methods.

The calculation 9 – ¾ might have been easier and an empty number line might have provided support (Figure 6.2).

8_____ 8¼ _____ 8½ _____ 8¾ _____ ____ 9 _____

Figure 6.2 Empty number line to support the calculation

Similarly, subtracting 0.3 from 7 would require knowledge of place value as well as familiarity with the value of the first decimal place.

The attempt from one child to scaffold a link between 70 – 3 and 7 – 0.3 appears seriously impressive and relevant to learner and peer mentor in terms of cognitive development (Figure 6.3). I haven't seen too much of this kind of mathematical discussion among primary children until fairly recently.

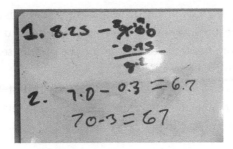

Figure 6.3 Attempt from one child to scaffold a link between 70 – 3 and 7 – 0.3

The link here with mastery is the concept outlined by Debbie Morgan (Director for Primary at NCETM). Discussing key points taken from Chinese maths teaching pedagogy she identifies the concept of letting the string of the kite unravel, to get it off the ground and in the air. Then the skill is to wind some of it back in to maintain control (Morgan, 2016).

So many issues emerge for these children from these tasks that the lesson becomes one of rich learning potential. Iona knows where the strengths and weaknesses of the children lie and what she is seeking to do. Here the string has certainly unravelled. The skill now would be to identify the ways to help gain control of the kite, to shore things up and to make learning explicit.

IONA'S CONTRIBUTION TO MASTERY

Iona manages many briefs within the school. She has a good broad understanding of what mastery could and should be. She has overcome the stigma of using concrete resources with a class who had not used them much for several years and this is having impact. What she shows clearly are two important features of mastery that are common to our Key Stage 2 classes. These are key issues that include:

1.   In many cases, our Key Stage 2 children have become quite spread out in terms of several features of their maths learning. This includes their fluency related to quick retrieval and recall of key information such as tables, number bonds and efficiency of mental calculations, and related knowledge linked to mental calculation. This also means that some children have quite secure knowledge while others don't.
2.   The weight of expectation of the Key Stage 2 SATs testing is still forcing really capable, committed teachers such as Iona to use the expected requirements of the end of year test to affect her day-to-day decision making with such a short space of time until they sit these tests.

She simply doesn't feel that there is time to go deeply into a range of themes in maths as a classic mastery approach would require. Her class management and organisational skills are of an extremely high quality. However, I know that this lesson alone threw up a number of features where learning could be moved forward and understanding developed more deeply through more explicit focus and more use of stem sentences. There could be more variation around structure to assist this.

Let us consider, for example, the question previously asked of 9 – 0.75.

Using an empty number line and then the column method several stems can emerge to guide and deepen understanding, including:

- 'Mixed numbers mean we have a whole amount and a part whole amount to deduct.'
- 'We must have our digits lined up in the right column so that we know their real value.'
- 'We can use addition to help us solve subtraction of decimals by bridging through the next whole number.' (So here we would start with Figure 6.4.)

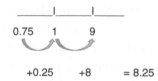

Figure 6.4 Using addition to solve subtraction of decimals

- 'We can use zeros to make sure each number has the same number of digits.' For example:

T	O	1/10	1/100
	9.	0	0
	0.	7	5

The question as to why we are able to use zeros to do this also requires careful scaffolding. It involves an awareness that zeroes as decimals at the end of the number have no value, e.g. 63.500. They merely indicate that there are no further part wholes. Elsewhere, the decimal acts as a placeholder emphasising the value of the other digits, e.g. 1203.05.

The whole process of understanding common fractions as decimals would have preceded this, for example:

- ¼ = 0.25
- ½ = 0.5
- ¾ = 0.75

The children would then become comfortable subtracting these amounts from one and then move on. Thus 9 – 0.75 would only appear several stages down the line. This is the long-term goal for Iona, in a couple of years' time.

IONA'S CASE STUDY: A SUMMARY

Iona indicates that elsewhere in the school, particularly Key Stage 1, a more standard mastery approach is taking place. There is time being devoted to a CPA approach, multiple representations, trying to allow key understanding to be agreed, clarified, said and retained by almost all children. Meanwhile, the race in upper Key Stage 2, for many schools, involves plugging the gaps in knowledge and understanding among cohorts for whom mastery-style teaching didn't begin in time. Iona seeks to bring a mastery flavour to a situation not of her making. Hopefully it will not be present in the same way in four or five years' time.

CASE STUDY 3: DAVID CUNNELLY, SHOREDITCH PRIMARY SCHOOL

David is the newly appointed maths lead in the school where we both attended a two-day workshop on mastery teaching. David and I were both keen to explore its place in the context of other principles we had held previously about what maths teaching should be.

I was already beginning to buy into the principle of learning being made very explicit, so long as this did not mean simply telling children what they needed to learn and remember. Explicit learning, for me, needed to come out of experiences and activities that the children participated in and made sense of.

David was looking for a manageable way in to staff dipping their toes into the mastery approach to learning and teaching. He settled on a Friday experience that all staff participated in where there was a mastery-style approach that related to investigational problem solving. In a school with quite high levels of deprivation and income support, David was fiercely aspirational for all children within his class. I observed two investigations, both of which we were able to unpick afterwards and have helped me construct an understanding of why whole class teaching has to work. I also feel I am clearer on where the issues that we have always valued highly fit in. This list includes challenge for all children, accessibility for all children, a belief in more secure children having a positive impact on those around them (Vygotskian, social constructivist style).

This particular problem solving lesson, I feel, helps us to evaluate the key issue about providing both depth of understanding for some as well as essential learning for all. I was indeed curious about this. Problem solving does appear among writings related to mastery (Yeap Ban Har, 2011; Posamentier and Krulik, 2015). However, the tightness of structure implicit in most training courses on mastery made me wonder how this would unfold.

REASONING

David's starter activity helped children to consolidate the link between minutes and hours from different perspectives, e.g. how many minutes in five hours? How many hours in 420 minutes? The explanations were valued even more highly than the answer, with reasoning being the important focus. This was linked to the main problem which also had a time focus.

Let us have a look at this problem:

Mr Scott's watch is broken. Mr Cunnelly's watch is also broken.

Mr Cunnellly's watch loses two minutes every hour. Mr Scott's watch gains one minute every hour.

They both set their watches from the radio at 6 am and then start their journeys to school. When they arrive at school at exactly the same moment their watches are ten minutes apart in time.

What was the real time at this point when they arrived?

What system can you use to solve this problem? What other differences and real times can you work out?

Reasoning stems:

- This is different because ...
- This is true because ...
- I already know that ... so ...
- It can't be because ...
- If ... then ...
- This is the same because ...
- I estimated that ...

The above problem was discussed, with children being asked to identify key information and redundant information. Redundant information to the mathematical problem included the names of the teachers. Quite a lot of the other information was relevant, such as the start time, the amount of time gained or lost and how far apart on arrival.

The children have a bit of time to think. David then guides them to a key scaffold, namely what the difference will be after an hour (Figure 6.5).

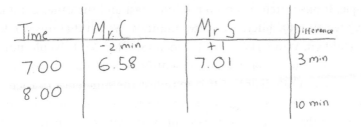

1. What is the rule?
2. What time is it on Mr Connelly's watch?
3. What time on Mr Scotts?
4. What system can you use to work them out?

Figure 6.5 Example of a scaffold to help solve the problem

As you can see, this scaffold helped to capture the problem. We could debate the issue of how much of a scaffold the children should initially have. Many, in fairness, had worked out that there was a difference of three minutes. Some knew immediately this was per hour and others realised this with the little prompt shown in Figure 6.5. Others beyond this were just able to accept this fact.

Many children began to work on this table, identifying that the difference got three minutes bigger every hour, similar to Table 6.4.

Table 6.4 Using a table to solve the problem

Time (o'clock)	Mr C	Mr S	Difference (minutes)
6	Correct time	Correct Time	0
7	− 2	1	3
8	− 4	2	6
9	− 6	3	9
10	− 8	4	12

So far, so good. The issue regarding the fact that there was a difference of ten minutes rather than nine was a stumbling block for a number of children, maybe three quarters of the class.

This may seem a small point, but here it was significant. When we chatted afterwards, I suggested to David that had the difference in the two clocks been different, then the actual mental calculation and connection needed to complete the problem may not have alienated some of the children to the extent that it did; something of a link once more with explicit learning and cognitive load.

For example, if one watch had been a minute fast and the other a minute slow, each hour would have meant a difference of two minutes. We felt that this would greatly have assisted the children. Why? The cognitive load (Sweller, 2011) would not have been so great. Thirds of an hour are far harder to identify and calculate than halves. Each hour would have created a difference of two minutes; the difference of each minute being reached every half hour. Even a gain and loss of two minutes per hour on the watches would have meant that a difference of a minute was achieved every quarter hour. The link between halves and quarters is more natural than the pathways involving thirds for most primary children, currently.

Although he happily contributed to our critiquing of the lesson, there was also some sadness for David. His aspiration that most children of differing attainment levels could access the main, intended learning did not come to fruition. He concluded that the children who stayed the distance and prospered were all higher-attaining children.

We both agreed that his clear early scaffolds allowed all children to access the problem in its early stages. Thereafter some children seemed to become disconnected as the challenge to keep control of the problem became greater.

David is not alone with this perception. Although I feel clearer about what mastery can achieve, I feel a sense of loss too. One of the strengths in the UK has often been the belief that all children can succeed if we genuinely communicate the idea that we have high aspirations for all.

What is starting to come through is the realisation that children are communicating something to us. Namely that unless the confidence level is there and knowledge is understood securely, then application of knowledge and depth of understanding will not be secure. Thus learning has to, in the main, be structured and understanding secure. The key learning about the changing difference and what it represented would, in all probability, have been easier to absorb with numbers that required less manipulation, that were cognitively less demanding. Rowland et al. (2009) identify precision examples to support explicit learning as a key feature of their knowledge quartet. This includes the following stem sentences:

- 'In every *hour* that passes the difference between the time on the two watches will *increase* by *three minutes*.'
- 'If the difference between the two watches is a multiple of three minutes this *means that an exact hour will have passed*.'
- 'If the difference between the two watches increased by only two minutes per hour this would mean each watch *was only one minute out (or one watch was two minutes different and the other stayed the same)*.'
- 'Because the two watches differ by three minutes as every hour passes this means that they differ by one minute when *a third of an hour passes (20 minutes)*.'

Clearly, the numbers would change if the adaptations were made to the difference but the concept would be the same. Indeed, David and I concluded, the gain and loss of only a minute on each watch might have created a more manageable initial problem that could have allowed less-confident children to become more secure. Children who had shown secure understanding on the original problem could then branch out to the problem that was given to secure greater depth of understanding.

SCAFFOLDS USED

Table 6.4 acts as a strong scaffold. Throughout the lesson, many children used this to try to solve the problem. Some were successful, others did not quite secure the solution but did understand what they were trying to achieve. A second visual scaffold was used (Figure 6.6).

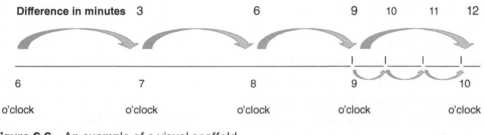

| Difference in minutes | 3 | | 6 | | 9 | 10 | 11 | 12 |

| 6 | 7 | 8 | 9 | 10 |
| o'clock | o'clock | o'clock | o'clock | o'clock |

Figure 6.6 An example of a visual scaffold

DIFFERENCE

From Figure 6.6 we can see that between 9 o'clock and 10 o'clock, the two watches have a difference of ten minutes at a point a third of the way between the two hours. Here, I believe, lies a root barrier to the focus being on establishing a solution.

Two things are becoming clear to me. One is that visual scaffolds and prompts are key to the mastery approach; they are the basis for both discussion and understanding. They are worthy of discussion as David and I did both before and after the lesson. We will all become more knowledgeable and confident in how we plan and execute ideas that help make understanding explicit and allow for depth of understanding, at least in some children. I believe this requires teachers to become comfortable with putting ideas and lessons out there for others to sit in on and join in with a community of learners, a community of practice (Lave and Wenger, 1998). It is a process of making what we achieve more robust. There are many reasons why some teachers would be reluctant to do this initially but there are signs already that these barriers can and are being broken.

POSSIBLE OPTIONS FOR STRUCTURING THE CLASS

In discussing the lesson over lunch afterwards, David and I felt some amendments might have allowed more children to have more accessibility to learning more of the time, although we might not fully know the extent to how being stuck can be a profitable solution. Some children emerged positively from being stuck; others, I feel, less so.

Things could have been different in this lesson. The task used in the lesson was a rich one as it *was* based around commonly experienced situations for Year 6 children, including teachers who they know, clocks or watches gaining or losing time, and a known experience of travelling to school.

However, whole class and mixed attainment exposure could have been used to solve the problem. With hindsight this was likely to have more impact across a range of children with the modified task about the gain and loss of the two watches each being one or two minutes. The numbers generated from the hourly difference would have been much easier to manipulate. Thus when it came to the point of discussing the problem, although some children (6 out of 28) would have been able to achieve the answer quite easily, the opportunity to analyse the structure through the stem sentences might well have secured their understanding of it enough for them to branch out on related but more challenging problems. This might have included a version of the one that they did. Supported by the two scaffolds explored, they could have applied these to similar problems with variations relating to the start time, arrival time, whether it was an o'clock start, as well as variations involving the two watches – for example, both watches gaining but by different amounts, both watches losing but by different amounts. Also, the differences would be varied to provide deeper understanding of transferring the difference in minutes on the two watches to the amount of time that had elapsed. Meanwhile, crucially, other children less secure in their understanding might stay with David for a while. This could be useful for several reasons, including:

- They could repeat a similar problem with a different starting time.
- They could have the same starting time, the same time difference on arrival but vary one or both of the gain or losses on the watch.
- They would or could have more time to apply the stem sentences.
- The shared task could be modelled and made explicit using the two scaffolds discussed: the table and the number line.
- Once they had completed another problem together they might try a third, similar one, independently.

At this point David would be keen to access the work of the rest of the children in the class. At some point a plenary would ensue reinforcing the key learning points common to the problems that had been experienced with appropriate variations. Some children would make connections very rapidly with the re-teaching. In some cases they might wish to join in with the independent group at this point.

IS THIS A MASTERY APPROACH?

It is very much so. The main teaching is explicit; linked knowledge is secured across the class or close to being so. Some children have been able to secure depth of understanding through controlled variations; this can be through consolidation and by experiencing problems that are related but are not the same.

A decision can be taken as to whether or not children who still remain unsure about key learning require further support at some point in the next 24 hours before the lesson theme is continued.

This lesson style also highlights the issue of ensuring the attainment gap does not widen too much among children with regard to achieving an understanding of the main learning. It is the depth and variation that will allow children who understand more quickly to take learning further.

We have to rethink and then internalise the key message. By letting go of the idea that differentiation by outcome can provide value added for all, we can focus more on making intended learning explicit. This needs to be achieved for all children to avoid the gap between strongest and least secure from widening further.

CONCLUSION

The notion of developing 'mastery in the UK' of some sort is, to my mind, essential. It is simply not possible to take an approach from another education system that is dependent on a quite specific pedagogy and impose it in its entirety on children whose experiences have been extremely different. It will take time. Thus many schools are seeking a more thorough mastery approach with younger classes and an adapted one with older ones, particularly those currently in Upper Key Stage 2. The strategies of concrete, pictorial and abstract may vary in implementation with older children. It should be less the case with younger ones and they will be happy to continue this process as they get older.

My discussions with these teachers allow my current position to be, in my opinion, that 'less is more'. It is vital to have more depth with less content around a very explicit approach to emphasising key learning. It is within this structure that understanding can be deepened through different ways of letting the kite out.

The explicitness of such learning has not always figured on our radar as much as maybe it should. One reason may be that many of us have held on to the idea that great things happen when we believe in all children as well as the notion of all children learning together. Quite so; however, we may need a little more tightness, more explicit learning and revisiting, if sound learning for all is to become a reality with deeper learning opportunities available around this.

CHAPTER 7:

TEACHING FOR MASTERY

What you will learn from this chapter:

- Further insight into small-step progression
- Clarity regarding how a mastery approach seeks to ensure that learning is made explicit
- Understanding of how multiple experiences around a given theme deepen understanding
- Awareness of how skilled teaching utilises questioning to ensure most children secure a basic understanding of the key concept within the lesson
- Appreciation that within a whole class approach some children are able to develop and show deeper understanding of what is being taught
- Evidence about how the four (or five) main features of mastery teaching are developed by skilful teachers and should, in time, be developed by us all

This chapter explores how experienced teachers in the United Kingdom go about their craft. Like any community of learners they all identify that it is an ongoing journey and they seek to learn themselves as well as allow others the chance to learn from them.

CASE STUDY 1: LESSON PLANNING WITH CONOR LOUGHNEY

Conor is just completing his training for mastery through the London Central and North West Maths Hub, having been to Shanghai in September 2017. He works with maths leads in six schools, guiding them to focus on and develop mastery techniques and practices within their schools. He has modelled lessons in Key Stage 1 and Key Stage 2 for them this year. He has attended NCETM sessions to write spines to support teacher planning that now appear on their website. By the end of the school year 2017–18, Conor will have completed his training and he will also have led a Teacher Research Group, working with other maths leads from the locality. Within this, he models lessons that are discussed, and has monthly meetings to discuss resources and ideas being used within the other schools.

PLANNING FOR AN INITIAL YEAR 2 LESSON ON DIVISION

Conor and I meet in his office a few days before I will observe him and we discuss the merits of division by grouping and/or sharing. Conor has already taught multiplication through groups, arrays, Numicon and repeated addition. Children are familiar with two, five and ten times tables. We both reason that this should be used to underpin the division work. 'There will be less cognitive load. It would be a wasted opportunity not to link it back to five times and ten times tables' concludes Conor. (In addition to Sweller's work, it is worth looking online at the references made to cognitive load by Dylan Wiliam, 2015.)

LESSON ON DIVISION

The idea of unequal groups goes alongside thoughts linked to bar models, arrays and matching of people to groups. Good planning can, and sometimes should, involve thinking through ideas and refining them. Conor thinks through division as equal-sized groups and draws some diagrams to show his thinking (see Figure 7.1). This includes allocating parts of arrays to different people.

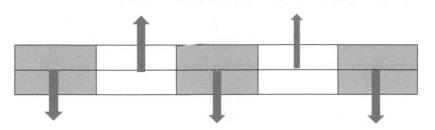

Figure 7.1   Showing some of Conor's early ideas thinking through work on arrays alongside the idea of division.

Some of the progression of planning ideas include:

- Division is when the whole is divided into equal-sized parts (whatever size the whole is).
- Proper fractions are part of a single whole.
- Division involves making equal-sized groups.

CONTEXTUALISING THE WORK

Conor ponders for a long time on how he can contextualise the work. He looks at two NCETM short teaching videos to help him focus. He has to work with the children to understand what division is by ensuring they know what it isn't. When he is happy, he will start with a section about distinguishing between equal and unequal groups. Why? He needs the learning to be specific. He has to ensure work spent discussing equal-sized groups is not going to fall on fallow ground. Children need to know what are not-equal-sized groups as well as what are. This makes a lot of sense.

He had been hesitant about focusing on grouping rather than sharing between as a model for division. For example 20 ÷ 5 is to be seen as 20 divided into groups of five (Figure 7.2) rather than among five (people) (Figure 7.3).

Figure 7.2 An array representing 20 ÷ 5 (divided into groups of five)

Figure 7.3 An array representing 20 ÷ 5 (divided among five)

We reach the conclusion that the NCETM video about grouping is useful but we are not sure the learning is made explicit enough for our purposes.

DELIBERATE MISTAKES TO DEVELOP UNDERSTANDING

The idea of clarifying 'what something is not', is often used by teachers to establish understanding and evaluate whether it has taken place. With younger children, teachers may use a puppet to make mistakes that the children need to look out for – the silly puppet who makes mistakes. Children are engaged by the puppet and the teacher can evaluate understanding by who is able to correct it (Thompson, 2008).

Conor is keen to develop knowledge of 'equal-sized groups' by building on the work he has done with the class on multiplication.

Figure 7.4 Array of three groups of five

Figure 7.4 shows three groups of five. It is also 15 shared into groups of five. The array can be seen in different ways but that is the link Conor is seeking to develop. He works on the plans along the lines that we discuss, including (see also Chapter 5 on small-step progression):

- Division as represented through equal-sized groups.
- Building on multiplication groups.

- Using known awareness of the five times table to reduce cognitive load. This allows the process of understanding division as equal-sized groups to be the sole focus.
- Starting with unequal-sized groups and distinguishing between the two.
- Emphasis on vocabulary with carefully thought priorities.
- The dividend will be referred to as the whole (amount). Later it will be called the dividend. It also allows for use with bar modelling at some point, which this class have already been introduced to. The divisor will be discussed as the 'equal-sized groups' and the quotient will be the number of equal-sized groups, sometimes called the answer.
- The division sign will be used but not overemphasised. Conor anticipates some children being familiar with it (which later proves to be correct).

Conor's taught lesson includes small-step progression within the tight framework outlined. The aim of both is to make intended learning explicit, an absolute necessity for a mastery approach. The basic learning needs to be explicit because it is only when the identified learning has been grasped that the deeper understanding can be developed.

DO ALL CHILDREN DEVELOP EXPLICIT UNDERSTANDING AT THE SAME TIME?

Obviously not and we need to confront the issue. The class needs to stay connected. Therefore, as some children are secure in new knowledge and are guided towards depth of understanding, more time is needed to allow all children to secure the original, explicit learning.

Conor uses a number stick with multiples of five, out of sequence, to commence the lesson. Children identified that it was indeed the five times table jumbled, and together they repaired it. He asked them how they knew it was the five times table and what patterns they saw, their reply indicating the numbers went up by five each time and that the last digits were five then zero each time. Most children understood, others at least heard the explanation and thought about it.

This activity developed fluency and recall as well as laying the foundation for the forthcoming link with division involving groups of five. They were then asked to identify which pictures represented equal- and unequal-sized groups (see Figure 7.5).

This carefully constructed activity involves five pictures, each of which has been chosen for a reason to clarify one of the key steps involving understanding equal-sized groups. The carrots have clearly equal-sized groups of two, the eggs likewise in groups of four. The sausages allow the stem sentence of unequal amounts to be clarified, spoken and heard. The Numicon pieces draw out the discussion about equal amounts though not repeated pieces; the one and two still total three.

Conor's *dong nao jin* (see Chapter 3 for an explanation of this term) involved the large carrot and allowed another discussion. There is an equal amount of carrots in each group even though the carrots' sizes are not the same, with one being larger than the rest.

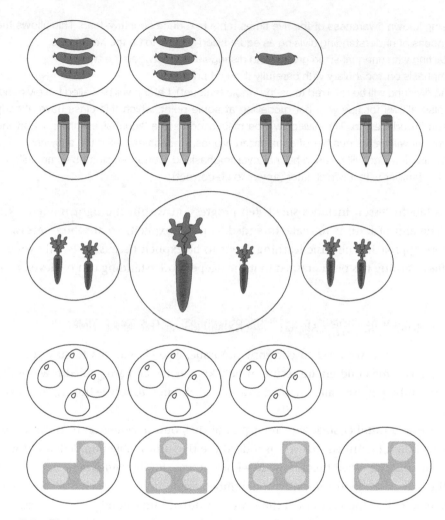

Figure 7.5 Pictures representing equal- and unequal-sized groups

Thus, it is agreed that this could go in either section depending on how the question is interpreted. These are rich discussions within a focused atmosphere. All children wrestled with the issues. The children are interested, they have repeated stem sentences appropriately to each other. Overall, Conor is happy that all children are grasping 'equal-sized groups' and are ready to apply this in a new context. Children were shown a group of 20 pencils and asked to use counters to represent the top ends of the pencils and to arrange them in equal-sized groups. They then grouped carrots into groups of five. Finally, they were asked by the character in the text to match five children to a car from a visual showing 30 children. The focus on five remaining as the divisor is a key issue here. Variation comes in the resources: carrots, pencils and children in cars. It also comes through in the resources being used: counters and Numicon that are representing these objects. It will be a professional decision as to when the divisor will change and how the discussion will go. This is mastery; small-step, specific variation to deepen understanding with multiple representations.

REPRESENTATIONS

Interestingly, within both the grouping-in-five tasks, the children frequently used Numicon-shaped groupings of five; this shows transferable learning and should be applauded. A possible drawback would be if they only saw the grouping of five in this way. It highlights the value of multiple representations of the same idea, a mastery requirement.

Using the division sign and the interpretations described earlier, children record calculations such as $15 \div 5 = 3$ to mean fifteen divided into groups of five means that there are three of them.

For those of you questioning the emphasis on seeing division as creating equal-sized groups as opposed to sharing between people, I would say the following: there is a place for both interpretations of division. The equal-sized groups concept underpins deeper understanding of division and part wholes including division by fractions. The calculation $2 \div \frac{1}{4}$ has little meaning as a 'shared between' algorithm. Two shared among a quarter of a person is a struggle to conceptualise. Two shared into equal-sized groups of a quarter is much more easily understood. There are four quarters to each whole and therefore the answer is eight.

The questions are again carefully graded, moving from words into symbols. The children working on question 6 in Figure 7.6 have begun to deduce the whole (dividend), the equal-sized group of five (divisor) and the number of equal groups (quotient). Finally, they are encouraged to apply the knowledge they have been securing by making their own array illustrating a division calculation. This active use of secured knowledge certainly provides depth and further development. It also allows time for Conor to secure understanding in some children who have only partly secured their understanding of the original problem.

The task here is followed by a game involving Figure 7.7. Two teams had to identify whether the left hand or right hand representation correctly showed the division calculation referenced. The variations in group size allow the original point to be emphasised. They make children look closely. A child in the first team (right hand side representations) or the second team (left hand side representations) has to say whether their side is correct or not and why. Discussion showed a high level of understanding and engagement. The articulation of the reasoning is the key part of a mastery approach emphasising explicit focus and reasoning. In point of fact the final line of Figure 7.7 shows two incorrect representations. The discussion with the children clarified this point.

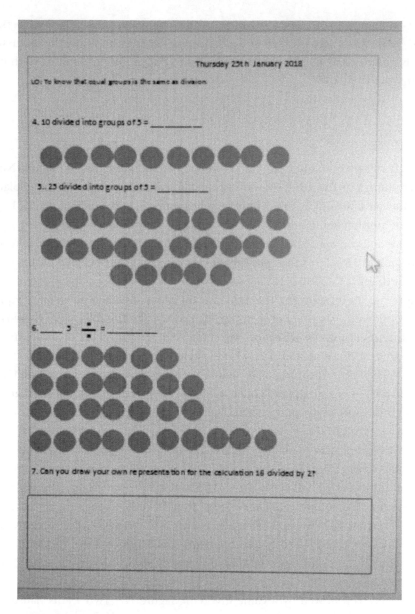

Figure 7.6 Division exercises

Afterwards, Conor discusses ways to move on. These will focus again on groups of five to start with to allow variation to the structure within a known number focus. There will be time to allow variations in group size. For now, the variation will focus on using arrays to write equations. As the lesson progresses, attention can switch to groups of two. This will be a key point that some children will be more than ready to tackle and some will

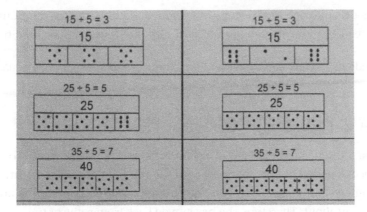

Figure 7.7 Game involving division exercises

need scaffolding and a little time. This will allow some children to apply knowledge in more depth as more basic understanding is achieved for all. The scheme work will draw in links with bar modelling.

Conor could ponder several ways forward, working with the four key features of mastery emphasised by the NCETM: fluency, variation, multiple representations and reasoning. Grouping with Numicon or Cuisenaire would work well here.

Let us look at the calculation 12 ÷ 3. This could be created as shown in Figure 7.8.

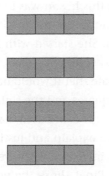

Figure 7.8 Representation of 12 ÷ 3

From the example above, we see the answer to the calculation would be four when we share 12 into groups of three.

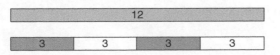

Figure 7.9 Bar model of 12 ÷ 3

The bar model approach here (Figure 7.9) would allow children to count out how many groups of three 12 can be divided into. A stem sentence that could be used here is:

- 'I can divide 12 into four equal groups of three because four lots of three equal 12.'

CASE STUDY 2: PINAL SHETH, ELMHURST PRIMARY SCHOOL

Pinal is a Year 5 teacher and maths lead at Elmhurst, where she has been working for five years. She spent a period of time involved with the work of the maths hub attached to the school. Her interest and passion is with the children. Maths is one of the areas that she feels passionately about. Therefore, she has moved back from some of the work in the hub to concentrate on leading maths in the school and class teaching.

Naturally, with training regularly on hand in the extended part of the school, she has acquainted herself with many of the ideas of the Shanghai and Singapore teaching methods. Chinese teachers have been based at the school for periods of time; she is comfortable in terms of what she is trying to do with the children in their learning. She is also comfortable about being observed, discussing issues related to maths teaching pedagogy and mastery principles. Thus both the observation of her teaching and the discussion with her provide instructive information about what we are aspiring to do in classrooms in the UK with maths mastery.

Her broad learning intention in this lesson was to deepen children's understanding of a half. This was to include understanding a square with regard to its properties, including sides, angles, orientation and area. She started with a question: 'If I have an area of 16 squares in my square what will it look like?'.

Children were cued in to articulate that it would have four sides with the same length, the area would be 16 same-sized squares and the square root would be four, the number multiplied by itself to make 16. This reason-based dialogue is common in her classroom. Children are used to being asked to explain and justify what they say as best as they are able to. The expectation for them increases as the year progresses and should be a continuation from the previous year. Pinal chose the visual theme of squares to make the concept easily accessible at the start of the lesson.

Square numbers are discussed in addition to the number 16 already mentioned. Pinal re-clarifies what a square number is and children reach the conclusion that 9×9 is 81. Pinal illustrates this as repeating rows of nine showing where 9×9 comes and extending to 12×9 (Figure 7.10).

Pinal looks at two multiplications:

- $6 \times 9 = 54$
- $12 \times 9 = 108$

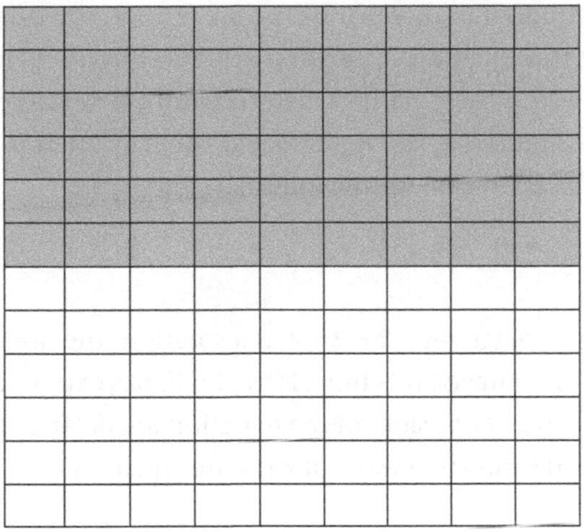

Figure 7.10   Illustration of 12 × 9

She asks the children to think about how the two facts are connected. The children notice that 54 is half of 108 and Pinal guides them to the idea that six rows of nine are half of 12 rows of nine.

Pinal and I have both spent time developing a range of ways to explore maths themes with children.

Afterwards, I ask her whether she would ever consider posing a problem, such as:

> If I want to halve the area of a square or rectangle (or any other two-dimensional shape) why do I only need to halve one measurement; why not both?

(Many trainee teachers, not having received mastery teaching or teaching based on reasoning are unclear that when the dimensions of a flat shape are doubled the area is in fact four times bigger (2^2).)

She agrees that this could have been a rich area. She had others to pursue, though, and this is the point where there are often many options or choices to pursue. There are so many interconnections; we will build up knowledge as we teach even if we are not initially familiar with them.

She explores the following questions:

- 9 × __ = 18
- __ × 9 = 36
- 108 = __ × 9
- 6 × 3 = __ × 9

The vast majority of children in this Year 5 class are engaged by this dialogue captured by the phrase 'balancing the equation'. They have used real balances in previous classes and earlier this year to develop these pathways for learning and understanding. The deeper understanding of = as signifying balance or 'equal value' is often understated.

Children are then asked to balance the following equation:

$4 \times \_ = 2 \times \_$

Although some children suggest $4 \times 2 = 2 \times 4$ as a solution, the use of inverse laws, which the children know, is discouraged this time. Here, Pinal has explored the idea of 'half' in a looser but connected sense. Both sides of the equation are balanced, they are equal. They are not formed in exactly the same way but they are equal, as two halves are equal. They have the same value.

Her next question asks the children to compare these two multiplication facts:

8×7 and 6×9.

Do they balance? No they don't, but it is a common error for children to use additive rather than multiplicative reasoning to deduce, falsely, that as nine is one more than eight and six is one less than seven that they might balance out. Not so. Later Pinal concedes that so many rich starting points to explore further need to be managed in a finite way. Thus she returns to her original theme of the 4×4 grid. Children draw two of these.

Figure 7.11 A vertical 4 × 4 grid

Figure 7.12 A horizontal 4 × 4 grid

They are asked to shade in half of each grid. Initially, there are only two variations within the room, shown in Figures 7.11 and 7.12. Pinal wants to explore this in much more detail. She makes a pedagogic decision to raise the bar. Until now children had only really focused on a block, on two congruent shapes with a different orientation. She engages the children in a discussion about how many small squares have been shaded in each square, deducing that it is eight out of 16.

'It is a half because the numerator is half of the denominator.' In other words, half of the squares have been shaded. She models this as numerator, vinculum and denominator: $\frac{8}{16}$

She then draws two more grids of 4 × 4 and gradually completes them asking the children to count with her as she completes them (Figures 7.13 and 7.14).

'Are these half shaded?'

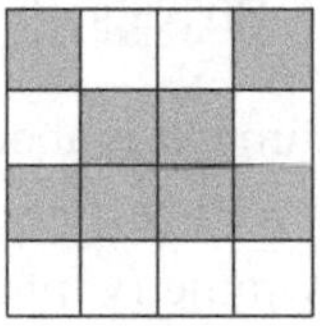

Figure 7.13   A shaded grid

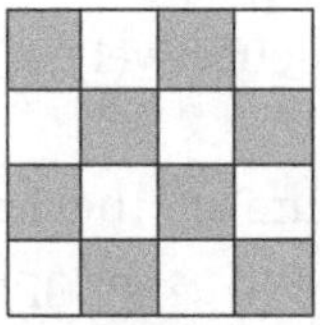

Figure 7.14   A further example of a shaded grid

Reluctantly, but then excitedly, the children cotton on. They accept that these are half shaded in, and return with more spirit to finding other ways to shade half. The differences in their second attempts are fascinating. Why do they create their original neat, tidy, block shadings for a half? Why have they become energised? Where could this move on to?

Pinal and I conclude, afterwards, that possibly neural pathways tend to be grown through exposure to ideas, visual and otherwise. Pinal also feels that the teacher's role, input and expectation are key. Here she had a clear expectation of what the children could achieve and was going to scaffold from whatever starting point they appeared to show to her.

Her second discussion not only started to grow pathways or reconnect children with previous ones. Given that there is a reason for most things, Pinal and I also feel limited exposure to shape and representations of, among other things, halves also contributes. Here, children came up with many new ways to represent halves.

Figure 7.13 is compared to a new design (Figure 7.15).

Figure 7.15 Another shaded grid

It is agreed that one is a rotation of the other.

TEACHING AND DISCUSSION POINT: THE POSSIBILITIES OF A MASTERY APPROACH

This is a key point about mastery teaching. It is about the art of the possible. Pinal agreed with me that if we use the analogy of 'letting the string out on the kite' then the idea of introducing rotational and reflective symmetry into a lesson about understanding halves in a more complete way was possibly a bridge too far. As Pinal pointed out, she was very much in charge, noticing the response and free to adjust as she saw fit. In fact, she chose to leave symmetry there for the moment and return to her original line of enquiry about different ways to represent what was effectively $\frac{8}{16}$, an equivalent fraction to $\frac{1}{2}$ in the context of a 4 × 4 square grid.

Why am I emphasising this feature of the lesson? Because is it fundamental to understanding what mastery is and this is an approach that allows a more complete understanding to emerge. Pinal makes her choices from a wide range of options; she has subject knowledge, pedagogic knowledge, knowledge of the necessary features of mastery and confidence. She makes her choices based on these options. Other teachers, including trainees, NQTs, fairly new teachers and less-confident ones use their pool of resources to shape their own teaching. We all aim to increase our options through experience, discussion, training and reflection.

IS THERE A RIGHT WAY TO TEACH MASTERY?

There are key features to effective teaching, as you will have worked out, such as developing fluency, multiple representations, variations in structure and concept, and making connections. Beyond this, it is the art of the possible. I believe it is why lesson study and publicly viewed lessons are so popular and important in China and Japan. It is an exchange of views among many people who, in the main, are doing a good enough job; it is an exploration of what might be possible and of alternative possibilities.

Many of our teachers are less experienced in maths teaching and knowledge than, for example, primary teachers in Shanghai. Nevertheless, they each have a pool of possibilities to choose from. The emergence of effective, mastery-based schemes adds to the pool of choices all teachers possess. However, the scheme should only be the starting point for teachers and not be seen as a job done. It has to be used as part of a growing understanding of what possibilities are there when planning mastery lessons. The active use of the scheme, including moments to break away from its content, are essential.

PINAL'S CHOICES

As the children's confidence grew, Pinal pushed more ideas their way. She had already scaffolded them to open up their thinking about what new variations there were on the original two they had come up with. Now she extends further, halving squares in different ways (Figure 7.16).

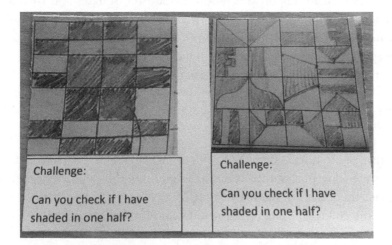

Figure 7.16 Different challenges used by Pinal

This is done diagonally and horizontally, and the children are energized by the possibilities.

'How many parts this size would it take to fill the whole grid?' she asks. 'What fraction of the whole would each part be?' is her parting shot as the lesson ends. Some children are there already, some are close and some are interested but not there yet. The lesson ends with energy and Pinal has plenty to evaluate about where to take the lesson next.

Pinal has many choices now. She dips into resource books, makes her own slides and resources, uses the school's chosen scheme, 'Maths – No Problem!' She uses all these possibilities to craft effective learning experiences. These are underpinned by National Curriculum guidelines but extended through her commitment to knowing what she knows in a way that facilitates, guides and ensures progress and the chance of deep understanding. It does not happen overnight but it can happen, eventually, to all of us.

Certainly, she will have noted the range of development within the lesson. Knowing a half as $\frac{8}{16}$ in a number of ways was the main goal for all children. The other connections and possibilities allow depth for a number of the class too.

CASE STUDY 3: CIARA SUTTON FITZPATRICK, WIMBLEDON PARK PRIMARY SCHOOL

Ciara is the maths lead at Wimbledon Park Primary School and is currently involved in mastery training. Wimbledon Park is a three-form entry school so the post includes a lot of responsibilities. Here Ciara teaches her Year 2 class a lesson related to understanding the significance of ten more, in our base ten. They have covered work linked to inverse operations of addition and subtraction.

The resources used to support this lesson include 100 squares and Dienes (Numicon would provide support, and later possibly bead string, number line and Cuisenaire, if it is marked in cm). I reference these to reinforce the idea of multiple representations to develop deeper understanding of specific intended learning.

The lesson starts with the following pairs of addition calculations:

- 30 + 4 and 30 + 40
- 2 + 50 and 20 + 50

Children are asked to discuss these and to clarify what is the same and what is different. This exposes the concept about the column determining the value of the digit and therefore the final sum of the two numbers.

Ciara asks the children to complete the following three short activities:

A. Add and subtract ten. Children use their 100 squares as a scaffold to count in tens, starting at zero. How much did I add each time?
B. They count backwards in tens (exposition of increase and decrease), focus on patterns involving the tens and ones. The following stem sentence is used by the children: 'The zero in the ones column stays the same'.
C. Using Dienes show me two and add a ten. Also, mark two on the 100 square with a cube.

The activities generate the following dialogue:

Martin: 'Every time we add ten it's one bigger in the tens'.
Ciara: 'The tens digit is increasing but the ones digit stays the same'.

This stem sentence is repeated throughout the lesson. Ciara then decides to take the concept further, by looking at the twos columns on the 100 square and getting the class to count together out loud, 2, 12, 22, 32, 42 all the way up to 92.

Ciara then asks, 'Martin, what comes next?'

Here Ciara uses her understanding that this will be on the edge of the comfort zone of some children and therefore a potentially rich area. Going across the 100 boundary will test their understanding. She throws it out there, noting the children who either answer or come close to understanding and moves on. This delving into depth of understanding will be returned to in a later lesson.

Now she gets the children to make 62 using Dienes blocks. Children take ten away each time in pairs, taking it in turns to say the new total. They say the following stem sentence:

- 'When I take a *ten* away the number of *ones* stays the same.'

In *Big Ideas in Primary Mathematics* (Newell, 2017) this idea is explored further, encouraging the partner to cover the Dienes as a ten is removed, growing the mental pathway in children's minds. The cover is then removed to confirm, in most cases, that they are correct.

POSSIBLE TEMPLATE FOR LESSON OUTLINE PLAN DISCUSSIONS

LO: resources, points to expose stem sentences, variation, re-teaching, consolidation, deeper understanding and assessment.

The children all take part in a game where Ciara chooses a starting number, for example 27, and gives them instructions: add ten, add ten, subtract ten, add ten, add ten, subtract ten. What number are you now on? This reinforces the two inverse concepts simultaneously, addition and subtraction. Not all children would always be ready for such variation but here it works very well.

Ciara exposes depth of understanding with her next key question, carefully timed:

If Kelly said she finished on 32 how would we know she was wrong?

The following discussion ends with a new stem sentence:

- 'We would know because the ones digit is not a seven.'

A similar journey follows when 83 is the starting point. The original stem is revisited related to it only being the tens digit that changes when a ten is added. The lesson continues with the following task to complete the number sequences:

- 2, 12, 22, 32, __, __, __
- 65, 55, 45, __, __, __
- __, __, __, 31, 41, 51, __, __, __

This is procedural variation in as much as the concept is the same but the ability to adapt the knowledge is required. In a different lesson there may be variation in these questions, they serve a different purpose – addition in tens, subtraction in tens, then both together where the given numbers of the sequence lie in the middle. Some teachers naturally struggle to create such small-step progressions in questioning. This is understandable, schemes are getting better at this skill.

This can be introduced to children by asking them to look at the numbers 43, 93, 36, 73, and consider, if you count on in tens from 23, which one won't you say?

Through the answer of 36, Ciara draws out whether children will be confused by there being a three in the incorrect answer (36). She reaches the conclusion that her class will benefit from this, while another teacher might assume this as being too early for the children to be tested in this way. Children struggle here and Ciara uses a scaffold to discuss this issue (Table 7.1).

Table 7.1 Scaffold to count in tens from 23

Tens	Ones
4	3
9	3
3	6
7	3

'The ones stay the same when we add ten.' This seems to do the trick. The time on this has been worth it. Possible ways in which depth of understanding can emerge include the following stem sentences:

- 'When we count on in tens the ones digit always stays the same.' (Does the tens digit always stay the same?)
- 'What numbers would cause more than one number to change, several numbers to change?' (This can apply to addition and subtraction.)

CASE STUDY 4: JACK CORSON, BYRON COURT PRIMARY SCHOOL – YEAR 6 CLASS

Jack has worked for the North East London hub, leading training sessions and developing a reputation for his work on bar modelling.

He uses the 24 card game in his class, which children have clearly played before a number of times, and they are motivated. To play this game, the children have to use the numbers on the cards to reach the total of 24 (Figure 7.17). For example, using a card with the numbers 7, 2, 6 and 2, the calculation would be $2 \times (7 + 6) - 2$.

Figure 7.17   24 card game

Children are nearly equivalent in this current skill. It is competitive, but in a way that is aimed at sharpening up their thinking and allowing information to be recalled and used with some haste. This assists the pursuit of *fluency*.

These children have spent quite a lot of time on bar model representations to explore part – part whole problems and relationships between fractional amounts. When do you need to shift the bar? And when do you need to cut the bar?

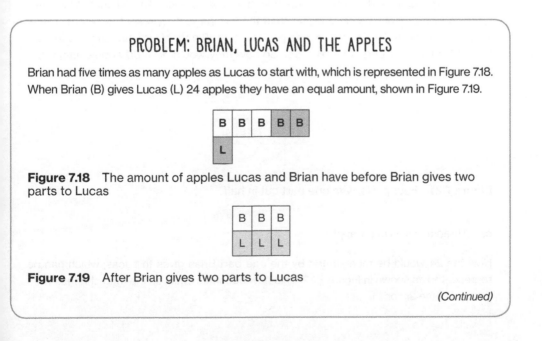

PROBLEM: BRIAN, LUCAS AND THE APPLES

Brian had five times as many apples as Lucas to start with, which is represented in Figure 7.18. When Brian (B) gives Lucas (L) 24 apples they have an equal amount, shown in Figure 7.19.

Figure 7.18   The amount of apples Lucas and Brian have before Brian gives two parts to Lucas

Figure 7.19   After Brian gives two parts to Lucas

(Continued)

(Continued)

a.   How many apples do they have altogether?

By giving Lucas 24 apples, Brian is giving two of his five parts so that they each have three parts. This means that if the two parts are worth 24, then one part is worth 12. Thus, originally, Brian had five lots of 12 (this makes 60) and Lucas had just 12. Thus the total is 72 (60 + 12).

What if Brian had:

b.   Four times as many apples as Lucas to start with?

To answer this question, a slightly different model is required, which is represented in Figure 7.20.

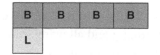

Figure 7.20   Model showing Brian had four times more apples

One of Brian's four parts has to be cut in half (see Figure 7.21). This means he now gives 1½ parts to Lucas and this leaves them with 2½ parts each. The 24 that Brian gave Lucas now represent 1½ parts rather than the two parts it represented before. These 1½ parts are worth 24. Therefore, one part is worth 16 and this is what Lucas originally had. Brian had four parts (4 × 16 = 64). So now they would have 80 apples altogether (16 + 64).

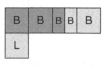

Figure 7.21   Four parts, with one part cut in half

c.   Three times as many apples?

Now the 24 would be represented by the one part Brian gives to Lucas, which can be represented as shown in Figure 7.22. This now becomes equal as the ratio changes from 3:1 to become 2:2 or 1:1.

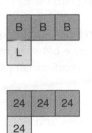

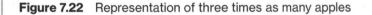

Figure 7.22 Representation of three times as many apples

d.   Twice as many apples?

If Brian had twice as many apples as Lucas, we could start by representing the amount as shown in Figure 7.23.

Figure 7.23 Brian has twice as many apples as Lucas

After we do this representation, we need to halve the part of the bar so that Brian and Lucas each have 1½ parts as shown in Figure 7.24.

Figure 7.24 Halving part of the bar

So now, having started with 48, Brian has given half a part to Lucas so that they each have 36. The original total now is 72. In short, the smaller the number of parts that the additional 24 represents, then the larger will be the combined total of the two original numbers for Brian and Lucas.

With this exercise, Jack is exploring two ideas:

- Redistributing the two amounts so that they are equal.
- Cutting the bar model if the difference between two bar models has an odd number of parts (effectively this means using a denominator that is twice as big).

Children tackle these four problems and then they are discussed. Jack does quite a lot of the modelling based on what he sees and what he wants to communicate. The first method used was shifting to make the amounts equal:

We can see that the amount that Brian gives to Lucas varies each time. When the difference between the two is an even number of parts, the transition is smooth. When the difference is an odd number of parts this creates different-sized part wholes which have to be understood, or changed. Possible stem sentences that are discussed and repeated include:

- 'All the bars must have equal-sized parts initially.'
- 'To make *two* differing amounts *equal* you must *halve* the *difference*.'

Jack looks to secure further understanding by asking: 'Can you have half a unit? Can you change the size of each unit?' The answer is yes. Bar modelling in this form works by making deductions based on, initially, equal-sized part wholes.

STRUGGLING, SECURING, SUCCEEDING, SOARING

Jack is looking to reach the securing stage with all children and going beyond this with as many as possible. The following discussion is about unit parts or part units.

- The visual act of equalling the amounts secures the understanding about half the difference.

Let us look at two problems that were used to discuss unit parts.

1. Hannah and David each have some money. The ratio of Hannah's money to David's is 7:4. If Hannah gives David £4.80 they will each have the same. How much did Hannah have to start with? What if the ratio were 5:4 and not 7:4, what would the answer to the question be then?
2. Ming had three times as many mandarin oranges as Nina. The ratio of Nina's oranges to Pedro's oranges was 2:3. After Ming gave a total of 28 oranges to Pedro and Nina, all three of them had exactly the same number of mandarin oranges. How many of these oranges did Pedro receive from Ming?

Let us now explain the answer to the first question involving Hannah and David:

Figure 7.25 Bar model for Question 1

Figure 7.25 demonstrates the 7:4 ratio between Hannah and David. The difference between Hannah and David is three units. If they are to have an equal amount these three units need to be split equally, so that Hannah keeps 1½ units and David gains 1½ units. We know that 1½ whole units or three half units make £4.80. Therefore a half unit is worth £1.60 and a whole unit is worth £3.20. This means that Hannah has £22.40 (which we can calculate through the multiplication sum: 7 × £3.20).

However, if the ratio were 5:4, then half a bar would be £4.80. A whole bar would be worth £9.60 and Hannah would have started off with £48 (5 × £9.60).

Jack then asks the children:

- We have found that 1½ bars are worth £4.80. How are we going to use this information?
- If we halve one bar, will we have to halve all the bars? Or will we need to remember to change when we identify the value of the whole bars?

To answer these questions, the visual representation is important. These children have been developing strongly for several months and they use the visual cue to understand Jack's questions. However, there are two issues:

- Structure: *variation* in the question is required, small variation around the same theme. In this case the theme has been using bar models and part wholes to interpret and solve problems.
- Arithmetic: the *fluency* is needed but only after the structure, visual or abstract have been understood.

So, easier numbers are used until structure is understood; here the children have worked at these kinds of problems before, hence there is some challenge in the numbers being used. The conceptual idea is still the main thing.

CASE STUDY 5: JACK CORSON, BYRON COURT PRIMARY SCHOOL – YEAR 5 CLASS

Jack starts the lesson with a problem from the previous day.

Figure 7.26 Number line to complete

The children had spent some time at the end of the previous lesson looking at the problem in Figure 7.26 and they had obviously discussed this with each other. It was reiterated that the two fractions had to be the same distance apart from the one recorded in the middle ($\frac{3}{8}$). The idea emerged that the denominator would stay the same. It had become secure knowledge within this group that one can count in fractional denominations, say quarters or eighths, and only the numerator would change, for example, $\frac{1}{8}$, $\frac{2}{8}$, $\frac{3}{8}$, etc.

Therefore, children suggested the missing numbers could be $\frac{2}{8}$ and $\frac{4}{8}$. These were added to a number line. Then a second pair was added ($\frac{1}{8}$ and $\frac{5}{8}$). There was some speculation that minus numbers might be used and also $\frac{0}{8}$, also known as 0 (Figure 7.27).

Figure 7.27 A completed number line

The big idea here was that the distance had to be the same going either way. Jack's next question had both a rationale and a line of inquiry and progression that he was seeking to develop. He asked the children to see if they could find other fractions that could be placed in the initial boxes with the same distance apart from the initial fraction, $\frac{3}{8}$. These were to have a *different denominator* to the eighths that had been discussed thus far.

He knew through previous work and assessment for learning that the children were familiar with equivalent fractions. Working in pairs, the children began to change the fraction $\frac{3}{8}$ into equivalent fractions such as $\frac{6}{16}$, $\frac{9}{24}$ and $\frac{12}{32}$ proceeding to record and discuss fractions equidistant from these. This had both engaged and challenged the children.

VARIATION AND DEPTH

Afterwards, Jack articulated the idea that many mastery teachers, here and in Shanghai or Singapore, will often attempt to make an adjustment to draw in one small amendment to the original learning. Here, the original task had been expanded to encourage use of equivalent fractions, by adapting the denominator.

Jack then re-introduced the children to an exercise from the previous day that referenced the following problems:

1. $\frac{2}{3}$, $\frac{3}{7}$, $\frac{4}{11}$, $\frac{5}{15}$, $\frac{6}{19}$, $\frac{7}{23}$, $\frac{8}{27}$, $\frac{9}{31}$, $\frac{10}{35}$, $\frac{11}{39}$, etc. In this fraction sequence there are various patterns. Some of the fractions will cancel down, which ones? What would the next fraction to cancel down be? What is a rule for the cancelled down fraction sequence?
2. $\frac{1}{4}$, $\frac{3}{7}$, $\frac{5}{10}$, $\frac{7}{13}$, $\frac{9}{16}$, $\frac{11}{19}$, $\frac{13}{22}$, $\frac{15}{25}$, $\frac{17}{28}$, $\frac{19}{31}$, etc. Which fractions in the sequence will cancel down? What would the next two fractions to cancel down be? What is a rule for the cancelled down fraction sequence?

3. $\frac{3}{4}$, $\frac{5}{9}$, $\frac{7}{14}$, $\frac{9}{19}$, $\frac{11}{24}$, $\frac{13}{29}$, $\frac{15}{34}$, $\frac{17}{39}$, $\frac{19}{44}$, $\frac{21}{49}$, etc. Which fractions in the sequence will cancel down? What would the next two fractions to cancel down be? What is the rule for the cancelled down fraction sequence?

Discussion had taken place and it had been clarified which fractions that could be cancelled down from the first sequence. So in sequence 1, $\frac{5}{15}$ and $\frac{10}{35}$ are cancelled and $\frac{15}{55}$ would be the next one to be cancelled. These would cancel down to $\frac{1}{3}$, $\frac{2}{7}$ and $\frac{3}{11}$ respectively.

Through discussion, rehearsal and prompting, the children were able to articulate that the numerator increased by five and the denominator by 20. They could also explain that the reason for this was that as the numerators in the sequence increased in ones, so the denominator had four added to it each time. Therefore, both increases maintained the link with the five times table. Some were able to see that if any fraction with a five as a numerator had been used, then the pattern would have been maintained as long as the change in the denominator had been constant and that the numerator had increased by one each time.

So, in the second sequence, $\frac{5}{10}$, $\frac{15}{25}$ are cancelled and the next number in the sequence would have been $\frac{25}{40}$. The numerator was increased by two each time which means that the next number in the sequence had a numerator of ten more (5 × 2) and a denominator of 15 (5 × 3) more.

Speaking with Jack afterwards it was clear, as he allowed the children to articulate what they were observing, that they had noticed a lot. Some things related to what he had seen and wanted to accentuate, and some had not been on his radar. He articulated this and emphasised he would like to pursue those conversations with the children and follow their thinking through.

CONTROL AND VARIATION

What he had been able to control was the children's ability to follow through the patterns and to articulate them using vocabulary they now had increasing understanding of. What he felt he had not been able to keep a lid on was the deductive reasoning related to the sequences and learning to predict what kind of patterns were appearing.

Given that he was seeking to develop children's deductive reasoning related to denominators, numerators and equivalent fractions, he moved into an area of new learning that built on what the children had already done.

- **Small-step progression:** A key feature of mastery-style teaching is to manage new learning so that it happens in each taught session but it is made explicit, articulated by the children and often revisited in several different forms (see Chapter 5 on small-step progression).

- **Managed learning:** Here Jack moved to a guided task that linked to his starter activity of identifying two fractions equidistant from $\frac{3}{8}$, one with a higher value, the other a lower value.

He listened to children's thinking giving credit for fractions that used eighths, identifying children's ideas that included different denominators. Thus, equivalent fractions to $\frac{3}{8}$ such as $\frac{6}{16}$, $\frac{9}{24}$ and $\frac{12}{32}$ emerged. We discussed afterwards whether this question might have been used: 'Why will there be more possible solutions when using sixteenths or twenty-fourths than eighths?' The reason for this is that the larger numerators and denominators certainly create more opportunities to find equal differences using the same denominator. Some children were beginning to see this.

Thus Jack varied the work he gave the children by choosing examples that gradually challenged the children. The variations were small but significant. Let us now consider two examples that are similar to ones that he chose:

a. Find a fraction between $\frac{1}{5}$ and $\frac{3}{5}$. Then find another. Then explain how you know they are between the two original fractions.
b. Find a fraction between $\frac{5}{7}$ and $\frac{3}{7}$. Then another. Then explain how you know they are between the two original fractions.

For example, finding the difference between $\frac{1}{5}$ and $\frac{3}{5}$ required finding halfway between the two numerators but nothing else. The first gradation was to find another fraction (apart from for example, $\frac{2}{5}$), that was between the two fractions. This requires knowledge of equivalent fractions so that changing $\frac{1}{5}$ and $\frac{3}{5}$ to $\frac{2}{10}$ and $\frac{6}{10}$ would allow $\frac{3}{10}$, $\frac{4}{10}$ or $\frac{5}{10}$ to be chosen. The switch to varying the denominators rather than the numerators requires reasoning that understands that the greater the denominator the smaller the value of each part relative to the same whole.

Jack knows the progression of understanding needed here; schemes are now replicating such progression. Clearly an understanding of the progression can be shared in schemes through teacher notes. Ultimately greater teacher knowledge will lead to more robust and efficient conversations.

STUDY CASE 6: GEMMA FIELD, WIMBLEDON PARK

There is a Year 4 team meeting at 8 am. Four teachers (three class teachers including Gemma, as well as a trainee), have a meeting on a daily basis. This is happening simultaneously in other year groups in the school for Years 1–6. Overall, the lessons for each of the three classes have been crafted by the year lead, in this case, Gemma.

Gemma has a passion for teaching for understanding and has embraced the mastery approach that values fluency, reasoning, variation and multiple representation within their own personalised approach to small-step progression, outlined in Chapter 5.

The Headteacher, Mr Paul Lufkin, indicated that 'succession planning' was an important issue for him, having someone ready to fill the shoes of an incumbent in a leadership role. Here Gemma is providing the lead and modelling but she is training and supporting too. Teachers are assisted and empowered to develop these skills.

In class, Gemma's initial question invites children to reflect on what these numbers have in common – exploring what is the same about them and what is different:

- 970, £0.99, 4,301, 1,028 and 100

It is agreed that they all include at least one zero. It is also agreed that the position occupied is not always in the same place value column. The value of the zero digit in that column is zero. In all cases, the presence of the zero changes the value of the other digits.

On the next slide, three other numbers are compared:

- 240, 204, 024

In the pre-lesson meeting, Alice has flagged up that a few of her children have struggled to understand why it isn't appropriate to record 024 as an answer in division problems.

For example:

$$\frac{024}{6)144}$$

There are many possible ways to overcome this, but the one that comes to my mind is by comparing 024 with 24 using Dienes. Zero hundreds, two tens and four ones is in fact the same as simply having two tens and four ones. Gemma gives the idea of discussing that it simply means 'no hundreds'. We later agree in the discussion about why this method of recording, e.g. 024, is not used: the zero is redundant.

In the lesson, Gemma has used her flipchart to show the Dienes representations to illustrate that the numbers have different values despite using the same digits. This is after the children have discussed how the numbers are the same and how they are different. She clarifies that 024 and 24 have the same value and asks if the same applies when the 0 is removed from the end of an integer, as in 240 and 24.

Table 7.2 Removing a zero from 240: does the value change?

H	T	O
2	4	0
2	4	

This is a clever route to take as she is seeking clarification that the 0 at the front doesn't mean the other digits have been moved, giving them a different value. This does happen when the 0 is at the end, as in Table 7.2. It is one of a number of conversations she might pursue. The point being that the depth of understanding can come through a number of different, interrelated routes that I feel is captured by the term *possible conversations*.

It is clarified that the answer would be different for 240 ÷ 2 as opposed to 24 ÷ 2.

Dienes again proves instructive, the power of the pictorial representation reducing the 'cognitive load' (Wiliam, 2017). The four divided into groups of two creates two groups of twenty in one calculation and simply two in the other.

$$\overline{)608} \quad \overline{)680}$$

Thus the two division algorithms include the same digits but the physical representation would be different. 608 has six hundred pieces and eight ones whereas 680 still has six hundred pieces but eight tens this time.

As we see above, the choice of questions opens up the exploration further.

There is a general feeling within the class that the presence of a zero in the dividend (starting total) means that there will be a zero in the quotient. Gemma cleverly explores this through this question. It is established that 680 ÷ 4 does leave a quotient (170) with a zero whereas 608 ÷ 4 does not (152). This then leads to the belief that if the zero is at the end of the number, then a zero will be part of the answer but again the opportunity to explore further disproves this.

I ask Gemma to explain her rationale behind the children she supports. She identifies four children who would struggle to achieve the main learning intention, which is to understand that division involving numbers with a zero in them creates different quotients when the number is whole (integers). They can lose momentum because their fluency is not strong and their tables are not secure. She articulates, crucially for me, that simply hiving them off makes them over-dependent on adult help. She encourages children to draw the integers using Dienes style representation coloured counters.

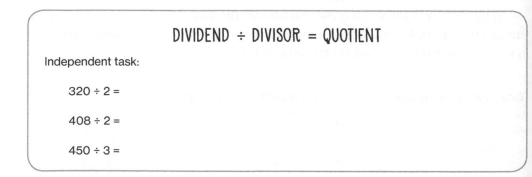

DIVIDEND ÷ DIVISOR = QUOTIENT

Independent task:

320 ÷ 2 =

408 ÷ 2 =

450 ÷ 3 =

$504 \div 4 =$

$603 \div 3 =$

1. What's gone wrong here? Explain the errors or assumptions that have been made.

$360 \div 9 = 4$

$708 \div 2 = 304$

Conjecture: If there is a place holder in the dividend, there will also be a place holder in the quotient.
    Do you agree? Convince me! Prove your answer using examples.

Beyond this point, some children have established that there isn't necessarily a place holder in the quotient and have started to think about defining and describing when there would be a place holder and when there wouldn't. This illustrates how depth of understanding can easily be achieved through focusing on small-step progression. It requires the subject and pedagogic knowledge to know how to go deeper with less content. It can help to have a more knowledgeable other close at hand. Here, Gemma achieved both of these things, I believe.

CONCLUSION

There are several features common to these lessons. All define intended learning quite closely and all seek to explore the themes using multiple representations, resources and experiences. They each seek to identify specific ideas to focus on that can lead to stem sentences that are used, repeated and often emerge from asking the children to complete them.

For example, the following stem sentence emerges from (comparing $\frac{2}{3}$, $\frac{2}{5}$ and $\frac{2}{7}$) using fractions with the same-sized numerator:

- 'The *larger* the denominator the *smaller* the value of the fraction.' (This is because ...) The stem focuses on reasoning that if equivalent wholes are cut into equal-sized parts then the parts of the whole cut into the fewest, equal-sized pieces will be larger.

The process of identifying small steps of progression is key. It allows emphasis to be placed on specific learning. Once this has been secured or is close to becoming so the teacher's role moves on. Depth of understanding can then be developed and articulated by some at the same time that other children are then being supported to understand the original ideas.

The reason why this latter feature of the lesson is common in such lessons is due to the fact that maths classes should not be ability grouped. The gap between the strongest and weakest should not become too great. This means engaging all children in relevant key learning; it also means revisiting that learning with some whilst others apply knowledge to develop depth of understanding. Most teachers believe in this philosophy, some require some help in securing the pedagogy of bringing this about. $\frac{2}{5}$

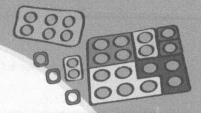

CHAPTER 8:

PLANNING AND SCHEMES OF WORK

What you will learn from this chapter:

- Knowledge about the style, content and intentions of the main current schemes related to maths mastery in primary schools and other related planning sources currently used to plan mastery teaching
- How mastery schemes differ from other schemes used previously in the UK
- Clarity on how to maintain a whole class approach to teaching primary maths or awareness of why this might not be possible
- Insight into issues and opportunities related to planning and pursuing mastery in different schools
- Confirmation about how the key points related to mastery teaching have to be regularly present in mastery planning and teaching
- Knowledge of the growing awareness that teachers either need to learn how to plan explicitly for mastery development or to understand how the scheme they are using is doing it for them
- Realisation that excessive use of a mastery scheme needs to be accompanied by adaptation to make it relevant to their class

MASTERY TEACHING FEATURES THAT A SCHEME WOULD NEED TO ADDRESS

Mastery in the UK, fronted by the NCETM and maths hubs around the country, emphasises that we are striving to achieve a decisive pedagogy in primary maths teaching that is underpinned by four key features: fluency, procedural and conceptual variation, mathematical reasoning and thinking, and multiple representations. These four areas are closely interlinked. Any planning being undertaken or used needs to ensure that these features are key components. In addition to this, they should be bound together in a coherent way. This combination is much more explicit than we have been used to in the UK. We have tended to focus excessively on a formal, procedural approach to learning with table knowledge and number bonds emphasised and pursued with tenacity, or we have taught for understanding with an awareness that fluency would support this process. In addition to this, we have assumed gaps between lower and higher attainment are inevitable and targeted providing value added for all children in the class, from different starting points. Often this has involved setting, streaming or flexible grouping within classes.

SCHEMES OF WORK

The Department for Education (DfE) in January 2017 set out guidelines as to the sorts of schemes they wished to be used in schools in England. The following criteria were met and approved in only one case:

- Textbooks with explanatory notes.
- Structured, thorough support through resources.
- Coverage coherence.
- Concept clarity and representation.
- Structure and language specificity and progression.
- Activities to develop progression.
- Practice opportunities.
- Assessment.
- Teacher guidance.

Publishers were invited to submit textbooks for review by an expert panel set up by the DfE. The government agreed to match fund up to '£2,000 to schools purchasing "Maths – No Problem!"'. The scheme, overseen by Professor Yeap Ban Har, is linked to Singaporean teaching texts and emerges from a revised approach to maths teaching in schools that began in the 1980s.

In 1982, the Curriculum Development Institute of Singapore (CDIS) started to develop its own mathematics textbooks and curriculum. The book *Primary Mathematics* was first published in 1982 and in the late 1990s the Ministry of Education opened the elementary school textbook market to private companies. The 'Maths – No Problem!' scheme emerges from this initiative as it meets the criteria necessary for a scheme. Let us consider why it exists and what purpose it serves.

KEY POINTS ABOUT THE 'MATHS – NO PROBLEM!' SCHEME

When you look at the 'Maths – No Problem!' scheme, it is fairly apparent that it does meet the government requirements. However, the consensus seems to be that there are a number of considerations to factor in when using the scheme.

The scheme would appear to be accessible and set up to teach for progression. Ben McClellan, a student teacher currently undertaking a PGCE, is familiar with the scheme and identifies that, in order to use it well, teachers need to know their class and to be alert as they teach. The online software can provide screenshots to use as part of manufactured flipcharts. The teacher guidance, complete with possible and likely misconceptions, certainly supports the idea of developing meaningful conversations with children. Many schools now promote a growth mindset (Dweck, 2012) and refer to 'good mistakes'.

Ben showed me how he uses the scheme in the classroom. He refers to misconceptions about the ordering of objects and how this differs dependent on the starting point used which causes some confusion. He uses the following exercise as the basis for his teaching:

There are five children in the queue (Figure 8.1). What is the position of each child in the queue?

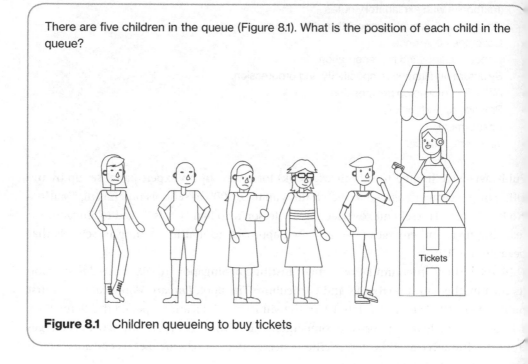

Figure 8.1 Children queueing to buy tickets

The position of the ticket seller in relation to the students would affect the order of the children. In the figure the rightmost girl is first in the queue, but if the ticket seller was to the left of all the children she would be the fifth. Ben pointed out that further awareness of your class builds credibility. In discussing this example with his class the ticket seller had Ben's own name and he used the children themselves initially with their own names acting out the scene. The concrete was preceding the pictorial and his content knowledge undoubtedly made the learning more explicit as the children saw its relevance much more quickly.

He feels that the scheme is tight and that there is little need to deviate too far from the prescribed content, other than to extend and develop greater depth. He feels the content there could, if needed, be extended further to ensure learning on occasions. Ben agrees that 'There is more than enough basic material' and that 'The textbook works well but the guidance section takes it further'.

We agree that simply dipping into a textbook will not suffice. This comes back to the coherence emphasised by the NCETM that teachers need to apply knowledge of children and that they need to adapt material, not change it. In Ben's view: 'There is a difference between adaptation and a pick and choose approach. The pitch is generally right. Questions tease out the misconceptions'.

Pinal Sheth, maths lead at Elmhurst Primary (who we first met in Chapter 7), agrees: 'Embrace fully or not at all. You won't see progress if you don't' she says and adds 'In the future we might not need books but we do at the moment'. By this she means that, in many cases, we are now thinking carefully about what and how we teach, even if the scheme provides the main content and progression. We, as teachers, still have to internalise what the scheme is seeking to achieve and adapt.

Pinal takes this point further: 'We still plan (at my school). You must make their lessons fit your class'. The staff at Pinal's school want to have an idea of where they are taking the teaching and learning. 'I need to see the journey we are all going to take. Where are my children currently; what will they cope with? Dipping in won't work.' Pinal does identify that pace and coverage are an issue. There are not enough days to teach all that the 'Maths – No Problem!' scheme would suggest.

CASE STUDY 1: ANNA WILLIS, REDLANDS PRIMARY SCHOOL

Redlands Primary School has been showing interest in mastery-style learning for a while. During the summer, they had a change of maths lead and the school decided to buy in the 'Maths – No Problem!' scheme. Anna Willis, Year 3 lead, describes the development since then in ways that have relevance to how real mastery teaching differs from methods taught previously.

Staff were encouraged to use this scheme as part of their planning, picking from it to supplement their other ideas about planning and teaching. By Christmas, this approach had been abandoned. They had bought the textbooks but not the online guides for teachers; fathoming progression was hard at times. Continuity was also difficult to achieve as a result of varying and sometimes slightly watered down implementation of the scheme. The idea of selecting from a range of resources has traditionally been seen as both creative and an opportunity to create momentum. However, in terms of ensuring learning and development in maths, planning has to be progressive and specific. Redlands committed to the full scheme after Christmas. The analysis, by Anna, is both instructive and, I believe, significant.

Understandably, as previously explained, the guidance for teachers creates greater knowledge and belief among staff. The amount of time taken to ensure children fully understand work covered is much longer with children who have not had related, secure previous learning. Anna points out that 'Maths – No Problem!' lessons take three times as long in Year 3 as they should and in Year 1 the time taken is much nearer to what is intended. This time-intensive element feels like another aspect of embedding mastery teaching, albeit one that, like others, may work itself through over a period of time.

Anna and the rest of the staff have chosen to cut parts of the curriculum with children in older classes to ensure that at least the number work can begin to reach the expected level towards the end of Key Stage 2. They still seek to develop problem solving through bar modelling as the scheme intends; shape and space along with data handling and some aspects of measure have been left fallow in the Key Stage 2. These have clearly been difficult decisions to make but can be seen as a valid attempt to provide a possible, coherent way forward.

The issue of dealing with children who fail to grasp key learning is tackled through a positive intervention; about 10–15 minutes of re-teaching or pre-teaching. Obviously that is at the expense of something else: guided reading or assembly. There is clearly an issue about how the children will access all of the standardised testing. Anna points out that the management in the school identify secure understanding as being vital, even if that cannot currently extend to the whole maths curriculum in Key Stage 2. Teachers use discretion to determine how lessons start and end. This decision is brave and, in my opinion, to be applauded.

Consequently, they are noticing in many years that children will not score as well as perhaps they could if fuller coverage had taken place. The management team have indicated that they realise that standardised test scores may suffer, but they would rather ensure that the learning is secure, even if this takes longer than is intended.

KEEPING A WHOLE CLASS APPROACH?

Children are taught as whole classes. In Year 3, Anna's taught class does have children who do not grasp the main learning that would develop mastery understanding. It is not always the same children in each different theme; some appear more than others. Anna's current approach is to find additional time in the day to teach them (perhaps 12–15 minutes) so that their understanding is more secure. Unless this happens, the gap starts to reveal itself further and the whole class approach becomes less sustainable. Although schools receive some match funding for 'Maths – No Problem!', Anna reports that the overall outlay regarding texts, practice books, online materials and resources is quite heavy.

AVERAGES AND DIFFERENCE: YEAR 1 AND YEAR 6

Looking at two themes, one from each key stage, we will see that 'Maths – No Problem!' draws the main features behind mastery together in a coherent way. Let us look at the statutory requirements that pupils should be taught on the 'mean averages' theme:

- calculate and interpret the mean as an average.

Non-statutory guidance on the 'mean averages' theme:

- Pupils know when it is appropriate to find the mean of a dataset.

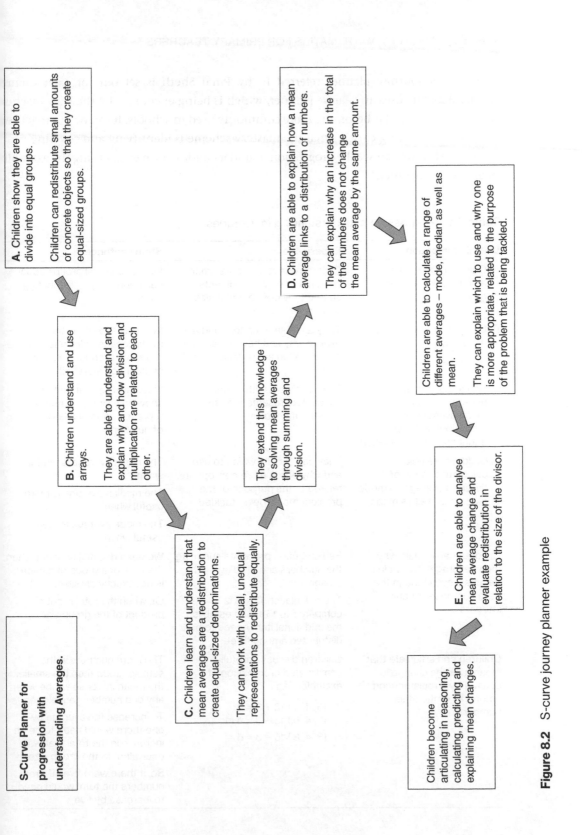

Figure 8.2 S-curve journey planner example

S-Curve Planner for progression with understanding Averages.

A. Children show they are able to divide into equal groups.

Children can redistribute small amounts of concrete objects so that they create equal-sized groups.

B. Children understand and use arrays.

They are able to understand and explain why and how division and multiplication are related to each other.

C. Children learn and understand that mean averages are a redistribution to create equal-sized denominations.

They can work with visual, unequal representations to redistribute equally.

They extend this knowledge to solving mean averages through summing and division.

D. Children are able to explain how a mean average links to a distribution of numbers.

They can explain why an increase in the total of the numbers does not change the mean average by the same amount.

Children are able to calculate a range of different averages – mode, median as well as mean.

They can explain which to use and why one is more appropriate, related to the purpose of the problem that is being tackled.

E. Children are able to analyse mean average change and evaluate redistribution in relation to the size of the divisor.

Children become articulating in reasoning, calculating, predicting and explaining mean changes.

The type of journey planner referred to by Pinal Sheth is set out for each theme (Figure 8.2). She uses an S-curve planner, which is being encourage by the Hub Teacher Research Group and is becoming more commonly used in schools. It can be put together simply by evaluating closely what the mastery scheme is identifying and covering.

In Table 8.1, we can see the progression of understanding in averages using the example of an S-curve planner.

Table 8.1 Progression of understanding in averages

Learning intention	Experience	Stem sentences
A. Children show they are able to divide into equal groups	Children can redistribute small amounts of concrete objects so that they create equal-sized groups	Making unequal groups equal can happen by redistributing them
B. Children understand and use arrays	They are able to understand and explain why and how division and multiplication are related to each other	My array shows me that multiplication calculations make the same product whichever number you start with
C. Children learn and understand that mean averages are a redistribution to create equal-sized denominations	They can work with visual, unequal representations to redistribute equally	Mean averages are about showing a single number as a representation of a larger group of numbers
D. Children are able to calculate a range of different averages – mode, median as well as mean	They can explain which to use and why one is more appropriate, related to the purpose of the problem that is being tackled	The mean average is useful when ... The median average is more useful when ... The mode average is more useful when ...
Children can explain why mean averages can include decimals even though the data comprises of only integers	Redistribution precedes summing the numbers and dividing by the divisor. The calculation 12 ÷ 3 is compared to 13 ÷ 3 to establish the additional item needs to be distributed among three	We get a decimal quotient when the total of a group of numbers is not exactly divisible. Or, when the total is not a product of the group size
Children can articulate that mean average change is caused by a redistribution among all of the other numbers	Children discuss carefully constructed progression of examples, e.g. (3, 4, 5,) 12 ÷ 3 = 4 (3, 4, 6,) 13 ÷ 3 = 4 r1 (3, 4, 8,) 15 ÷ 3 = 5	The more numbers in the sample group then the smaller the mean increase will be when any one number gets bigger. To increase the average by one there would need to be an increase in the total that was equivalent to the group size. So, if there were five different numbers the total would need to increase by five

MODE

The mode would allow a decision that is reasonably well-received, such as choosing an ice-cream flavour in which each child has three choices. A first choice would get three points, a second one would receive two points and there is one point for third choice. This allows children and adults to be happier with decisions or choices. The mode can also be useful when we are finding out what the most popularly liked thing within a range is, such as names, flavours, drinks and books. These can inform decisions made on behalf of larger groups or business decisions about production and sales strategies.

MEDIAN

The median could be used in test scores to determine groups in the class as it would show where the middle child in the class was and what kind of targeted teaching might prove useful. A useful discussion concerns which middle point is most beneficial in a given circumstance. Is it better to know the child with the score half way between the highest score and the lowest score, or is it more useful to know the score of the child halfway down (or up) the class in an ordinal sense? For example, the 5th out of 9, the 11th out of 21, or in the latter example the 25th percentile, 50th percentile, 75th percentile or any other percentile. Three equal-sized groups would necessitate 33rd and 66th percentiles. It is the latter piece of information that represents the median, the data amount that occupies middle place in a range of data or scores.

MEAN

The mean might prove useful in looking at a set of scores in one subject by a child. An overall average of a range of assessment tests would give a broad indication of strength or weakness. Most formative assessment deals with detail. Therefore, information about which areas were answered incorrectly and analysis of whether there were mistakes or misconceptions at the root of those mistakes would assist thinking. In the end, we might want children to identify stem sentences related to averages. Let us consider the example of the wages of four brothers and their average earnings. If all four earn £20,000, how much more would one of them have to earn until the average was £25,000?

A stem sentence that could be used in this example is:

- 'The increase in one brother's earnings is not the same as the average increase for all the brothers. This is because the single increase in salary has to be distributed equally among the four of them.'

PROGRESSION ACTIVITIES

The progression is similar to the journey planner shown in Figure 8.2. Carefully thought through, the examples draw out the key issues identified. Family age averages give the opportunity to explore outlying numbers, for example, an elderly relative will change the average age significantly. The scheme guidance identifies what to emphasise to allow first mastery and then greater depth of understanding to emerge.

These are not the only 'Maths – No Problem!' activities that are valid. However, it is a good example of clear progression and a recorded thread of possible, productive conversations with your children. Pinal and other teachers would say that knowing your children and gaining increased confidence in your own understanding will allow you to adapt your focus as you realise particular issues need more or less time.

Table 8.2   Statistics – Year 6 (Askew et al., 2015b)

Mastery	Greater depth
Ten pupils take part in some races on Sports Day, and the following times are recorded.	Three teams are taking part in the heats of a 4 × 100 m relay race competition on Sports Day.
Time to run 100 m (seconds): 23, 21, 21, 20, 21, 22, 24, 23, 22, 20.	If the mean average time of the four runners in a team is less than 30 seconds, the team will be selected for the finals.
Time to run 100 m holding an egg and spoon (seconds): 45, 47, 49, 43, 44, 46, 78, 46, 44, 48.	At the start of the last leg of the relay race, the times (in seconds) of each teams' first three runners are:
Time to run 100 m in a three-legged race (seconds): 50, 83, 79, 48, 53, 52, 85, 81, 49, 84.	Team Peacock: 27, 29, 31
Calculate the mean average of the times recorded in each race. For each race, do you think that the mean average of the times would give a useful summary of the ten individual times?	Team Farah: 45, 43, 37
	Team Ennis: 29, 30, 25
	Which of the teams have the best chance of being selected?
Explain your decision	Explain your reasoning

Reasoning is explored in both tasks in Table 8.2. Children are expected to show how to interpret the data and complete the task in the greater depth example. This is the part where some teachers may struggle: creating problems that allow opportunity to show greater depth. The reality is that this is important. There have always been good resources related to exploring depth through websites, such as NRICH. If the core structure to teaching is provided, the research focus can be on the supporting application of knowledge materials, such as NRICH, 'White Rose', NCETM and other sources. In time, teachers may create their own, and some already do. Some school maths leads have set up resource banks so that ideas can be shared; this process and strategy is also being shared among schools, a learning community developing resources for collective use.

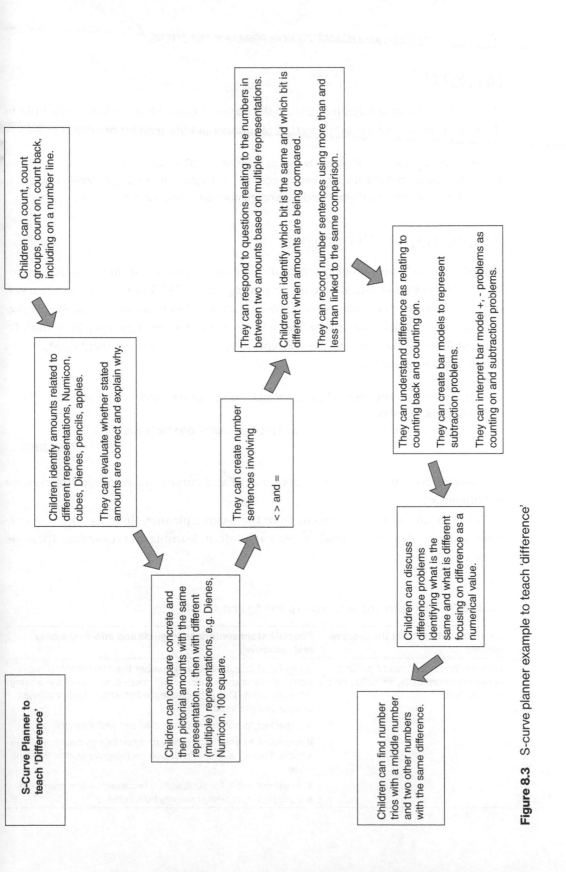

S-Curve Planner to teach 'Difference'

Children can count, count groups, count on, count back, including on a number line.

Children identify amounts related to different representations, Numicon, cubes, Dienes, pencils, apples.

They can evaluate whether stated amounts are correct and explain why.

Children can compare concrete and then pictorial amounts with the same representation... then with different (multiple) representations, e.g. Dienes, Numicon, 100 square.

They can create number sentences involving

< > and =

They can respond to questions relating to the numbers in between two amounts based on multiple representations.

Children can identify which bit is the same and which bit is different when amounts are being compared.

They can record number sentences using more than and less than linked to the same comparison.

They can understand difference as relating to counting back and counting on.

They can create bar models to represent subtraction problems.

They can interpret bar model +, - problems as counting on and subtraction problems.

Children can discuss difference problems identifying what is the same and what is different focusing on difference as a numerical value.

Children can find number trios with a middle number and two other numbers with the same difference.

Figure 8.3 S-curve planner example to teach 'difference'

DIFFERENCE

We will now look at another theme from the National Curriculum for Year 1. The links to the concept of 'difference' in the section of number (addition and subtraction) include:

- Add and subtract one-digit and two-digit numbers to 20, including 0.
- Solve one-step problems that involve addition and subtraction, using concrete objects and pictorial representations, and missing number problems such as 7 = ? – 9.

NOTES AND (NON-STATUTORY) GUIDANCE

They discuss and solve problems in familiar practical contexts, including using quantities. Problems should include the terms: put together, add, altogether, total, take away, distance between, difference between, more than and less than, so that pupils develop the concept of addition and subtraction and are enabled to use these operations flexibly.

In addition to the links to the concept of difference previously mentioned, pupils should also be taught to:

- Read, write and interpret mathematical statements involving addition (+), subtraction (–) and equals (=) signs.
- Represent and use number bonds and related subtraction facts within 20.

(DfE, 2013)

In Figure 8.3 we can see an example of the use of an S-curve planner to teach the concept of 'difference'.

To help with the learning outline from the S-curve planner, there are some possible stem sentences that can be used to guide and inform learning and reasoning. These are shown in Table 8.3.

Table 8.3 Stem sentences linked to planning and activity

Learning outline from the S-curve planner	Possible stem sentences to guide and inform learning and reasoning
Children can count, count groups, count on, count back, including on a number line	When I add or subtract on a number line I immediately move from my starting number: I don't count it as part of the adding or subtracting. This is because *the first number I add or subtract will change the amount.*
	It is quicker to count on rather than recount everything.
	It Is quicker to start with the bigger number to count on when adding. This is because *the total of the two groups will be the same anyway.*
	This will not work for subtraction because *we aren't combining two groups; we are taking one away from the other*

Learning outline from the S-curve planner	Possible stem sentences to guide and inform learning and reasoning
Children identify amounts related to different representations, Numicon, cubes, Dienes, pencils, apples. They can evaluate whether stated amounts are correct and explain why	I know that there are nine because *there is only one more needed for the tens frame to be full.* I know there are 12 because *there is a two and a ten. So starting at ten it goes 11, 12.* It is 12 because *it is two rows of six. Double six is 12.* It is 29. *There are two tens and if there was another one it would make another ten. One less than 30 is 29*
Children can compare concrete and then pictorial amounts with the same representation and then with different (multiple) representations, e.g. Dienes, Numicon, 100 square	23. These two ten rods are the same as the Numicon tens. *The three ones is the same as the three.* No. I don't think it is the same as 24 on the 100 square. *All the numbers in that column have four ones. Here there are only three ones*
They can create number sentences involving '<', '>' and '='	$6 = 4 + 2$; $6 = 8 - 2$ $6 > 4 + 1$; $6 < 4 + 3$ • The = sign tells us that the numbers or calculations on either side have the same value. • The < and > signs show us that the number or calculation on the open side is larger. • We read calculations from left to right and so < shows us that the left hand number is smaller than the right, e.g. $3 < 5$ • > tells us that the number or calculation on the left hand side has a greater value than the one on the right hand side
Children can respond to questions relating to the numbers in between two amounts based on multiple representations. They can identify which bit is the same and which bit is different when amounts are being compared. They can record number sentences using more than and less than linked to the same comparison	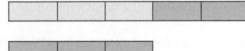 'Five and three are different. The three bit is the same but five has two more.' 'Three is two less than five.' 'I can count on from the bit that's the same to find the difference. Or I can count back from the bigger number until I get to the bit that's the same.' 'The difference is the same whether you go forward or back.'
They can understand difference as relating to counting back and counting on. They can create bar models to represent subtraction problems.	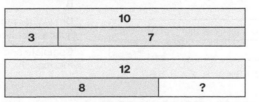 'The difference between 12 and eight is four: 12 is four more than eight. Eight is four less than 12.'

(Continued)

Table 8.3 (Continued)

Learning outline from the S-curve planner	Possible stem sentences to guide and inform learning and reasoning
They can interpret bar model +, – problems as counting on and subtraction problems	(Also: 'I found that I need the Numicon four to add to eight to get to 12. That is the difference.')
Children can discuss difference problems identifying what is the same and what is different focusing on difference as a numerical value	'13 and ten. They both have a ten but 13 has a three too. That is the difference.' 'The seven has a five and a two' (Numicon, cubes or Cuisenaire. 'The five just has the five; so two is the difference.' 'When I place the Numicon three over the Numicon five I can see that two holes aren't covered up. This is the difference between three and five.'
Children can find number trios with a middle number and two other numbers with the same difference	 'If there is a difference of two between two numbers and one of them is four, one number will be two bigger and the other two smaller.'

Let us now look at assessment examples from Year 1 from NCETM.

Table 8.4 NCETM Assessment examples from Year 1 (Askew et al., 2015a)

Mastery	Greater depth
A. $3 + \_ = 10$, $10 – \_ = 3$, $13 + \_ = 20$, $20 – \_ = 13$	A.
B. $3 + 2 = 5, 2 + 3 = 5, 5 – 2 = 3, 5 – 3 = 2$ Write the four number sentences for the picture above	B. Draw a bar model for $7 + 2 = 9$ and write four number sentences. Complete and write the number sentences using this model

Mastery	Greater depth
C.	C.
Robert has five more cherries than John. John has 11 cherries. How many does Robert have?	Together Sam and Tom have 19 football stickers. Tom has eight stickers. How many stickers does Sam have?
Write a number sentence you would use to solve the problem	Write a number sentence you could use to solve the problem

In the assessment examples shown in Table 8.4, compiled through NCETM, it is clear that some thorough work would need to be taking place in class to allow the vast majority of the class to be able to tackle, successfully, these questions, in both left or right hand columns.

To be able to answer the A questions, the children will need to have had significant experience and discussion around multiple representations exploring the links between addition and subtraction. The greater depth questions explore the extent to which the children can apply the inverse operations and connections independently. This takes time for teachers to familiarise themselves with resources, manipulate, and create variations in the experience and questioning.

The B questions indicate the progression needed to move to a more pictorial form of representation that will draw on the depth of knowledge gained through manipulation of concrete resources around carefully structured questions. In applying greater depth questions, children interpret the question, carry out the operations and apply them to the part – part whole structure shown. In Year 1 that may appear to be asking quite a lot of the child. However, the schemes being vetted and approved now have carefully crafted progression that spends more time securing fundamental knowledge of structure of small numbers. That is the real gain. We have to resist the real temptation to overload the curriculum at this age as it will compromise the depth of fundamental understanding that can be achieved.

'INSPIRE MATHS'

Although yet to achieve government approval in England, the 'Inspire Maths' scheme is used in many countries and represents the scheme used in Singapore which has underpinned the secure understanding many children in that country gain.

Earlier in this chapter we looked at the criteria schemes need to meet to get approval. In this particular scheme, some teachers feel that the coverage and concept clarity are a little harder to fathom in places. This might be true, but it is a strong scheme and with feedback from schools ongoing, I would expect the scheme to be approved in the near future. The government has made it clear what it is seeking.

Long-term planning and medium-term weekly outlines are clear in their content. This is supported by guidance per question and rationale behind each question to be shared and worked through with the children. In addition, the practice books consolidate and develop understanding.

Dr Fong Ho Kheong, in the introductions to the 'Inspire Maths' books, emphasises CPA progression and acknowledges building on the ideas of theorists such as Piaget and Bruner, where children construct their initial understanding of the world through interacting with it in physical form. From this, the representations, patterns and articulation can be fine-tuned to support children in being able to discuss patterns based on prior experience, whether in abstract, pictorial or concrete form. The 'Inspire Maths' scheme (2015) holds as important the teaching for understanding as upheld by Richard Skemp (1978). David Ausubel's articulation, referenced in the introduction, about striking a balance between consolidating established understanding and exposure to new understanding is also fundamental to the progressive, tightly structured development of the scheme. It fully acknowledges the work of Vygotsky (1978) through the use of words to capture thought and debate what one is thinking or beginning to understand. This is the essence of mastery. Children have to be able to evaluate their own thinking alongside what others are sharing. This requires a culture in the classroom that has been inconsistent at best in the UK to date.

The 'Inspire Maths' scheme holds problem solving in high esteem as the way to consolidate and extend the work being done in understanding fundamental maths. There is some talk that the reason that the scheme has not yet won government approval is because it has not yet been adapted to fit the National Curriculum in maths. If so, this appears to be a thorny issue to me. Why would we feel the structure of the Singapore curriculum needed adaptation when we have upheld the value and success of it in the first place? Interestingly, the 'Maths – No Problem!' scheme has been adapted to include the expanded curriculum in England, while the 'Inspire Maths' scheme has not.

'MATHS MASTERY'

The 'Maths Mastery' scheme was founded by Dr Helen Drury, who wrote the book *Mastering Mathematics* (2014). Her long-term analysis of Shanghai approaches to mathematics has been a big part of the journey towards mastery in the UK. The scheme is used by almost 500 schools across the country. The team behind the scheme and resources for it have grown.

The scheme is linked to the Ark academy chain, which has a number of schools across London and now further afield. Given the detailed link with Shanghai and Dr Drury's knowledge about learning maths and the issues faced in the UK traditionally, many Ark teachers have visited Shanghai and there are strong links with the style of teaching there. Ark schools have hosted many Shanghai teachers who have come to schools to teach and demonstrate a mastery-style approach to teaching maths. Part – part whole knowledge underpins a lot of teaching in numberwork. The lessons are carefully graded with discussion and key learning consistently drawn out through small variation and discussion as fluency is developed. Initially, the resources for younger children (early years) were thought to resemble Key Stage 1 materials but this has now been amended. As we will see in Chapter 11 on early years, there are now very relevant, accessible resources. The work at that age is clearly underpinned by a commitment to early learning principles in number that are discussed in that chapter.

The online resources have clear explanation about teaching progression and include electronic resources to underpin activities. Here, there is also a focus on games, problem solving and application of knowledge. Games appear where the strategies can be effectively discussed and learning remain explicit. This is the one big idea that is likely to mean that mastery maths features are here to stay. If Dienes equipment is used to explore grouping, then it is done clearly and thoroughly. It is not the only resource, but time and attention are paramount. Teachers learn to have meaningful conversations around the work. Maths leads set the tone and clearly it helps when there are several classes in each year for deeper discussion and observation to take place to support teacher development.

Reasoning is present throughout all lessons. The answer is of some importance, and the explanation and justification even more so. I expect this group to be close to gaining government approval. Now the criteria are clear and time is passing, the scope is there for several schemes in addition to 'Maths Mastery' to fine tune their work to meet requirements specifically. 'Maths – No Problem!', 'Inspire Maths' and 'Maths Mastery' must all use feedback from their schools alongside their dialogue with the government. I am not aware of any disputation about the criteria; I would think it would be to the advantage of these three providers to each have the accreditation currently given only to 'Maths – No Problem!'

'WHITE ROSE' MATHS RESOURCES

There are currently 35 maths hubs in England; they deliver training and professional development around mastery in maths. They also oversee development of mastery across schools through trained mastery teachers leading and mentoring groups of other schools each year (see Chapter 9).

The 'White Rose' maths hub in Yorkshire had a resource base with mastery-style ideas to support a mastery approach to teaching: developing fluency, multiple representations, variation in concepts and procedures and reasoning and articulation. Clearly, the thread to lesson teaching may not be as precise as in the schemes but many schools are reluctant to use the commercial schemes. This is often for a combination of two reasons. One is cost, as setting up a new scheme with resources is expensive, even with government match funding. Secondly, the traditional desire by teachers to be creative is hampered by the need to follow schemes in what can be seen as quite a rigid way.

Pinal Sheth, at Elmhurst School where the North East London maths hub is based, is quite clear about this: 'You have to follow the scheme tightly, as prescribed. There may come a time when we, as teachers, understand mastery well enough to craft lessons ourselves but not in the near future'.

I would tend to agree. I think school creativity can only come in on top of the prescriptive yet sound approaches of tight structures such as the 'Maths – No Problem!', 'Inspire Maths' and 'Maths Mastery' schemes. 'White Rose' plans, free to use until now, provide assistance that helps teachers in schools without a scheme get into decent situations where good learning can take place. However, it can be argued that progression is less assured.

OTHER RESOURCES

There are obviously many more online resources to use. For example, 'Hamilton Trust' is subscription-based and is quite popular. 'Lancashire', with some free resources, is used by some. Overall, the thinking is that if we are to create assured understanding of mathematical concepts we need to understand what these concepts are and teach them with rigour. This process may be best served, ultimately, by learning to craft our own lessons..

Another resource, already mentioned, regarding mastery definitions as well as assessment materials, is NCETM. This organisation is the key facilitator of mastery development in the UK. Their videos of taught lessons provide useful dialogue about how mastery teaching has to achieve particular targets. This includes ensuring understanding is specific and evidenced through children's work through their thinking, reasoning and articulation.

CONCLUSION

Developing the confidence to plan mastery-style lessons independently is not going to be a quick fix. Our teachers, who have been trained and are being trained, point out that planning still takes a long time. For non-trained teachers, it will take much longer; therefore the carefully crafted schemes or team-planning initiatives may need to suffice for the moment. What we should all be striving to do is to evaluate closely the schemes we use, their teacher notes and progression. This will inform the discussion we have with our children. The phrase 'possible conversations' is one that I would like to promote; many good conversations around key areas of maths may take place. We need to keep our heads and try to link ideas up coherently in manageable learning chunks to assist this process.

CHAPTER 9:

SCHOOL MODELS FOR TEACHING MASTERY

What you will learn from this chapter:

- An idea of the different challenges being dealt with in implementing a mastery-style approach to maths teaching and learning
- An awareness of the issues related to planning regarding content, ethos and depth of understanding
- A realisation that there is no one single method or lesson that is right for all children, classes or schools all of the time
- An acceptance that continuity regarding teaching styles and learning could be beneficial
- That not all children will develop in the same way through the same input, and assessment needs to notice and act on this as well as measure progress

INTRODUCTION

The aim of this chapter is to put into context some of the many different models that might be seen in primary schools. The features that underpin a mastery approach are not necessarily new or untried in our schools. The combination of features related to it may be approached slightly differently. For us to consider the approach as a mastery one, certain criteria would need to be present:

- Whole class teaching and new learning accessible to the vast majority of the class is key.
- The features of developing fluency, procedural and conceptual understanding and reasoning through an approach valuing multiple representations need to underpin teaching and learning.
- The opportunity to tackle mathematical themes in depth needs to be offered consistently for children to develop secure knowledge in what is being taught.
- Learning needs to be made explicit and relate to understanding rather than, solely, remembering.
- Care is taken to ensure that virtually all children achieve the skills and knowledge required to attain fundamental understanding.

It could be argued that there is one more criterion needed for a mastery approach to be truly present, which relates to the belief that so much of mathematical knowledge is interconnected; for example, fractions relate to division. This has inverse links with multiplication. The list is endless. Thus, this creates multiple possibilities regarding the ongoing development of understanding. Plans for learning can tackle development in different ways. Teachers can plan different but effective learning. Let us now consider what supports or affects development in mastery teaching.

TIME-RELATED ISSUES

Lack of time is the key issue for so many maths leads and class teachers. While resources support planning and teaching to develop deeper understanding in a more measured way, the planning required to fit this to a class, within which there are many different considerations, is both time consuming and not without challenge. We can look longingly at Shanghai models of teaching that often see maths teachers teaching three 35-minute lessons, with the rest of their day potentially spent on preparation, lesson evaluation, follow-up teaching and other assessment- and planning-related issues. It may be that Shanghai teachers do teach a little more than this, certainly on some days. However, there is also a message here for us all. Effective planning has to build on where a class currently is in their understanding, and good planning takes time. Not so much the broad content or resourcing the lesson, but working out which conversations to have, which key learning to emphasise and which representations to use to bring the connected understanding together. In addition to this, it is also necessary to plan for the ways deeper understanding can be built onto the main, whole class intended learning.

TEACHING UNITS OF WORK

Jack Corson, the Teachers Research Group lead in the London North East maths hub, has been developing the skill of teaching units of work. This is one way to overcome the age-old problem of a whistle-stop curriculum that only achieves superficial understanding, the exact opposite of mastery teaching and learning. Members of the group have been encouraged to spend more time on a given unit with the aim of building deeper learning opportunities and greater opportunity to reason; to articulate and discuss their findings and understanding. In Jack's opinion, 'Finding the activities was fairly easy; thinking of the reasoning and discussion was good, but harder ... also thinking about the different kinds of representation to use'.

Other teachers question whether the variations they have created are correct. Have they left important things out? This is certainly worth debating with colleagues and mentors if you can. There is no single right progression and development, although there are some that do not really work; for example, tackling multiplication before addition. In the main, though, it is whether another suggestion would work better than the one you have got, or have tried.

We have to get used to the idea of something being good enough (rather than perfect) and we also need to be ready to reflect and adjust our focus and plan as we go in light of what happens.

The 'Maths – No Problem!' scheme has been carefully developed regarding progression and variation. At the end of the day it is a 'one size fits all' approach and most agree that it is used with an eye on whether the class are ready for all or some of what is being planned and focused upon. As examined in Chapter 8, the actual progression in the work is dependent on having sound prior knowledge and teacher confidence in understanding.

CAN WE GO OFF SCRIPT?

Traditionally, the idea among many teachers in the UK has been that we are always seeking ways to bring ideas and comments that come from the children into the lessons. Many of us believe that children are capable of using prompt ideas that we have given and coming up with some applications of these that we had not thought of. We like the idea that they will have lightbulb moments that they use to come up with original thinking that we have inspired.

The belief in small-step progression and explicit learning would suggest we be wary of the possibility of losing our original focus. The other side of the argument is that sometimes we really cannot tell how the children will react to our teaching. We are going to be well served by acting on their responses as this will be likely to maintain engagement or create or develop it. An example of this might be the Year 1 or Year 2 teacher seeking to focus on pairs through, for example, socks, shoes or line partners for assembly. If the children normally group in threes at tables or in the line, and a child remarks that every day three children are chosen to take part in assembly, maybe the teacher would be tempted to run with that theme for a while. The teachers and trainees that I have spoken to vary in the extent to which they feel that pre-planned material can be adapted. Most, if not all, would agree that a big deviation away from the planned progression is, in general, to be avoided.

HOW WELL DO WE NEED TO KNOW OUR KNOWLEDGE?

The answer is we need to know it as well as we can. However, we are not qualified primary specialists to teach only maths, therefore confidence and knowledge will vary. We need to develop the skill of noticing what we are not completely sure of. The journey will be a longer one for some teachers. There is no correlation between our initial confidence levels in the classroom and where we end up. Most of us learn through experience and some of us utilise our experiences well regardless of our starting point. The examples from Chapter 7 should indicate the increased confidence and assurance that are prevalent in teachers working at an advanced level. The goal for us all is to develop some of those qualities and to understand what good quality mastery teaching is seeking to emphasise, and we are all capable of achieving this.

Good quality mastery teaching can be achieved with support. We have a right to expect support within the schools that we work in. Sometimes this is through mentoring and from more experienced colleagues, sometimes it is simply the idea that we support others more in some areas and learn from them in others. This notion of 'communities of learners' is essential to all schools developing.

What models of planning, development, support and implementation of mastery-style teaching are there?

PROBLEM SOLVING FRIDAY AT SHOREDITCH PARK

This approach, led by David Cunnelly, first introduced in Chapter 6, is an inventive idea from a not uncommon base. The school has had a fairly traditional approach to learning but was looking to move away from scheme-based approaches that have not developed understanding as much as David, in particular, would like. He felt that the idea of a problem solving approach on Fridays meant that a dialogue could begin about how we develop reasoning skills. He has been proactive with resources and colleagues have come in to watch his lessons. He is currently working with colleagues willing to share thinking. The 'problem solving Friday' has meant that whole staff dialogue has begun regarding the kind of work that children can do to allow understanding to emerge. In discussion together, we both have highlighted the roots of existing practice and how the future might play out.

The current existing practices include:

- Only a little time for team planning and discussion around pedagogy and practice.
- Enthusiastic teachers but a wide range of confidence in teaching for understanding.
- Children whose fluency across the school is underdeveloped, compromising the speed at which new material can be accessed and the extent to which learning can be developed.
- Some mastery knowledge from the maths lead but only emerging spread of mastery understanding related to developing fluency, reasoning and depth of understanding.

The practices that might be featured in the future include:

- Select a scheme to support planning.
- Continue to break down barriers regarding a dialogue about pedagogy and working together to move understanding forward.
- Targeted work to increase fluency regarding secure knowledge in number, particularly in the younger years, to provide a platform for depth to be developed more easily. This is harder to achieve in older classes, where currently the range of understanding has become so vast.

'TAKE TWO' AT TORRIANO PRIMARY SCHOOL

Conor Loughney is currently the maths lead at Torriano Primary School, and he is in the second wave of mastery-trained teachers. He visited Shanghai for two weeks and after being put forward by the hub, he now trains and works with the NCETM. He has studied and discussed mastery teaching closely with Chinese teachers in Shanghai, with those who have visited here and with his own staff.

The areas that he has focused on developing with staff so far relate to planning, questioning and identifying small but significant ideas to develop using multiple representations and stem sentences. Above all, he prioritises the need to reason and prove why the stem sentences are valid.

When he plans, Conor considers ways that will make learning explicit. For example, in order to understand divisions as relating to equal parts, we have to identify what are unequal parts and why. In order to identify odd and even numbers by their last integer (ones or units), we have to understand why this is so. As we internalise the impact of multiplying by multiples of ten, we also have to explore why these patterns relate to the fact that our base is in fact ten; our grouping and place value system creates these patterns. There is no magic about ten; similar patterns occur when numbers are multiplied by the base, be it two, six, 20 or 1,000.

He has modelled joint planning with other staff and taught a range of classes around the school for Torriano staff development. He has also supported heavily maths leads from schools who form part of his own development group for the year.

The 'Take Two' theme is worth exploring and it refers to the school's decision to allow staff understanding and development to emerge together. As a two-form entry school, there was the chance for teachers to plan lessons together and to debrief once the teaching had taken place – rather like the approach to lesson study that has emerged from Japan. This has become popular throughout South East Asia since the Trends in International Mathematics and Science Study (TIMSS) video study in 1999, and more recently in England as we have become interested in mastery teaching. In short, several teachers use a taught lesson as a basis for personal and professional development.

Lewis (2002) describes the lesson study cycle as having four phases:

- Goal-setting and planning, including the development of the lesson plan.
- Teaching the research lesson, enabling the lesson observation; Japanese lesson study – teacher professional development through communities of inquiry.
- The post-lesson discussion.
- The resulting consolidation of learning, which has many far-reaching consequences.
  (See also Lewis and Tsuchida, 1999 for teachers' comments on the impact of research lessons on their understandings about science teaching.)

Torriano have taken this further. They have funded a scheme where teachers would observe their year partner teach the lesson that had been co-planned. This meant that an opportunity to reflect (together) preceded the stage that followed. The second teacher was then observed as part of the appraisal cycle by senior staff teaching this rehearsed, analysed lesson. The school have since refined the process. Teachers, including senior managers, felt the process to be worthwhile but thought that the appraisal nature of the work affected relationships. The appraisal aspect has now been removed.

Learning communities such as the ones described in Japanese lesson study take place in a context. Doig and Groves (2011) go on to emphasise the relevance of such shared professional work as a means to allowing shared understanding of teachers to emerge at a deeper, maybe transferable, level. In China, the more developed maths teaching knowledge of most primary phase teachers leads to what Ma (1999) describes as 'profound understanding of fundamental maths (PUFM)'. We are all seeking that to a greater or lesser degree.

In Japan, the model lends itself well to a group (staff) of teachers developing together through discussion, shared experiences, reflection, research and input from those with more experienced pedagogy. The whole idea of sustaining professional development to develop confidence in subject knowledge and teaching pedagogy is crucial to the success of mastery in England.

The issue about the context of development is interesting. Senior teachers within the school feel the pressure to demonstrate progress in children and, indeed, they are often heavily responsible for ensuring that this is so. However, the process seems to be quite subtle. The way maths has been experienced for many teachers as learners means a nurturing, supportive process is what is needed. What helps to create an effective, nurturing environment? In my experience, deep confidence and knowledge from the nurturers, and a commitment from the school leaders to ensure they can affect change within the school through having time to support, advise and model, help to create this environment. These features are not easily achieved; they also take time and patience.

SUCCESSION PLANNING AT WIMBLEDON PARK

The sustained development of primary schools with regard to maths teaching has always seemed slightly vulnerable. Even in two-form entry schools and schools that appear to be progressing well, this can be changed by the departure of key staff, including maths leads, who value maths and facilitate change, and who have championed a commitment to development, time and resources, or the emerging of a new curriculum. One-form entry schools can be the most vulnerable to these changes, with the staff most needed to ensure change and development to maintain momentum being the most likely to leave.

The default option of many capable primary teachers can be to play it safe unless supported, encouraged and challenged to do otherwise. As such, the approach of the three-form Wimbledon Park School is interesting. In time, it is possible that the approaches being used may become more widespread.

The characteristics of the school's approach include:

- Headteacher Paul Lufkin, wise to the vagaries of staff changes, sees the need to plan for succession to overcome changes and departures that can otherwise undo good work.
- Two teachers, Ciara and Gemma, both accomplished enough to be mastery trained through the London South West hub, are the maths leads. Ciara can be chosen for the training and Gemma is involved with organising training for other teachers through the hub.
- A Teacher Research Group within the school involving a teacher from each year develops expertise within the school that can allow Vygotskian styles of interaction, as understanding is both imparted and developed among staff.
- Ciara and Gemma generate momentum among the rest of the year leads to oversee the development of their year group staff, and to ensure consistency and dialogue within years.
- Daily 8 am team meetings take place within year groups to discuss the lesson for the day (see Chapter 7). Year leads have tended to put together the weekly outline, flipcharts and adjustments. However, when talking to Gemma, it became clear that they also have a responsibility to develop staff. As the year progresses, other members are also supported in preparing resources. This is where the commitment to succession starts, as teachers who carry out their responsibilities effectively often have to move schools to gain a promotion. Therefore, it is important to have maths leads and year leads ready to step up to a new role if this happens. The end of the academic year can clearly bring up that situation.
- The nurturing of teachers within planned team groups helps confidence elsewhere. At Wimbledon Park, meetings have been held for parents to communicate and give examples of the school's commitment to fluency, reasoning and depth of understanding. An attendance of around 150 parents (albeit among a quite large school community) is a significant response and generates good dialogue. Many parents will not be familiar with mastery features. For example, themes covered can and will include progression, reasoning or the use of manipulatives. The answer for many parents, when they were at school, was the be all and end all of the work, really. Procedures were taught; the answer rather than the reasoning and understanding that lay behind it was the main goal.
- Alongside these features of school life, the opportunity to observe in one of the 18 classes from Years 1 to 6 (three per year) goes a step further in allowing parents to support the school's priorities in teaching maths to their children. If school and parents are both committed to the same goal, then progress is much more likely. The willingness of the staff to put their skills on public show can only come about through feeling supported rather than exposed.

There are ways in which teething troubles have to be negotiated. Parents who are allowed access to lessons sometimes focus on their own child rather than examining the big picture of the philosophy behind the lessons. A commitment to reasoning and depth is a choice against this, which emphasises linear progression. Traditionally, children achieving success are given problems involving larger numbers and a curriculum aimed at older children. This is not mastery. Mastery requires depth of understanding, the emphasised features of reasoning, and it also requires that key learning is made explicit and utilised by exploring key concepts through multiple representations.

The Wimbledon Park model demonstrates the opportunities that larger schools with year teams bring. They have the chance to create models of working that can sometimes withstand the changes that seem to be part of primary school life. Certainly, change seems to be very common in schools in large cities.

A LEARNING COMMUNITY WITH A MATHS HUB FOCUS AT ELMHURST PRIMARY SCHOOL

It is worth mentioning schools that are directly linked to maths hubs, such as Elmhurst. Clearly, the funding to organise, train and research that has been designated to hubs can impact on the development of maths within the school.

London North East maths hub list Elmhurst as their Teaching School Alliance and cite strong links with a range of organisations across primary schools, secondary schools, University College London, industry and beyond. Based in the same location, the heads of the school and the hub work closely together. Shared premises mean that attending the many training courses provided through the hub, many of which are free, is far easier, logistically, than for teachers in other schools. The close association with the maths hub and a commitment to developing the practice of all teachers within the school makes Elmhurst and other hub-linked schools attractive for new and experienced teachers seeking to further their achievements in teaching maths. For those committed to involvement in developing their maths teaching and that of their colleagues, schools such as these do appear as attractive places. However, again, commitment and knowledge within senior management and succession planning add to sustained growth.

SUKWINDER SAMRA, HEAD OF ELMHURST PRIMARY SCHOOL

In an interview with Sukwinder, it was interesting to hear her view on the development of other schools like Elmhurst, and how her model could become a blueprint. The maths hub initiatives in England only began in 2014. She feels a visit to Shanghai opened their eyes as to how current procedural approaches, even at a forward-thinking maths school such as Elmhurst, gave too much emphasis on unexplained methods that were not completely understood.

Sukwinder acknowledges that, in terms of resourcing and training, there were real opportunities that the school took advantage of. However, in time, that opportunity could be extended to all schools; certainly, there is a programme underway to try to achieve this. Sukwinder also feels that the trip to Shanghai highlighted several other key things, such as bar modelling, the value and importance of reasoning, teacher subject knowledge and depth of understanding.

When asked about the challenge of delivery of lessons to the whole class, Sukwinder distinguishes between 'catch up' and 'keep up'. There are medium-term catch-up groups in Years 3 and 4, although the group is larger in Year 3 where there are eight children currently being taught independently. The aim will be sustained input until those children can keep up with whole class delivery. She is excited that the current evaluations of the Year 4 cohort look so promising as this is the first year group that has experienced a mastery-style approach in maths from Year 1, and this is a four-form entry school.

She acknowledges the driving passion for maths from the Executive Head, Shahed Ahmed. He is a passionate mathematician, which helps. However, Sukwinder and I both agree that a head who completely empowers the maths lead can also oversee significant development in their school.

Staff training is obviously aided by the school being a lead school. Sukwinder acknowledges that transition when staff leave is a challenge, as it is anywhere else, and the fact that the commitment to maths is such a high priority does attract teachers who are both confident and interested in maths.

She is committed to 'Maths – No Problem!' as a scheme and staff training on this has been ongoing, particularly on how progression in work is structured. Sukwinder feels a national breakthrough is possible. The mastery training of 700 teachers by 2020, together with the rollout of support for schools from these people, should be reaching half the primary schools in England by that point. We both voice the opinion that more money could hasten the speed at which the transition to mastery teaching can happen, as it is important that momentum isn't lost. For example, newly trained mastery specialists only work with schools to support them for a year. There is currently no ongoing support after that. This will inevitably lead to some slippage.

She speaks positively about the 'White Rose' resources and particularly the NCETM resources that are constantly being updated and added to. We both worry about children in environments where mastery is not being developed and this includes secondary schools, where Sukwinder reports quite mixed approaches. For example, there is still reluctance to use CPA in situations where it is most needed to reduce cognitive load and to aid reasoning. She aligns herself with Professor Yeap Ban Har in stressing that the key thing is that tables have to be understood as well as memorized. She is keen to draw attention to the importance of bar modelling and also to the development of mastery principles within early years.

I can see Sukwinder feels much progress has already been made. If it is not yet enough, the development of Elmhurst and schools like it does show that establishing a learning community within a primary school can drive forward achievement and understanding in maths.

SETTING AT BYRON COURT

There are many models of grouping related to primary schools. The issue is not completely straightforward. There is no prescribed method of similar attainment grouping or the avoidance of such an approach. However, given the esteem in which Shanghai and East Asian maths teaching is held, there is a clear structure to much of the teaching that takes place there. There, they do not have an obvious ability group. There is a belief that the teacher input is accessible by the whole class. The outcomes, too, should be positive for the whole class. Broad-based understanding and sound knowledge should be developed by all. That is mastery.

The prospect of this being achieved can cause some doubts. Leaving aside the debate about the nature of the testing we use, the achievement of expected levels of the cohorts of recent years tends to have plateaued at around the 70% mark. Although it is higher in a number of schools, the overall national average has been around this mark. The causes of such a statistic have been debated and some common discussion points are as follows:

- Teaching to the test has elevated scores to an extent. However, the application of knowledge required in a number of questions means that it is not possible to simply practice questions and replicate them in a test. There has to be understanding that can be used flexibly.
- Teachers' own confidence and lack of development in achieving deep knowledge themselves limits the conversations, interactions and focus of learning that take place, and teachers are certainly capable of moving their knowledge forward. However, the curriculum is busy, the teaching loads are heavy, the staff make up is transitory and the school development plan and professional development extend to more things than developing teaching and learning in maths.
- Schemes can provide some good structure and support but even the good ones can struggle to bridge the gap between a pre-prepared lesson or sequence of lessons and the need to evaluate children's responses to what they are being taught. For example, where are they insecure? What did they fail to understand? What misconceptions affect their understanding? The extent of their fluency, or lack of it, undermines the work being covered. In short, teachers need to understand and follow the thread of well-constructed schemes but also know when and how to adapt and supplement effectively.
- The gap between the lower-attaining and the higher-attaining children has historically grown with each passing year in primary school: maybe this has been in part due to the tendency to create 'attainment groups' within classes from as young as reception (aged four). Jo Boaler captures this debate well in *The Elephant in the Classroom* (2009).

Jack Corson arrived at Byron Court in September as Assistant Head, having worked within Newham for a number of years. With regard to maths teaching and learning within the school, he discussed the school situation with the Head and staff and opted for the following model as a stopgap method. Across the top years, there is a group for higher-attaining children. The other three groups within the year are mixed-attainment groups. The philosophy behind this is historical in as much as children learn from and with their peers who are similar in attainment but not at the same point. Vygotsky cites the 'more knowledgeable other' as the model supporting development. Jack also concludes that in set groups the higher-attaining children benefit to an above expected level. The rest gain little benefit from setting by attainment. The lower-achieving children can regress. The reasons for this can vary, including teacher subject and content knowledge (Gudmundsdottir and Shulman, 1987), choice of teacher for higher and lower sets, and lowered self-esteem of some children, which may all contribute (Boaler, 2009).

Jack's feeling is that in the short term the higher-achieving children need to be targeted because the challenge to meet the needs of all children efficiently within a spread out class becomes excessive by upper Key Stage 2. Thus, in the short term this model of grouping is used. He is an experienced and able teacher; perhaps the good progress being made by the higher set he teaches is no real surprise. However, his medium-term goal is to increase the confidence levels of staff around effective use of the 'Maths – No Problem!' scheme as a basis for staff development and teaching, moving towards a goal of whole class teaching without attainment groups in a few years' time. It is likely that this process will start with younger children before the gap becomes too great. The thinking here is that whole class teaching has to start young, for example at Year 1, and be maintained. Within these groups, schools must be proactive to ensure all, or nearly all, children grasp the learning related to the curriculum and that some children are given the opportunity to gain a greater depth of understanding.

Thus, Jack's goal in a few years' time, when in fact the school will be a four-form entry school, will be to operate like Wimbledon Park: to have confidence within each year group, access to support and guidance, and succession planning options to deal with staff changes.

WHAT HAPPENS WHEN CHILDREN DON'T UNDERSTAND WHAT IS BEING TAUGHT?

Most children will misunderstand some initial teaching; a few will not initially understand very much of it. What happens then? It is crucial that there are plans in place to allow the gap not to grow too far. This is not to be achieved by putting a ceiling on the level of understanding achieved by children who understand well. It has to be about supporting those who may struggle initially. There are several options to support this, including:

- Tight lesson structures achieved through following some schemes (see Chapter 10 for further details on this).

- Intervention groups: In classic mastery schools in East Asia, there are often support groups in children's early school careers. Young children who don't seem ready to access whole class teaching effectively are taught separately for a while to allow them to develop basic knowledge and early fluency thought to be essential to make suitable progress. When this has been achieved, they return to the regular classroom to access whole class maths. Clearly, it makes more sense to intervene early to allow children to keep within reach of their peers.

Although the previous points could help support struggling children, we are not using this in the UK. We don't have the funding and our approach is a little different. We are pinning our hopes on tight provision through the early stages; we do try to provide additional support within the classroom. However, this cannot simply be a teaching assistant being loosely assigned to work with children who aren't achieving. Blatchford et al. (2012) critique the negative impact on learning that this can often, but not always, have.

Repeated focus teaching is now much more common. Children who are not understanding key learning spend more time being supported by the teacher once the main bulk of the class have experienced the whole class teacher input and moved onto independent work. This model is being used more commonly in schools now. It is a form of re-teaching.

RE-TEACHING

Many schools now use re-teaching, although it may be in a later stage within the lesson. Some re-teaching takes place before lessons or during assembly times. Whenever it happens it is likely to be when the class is doing something else. If it is within the maths lesson, then obviously this has implications on where the teacher's focus centres; it can make it harder for the teacher to move other, more secure children, towards understanding of greater depth. These are age-old problems.

INTERVENTION GROUPS

Some schools will set up intervention groups aimed at either narrowing the gap of attainment or stopping it from getting bigger when traditionally this is what has happened. Elmhurst Primary is one such school. Sukwinder Samra, introduced earlier in the chapter, is very excited by the Year 4 cohort at Elmhurst. Having experienced mastery-style teaching for several years, the informal and formal assessments of the group show significant promise, possibly pointing the way forward for what can be achieved. Other schools are also optimistic about children who have had promising Key Stage 1 experiences. Interestingly, at Elmhurst they have also identified gaps in learning among their

Year 3 class. These children are currently in an intervention group along the lines of the East Asian models in the early stages. The idea is that when they have secured sufficient understanding, they will return to the main class for maths lessons.

These are big problems, as one of our beliefs is that we shouldn't ability group. Here the idea is being turned on its head. We may need to organise focused 'attainment groups' to fast forward learning, to reduce gaps and to ensure whole class teaching is accessed effectively by all. We have not been averse to short-term targeted teaching, particularly in Year 2 and Year 6. This form of intervention can, and has, run for periods of time so that whole class approaches can be secured.

The assessment procedures at Elmhurst, as well as the high priority that developing mathematical understanding for all children has, means that it is likely this will succeed. Can the approach work across the UK? It could, but there may be some hurdles to over-come, including:

- Rigour of teaching approaches.
- Money, if medium-term, additional teaching groups are being created.
- Teacher confidence and knowledge.

Progress is being made on all of these points. The last problem might relate to question-ing that maths takes such a large priority over such a long period. In order to establish a system of mastery teaching, this might need to be the case. Maybe for a while, some other areas of study would be held back a little for some children.

WHOSE NEEDS COME FIRST?

Teaching effectively has long been something of a juggling act. We seek to teach and to intervene to maximise the impact on as many children as possible but we also have to be smart. We have to keep all children on board. The most vulnerable are the least secure. However, ignoring the needs of the higher-attaining and secure children is also a big over-sight with sad consequences, so the juggling act isn't always easy.

The needs of the most vulnerable must come first. They are the least independent. Prior to mastery schemes and planning, it would not be uncommon for class teachers to give whole class input and support less-secure children on Monday and Tuesday in a week, possibly Wednesday too. Some teachers will allocate a teaching assistant to support weaker children regularly. Although there are exceptions, this is not a valid strategy. The class teacher should be the lead practitioner. It would even be worth having the teach-ing assistant observe how the class teacher intervenes and teaches on Monday, ready for that input to continue on Tuesday. All things could be possible. The big idea would be that at some point in the week these less-secure children have to try to 'fly'. The inverted commas are to express what we are trying to achieve, namely to avoid smothering children by constantly telling them what to do as we need to let them begin to work independently after good-quality input.

Gemma Field (Year 4 teacher), first introduced in Chapter 7, is quite explicit about using this as a strategy. She explains that she feels that the lack of fluency is at the heart of the struggle of a handful of her Year 4 class. She works with them to make sure that the broad understanding is there that they can try to apply; their progress is slower for the reasons stated and they can sometimes lose heart. However, she would rather scaffold the work so that they use strategies that take longer but work for them, than smother them with an adult permanently on hand. Crucially, in addition to this, she is trying to develop their fluency so that this gap, which is affecting their ability to access whole class teaching, is reduced. This is done through directed support at home, some additional small focus group slots in the week and online resources. She feels that the aim in the future is to stop the gap growing so big at an earlier stage, much as the Shanghai, Singapore and East Asian strategy emphasises, through early targeted support and intervention.

MISCONCEPTIONS

The awareness of likely misconceptions has been a key part of enlightened primary maths teachers' pedagogy for some time. The works of Hansen (2014), Shulman (1986) and Rowland et al. (2009) all relate to the common misconceptions that are likely to be part of the primary classroom. For example, it is a common belief that numbers get bigger when we multiply and smaller when we divide. Whilst true in a number of cases, this is inaccurate and creates confusion when found not to be so.

Similarly, the equals sign is often used in limited circumstance so that it comes to mean 'make'. The calculation 6 + 4 = 10 is often seen as meaning 'six and four makes ten'. Therefore, when exposed to the statement 10 = 6 + 4, there is often confusion. The aim is to emphasise that '=' refers to something that is balanced, that has a similar value. This is not only accurate, it starts to form the basis for understanding that underpins more complex maths related to balanced equations and how they can be manipulated to deduce unknown values.

There are many similar notions across the entire primary curriculum at all ages; we don't need to feel bad about this. Misconceptions occur all the time with any subject, although science and maths understanding have often been developed by using the commonly held misconceptions as the starting point to move thinking forward.

Crucially, this awareness of misconceptions seems to underpin approaches that can be termed as a 'classic' approach to mastery, as shown through the teaching of Conor and Pinal in Chapter 7. It is also present in the thinking of the teachers such as Iona Mumby in Chapter 6, who promotes the use of misconceptions as a basis for teaching with older children in classes where the attainment levels have become more spread out, in a way that we are striving to eliminate at earlier stages in the school.

Conor identified possible misunderstanding and exposed it through activity and discussion with fractions by focusing on fractions that weren't correct. In the activities, he included unequal parts as well as different-sized wholes. This was showing an awareness of likely ways that children misunderstand. Whereas well-constructed, early teaching of maths can make misconceptions less likely to be held, they will always occur to a degree. The experienced teacher learns to have discussions that expose them and moves learning and understanding forward as much as possible. Iona, working with older children (Year 6) is regularly feeding misconceptions back into the lessons. She meets on a regular basis with her year partner to discuss the misconceptions that are prevalent and how these can be fed back in.

WHICH APPROACH WORKS BEST?

This is a good question. The classic approach from Conor is aimed at developing early secure understanding that can then be built on. Iona would subscribe to this view also. However, working in a Year 6 class, whose journey through the school hasn't consistently been supported by deep emphasis on understanding and reasoning, there is a short-term job to be done. Although this may take away from some mastery-style lesson planning, there is a deadline of May when the SAT captures the progress children have made. This is achieved through a one-off exam, not teacher evidence of the kinds of reasoning children have shown. She hopes, in three or four years' time, to teach differently as the impact of a mastery approach through the school creates Upper Key Stage 2 classes where the gap is not so great and the range of misconceptions is not so wide and varied.

The middle ground might be as at Elmhurst, where Pinal adopts a classic mastery approach with a Year 5 class. Here there has been greater exposure to teaching for depth of understanding for longer. We live in an interesting time. The ability to move the overall understanding of a wide range of children forward seems tantalisingly close. However, the situation is vulnerable due to the following reasons:

- It may not be possible to sustain maths being the main focus of school development indefinitely.
- Teacher turnover, particularly in one-form and even two-form entry schools, makes succession planning difficult.
- Teacher subject knowledge and awareness of how to use this to have good conversations is varied; the support systems emerging in schools need to be maintained and extended. The hub-initiated mastery training programme development should assist this.

CONCLUSION

We can see that although there is a lot, potentially, to gain from adopting the content and style of teaching of East Asian countries, through what has become known as a mastery approach, there are some real dilemmas to overcome. We do not have our primary children taught by maths specialists. We have had wide-ranging levels of attainment across classes and schools and mastery understanding has to be for everyone. This chapter has covered many positives that are emerging in the light of the challenges we face. We have to have maths as a key school focus for several years now. We have to fund new training beyond 2020 as well as maintain the progress that is already being made. We have to ensure there are communities of learning and support within every school to allow confidence to grow and momentum to be maintained. It can be done, but it requires a full commitment at national level that filters down.

CHAPTER 10:

ASSESSMENT AND MASTERY

What you will learn from this chapter:

- How key, planned learning is developed through multiple representations around discussion and activity
- Mastery teaching involves developing an understanding of how to build and develop understanding through progression and variation
- An awareness of how understanding can be demonstrated and developed at greater depth through deliberate focus on reasoning and articulation
- Success in standardised assessment tasks alone does not ensure mastery of understanding; we can ensure that our teaching allows both of these things to emerge
- Assessment is necessary to evaluate whether the planned learning has taken place or needs further support and reinforcement
- Assessment of greater depth of understanding can be present, partly present or not present at all for any child. It may need evaluation of several pieces of work to decide if it is an overall fit for any one child

INTRODUCTION

We have assessed children in terms of their ability to answer questions where some application of knowledge is required for quite a while now. There have been variations in the way that the questions have been framed. Some teachers and schools have attempted to teach effectively across the school in order to allow children to feel comfortable in this work, regardless of how the questions are framed. However, in many cases the game has played out a little differently. The most common approach has seen a particular drive towards achievement in the standardised tests at Year 2 and Year 6. In many cases, teachers in those years have been charged with the task of ensuring children are familiar with particular kinds of questions. Such familiarity has, at times, been instead of developing deeper understanding in children through good conversations and ensuring that key mathematical points have been understood and articulated by the children. The redesigning of the SATs in the last two years has meant this is now not so much of an option. Without the kind of understanding referred to as 'mastery', children will not really be able to rely on mere familiarity around content. Certainly, teachers should be striving for mastery of understanding. Fluency may use memory and recall but there should, overall, be a focus on understanding. How might we hope these areas of study would be both understood and answered?

SATS TEST QUESTIONS IN YEAR 6: ARITHMETIC

Let us now have a look at some of the questions used to assess children on arithmetic:

Q1

40 + 1,000

This is a place value question. Children would have needed to be comfortable understanding about ten in one column being worth one in the next column to the left. The zero is used as a place holder. Thus digits used in different columns have different but related values, e.g. four, ones, four tens and four hundreds. Early representations of tens and ones with suitably scaffolded ways of recording would have built up the knowledge that powers of ten are recorded as a single digit. Thus 30 + 400 means that four hundreds and three tens are recorded thus:

H	T	O
4	3	

The zero is needed to demonstrate the column value of the digits:

H	T	O
4	3	0

Let us look at another question:

Q2

__ − 100 = 1,059

As with the previous example, this is also a place value question. However, it also relates not only to understanding addition and subtraction as inverse operations, but also to seeing this concept as a part − part whole link that could be represented as a bar model (Figure 10.1).

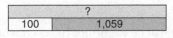

Figure 10.1 Bar model representing __ − 100 = 1,059

The 100 is being subtracted and the 1,059 still remains. So the original total (1,159) is the sum of the two numbers.

Q3

30 × 40 = __

The base system we use (base ten) means we regroup when we reach this number. Thus there is a connection between these multiplication calculations:

3×4 12

3×40 120

30×40 1,200

Three lots of four is going to produce 12 of something whether it be tens, hundreds or thousands. Thus $3 \times 400 = 30 \times 40$. One number is made ten times smaller and the other ten times bigger.

Q4

$581 \div 7 = \_$

Whether the connection is made through chunking or a more traditional method, it is essential that children develop an understanding of division as a grouping procedure rather than simply the 'share between' approach. This question, in essence, is asking how many groups of seven are there in 581. The task can be calculated by chunking groups away from 581 or building up to that total.

```
   083                          083
 7)581-                       7)581
   560   (80 × 7)             581    (83 × 7)
    21-                        21    (3 × 7)
    21   (3 × 7)              560    (80 × 7)
     0                         0
```

(add 21) 581   (**3** × 7)

(add 210) 560   (**30** × 7)

350   (**50** × 7)

The answer to the calculation will be 83 groups of seven which will equal 581. Obviously this can be refined for convenience.

Q5

$9 - 3.45 = \_$

To be able to do this calculation, knowledge that ten tenths make a whole would be refined through number lines involving tenths.

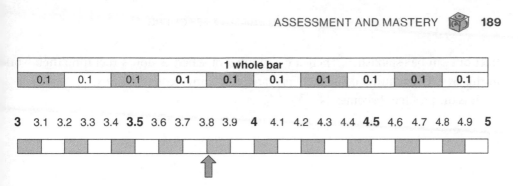

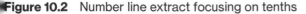

Figure 10.2 Number line extract focusing on tenths

The number line extract in Figure 10.2 will help us to have a productive conversation with children about decimals linked to pictorial representations. For example, what do the two digits in the number 3.8 tell us? Which whole number would we round to and why?

The use of Dienes equipment scores well here as the wholes (100 square or tens) are a known resource.

On the empty number line (Figure 10.3), partitioning of numbers is important. Surrounding the use of decimal columns is the extended idea that ten in one column is worth one in the column to the left. This is how grouping in our base ten happens.

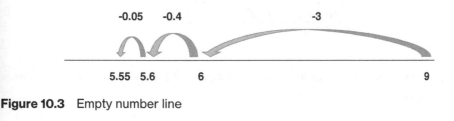

Figure 10.3 Empty number line

Q6

$$\frac{3}{4} - \frac{2}{8} = \underline{\quad}$$

One might be looking for an understanding that quarters can be converted into eighths (as shown in Figure 10.4).

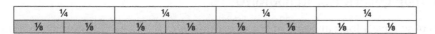

Figure 10.4 Example of a bar model

This should have emerged initially through concrete and pictorial form. It should then have been refined to focus on the fact that four is a factor of eight and therefore equivalent fractions can be established. There are a number of schemes now structuring their work in this way. They cannot completely prepare pre-planned conversations.

Thus the problem becomes $\frac{6}{8} - \frac{3}{8} = \frac{3}{8}$.

Q7

$418 \times 48 = \_\_$

The worry would be that this would be rote learnt as a procedure, known, remembered but not understood. Hopefully, it would have emerged from a grid multiplication focus where place value knowledge is assured (Table 10.1). Then it can be refined to efficient procedures that are also understood.

Table 10.1 Representation of 418 × 48

		4	1	8
			4	8
	3	3	4	4
1	6	7	2	0
2	0	0	6	4
1	1			

A left-field idea would be to multiply 418 by 100, then halve it and subtract two lots of 100. For example:

$418 \times 100 = 41,800$

$418 \times 50 = 20,900$

$2 \times 418 = 836$

Answer: **20,064**

SATS TEST QUESTIONS: REASONING

Let us now have a look at some of the questions used to assess children on reasoning:

Q1

What number is ten times greater than 907 (Table 10.2)?

Table 10.2 Representation of question 1

Th	H	T	O
	9	0	7
9	0	7	0

It has been the case that if children could say that, in order to multiply by ten, you moved the digits one column to the left that this was thought to indicate depth of understanding. Now, it is felt that there is still room for further discussion and understanding. Why does this mean the digits stay in the same order? Multiplying by one or ten, or indeed any power of ten, maintains this sequence of digits because these powers of ten are our column heading. We multiply by the constituent parts of a number. We can break this down into steps; for example, Table 10.3.

Table 10.3 Representation of 127 × 10

100 (× 10)	=	1,000
20 (× 10)	=	200
7 (× 10)	=	70
	Total	1,270

Q2

Complete Table 10.4. One row has already been done.

Table 10.4 Adding 1,000

Number	1,000 more
3,500	4,500
85	
	9,099
	15,250

This exercise has a clear mastery feel about it. Children will need to be made familiar with the effect of addition and subtraction as inverse operations. Hopefully, the discussions and experiences would allow them to be able to articulate the following:

- 'I put 1,085 here because that is 1,000 bigger than 85.'
- 'I put 8,099 in the left-hand column as it shows that 9,099 is 1,000 more than the number I am seeking.'

Q3

In Figure 10.5 tick two shapes that are ¾ shaded.

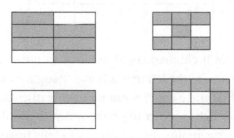

Figure 10.5 Four shaded shapes

As we will see when evaluating whether children are working at greater depth, we need the chance to see whether they can reason effectively. In this exercise, the chance is not present yet. A stronger question would be if children had been asked to explain why they made their choices. This exercise has clear links with the lesson taught by Pinal Sheth in Chapter 7. We just need to go further with the conversations we are having with our classes. We should spend more time reasoning about equivalence and difference; debating, explaining, questioning, reaching agreement. Maths leads can, and should, generate such discussions around staff; many of us have not spent enough time ourselves in such discussion. It will take time.

Q4

Round 84,516 to the nearest 10, 100 and 1,000.

The understanding required would centre around being able to identify the given column heading that the rounding should link to, for example, 'hundreds'. Anything after this column would need to be a zero. In this case, 84,516 will lie between 84,500 and the next multiple of the given column heading, 84,600 (Figure 10.6).

Figure 10.6 Representation of 84,516

Such work will have begun initially through the nearest multiples of ten with numbers between 10 and 90. Variation and progression will have taken the focus through the barrier of 100, between 0 and 10, decimal rounding, hundreds, thousands and beyond. This may be a journey across several years. Children will have had extended opportunities to ascertain key understanding before the kind of work here is tackled.

The following stems could be used for this example:

* 'When rounding to a power of ten you need to identify the two values of such a power either side of the number you are dealing with.' The stem here is capturing an abstraction, an explanation showing deep understanding of place value. It would have been borne out of much earlier work across time that might have begun several years before.
* 'We often round to a power of ten to allow us to estimate more easily.' For example, 49 + 32 will be roughly equivalent to 50 + 30.

Q5

Layla completes one-and-a-half somersaults in a dive. How many degrees does Layla turn through in her dive? (See Figure 10.7.)

Figure 10.7 Layla completing one-and-a-half somersaults in a dive (Crown copyright, 2017)

Progression to this point would involve some of the following:

a. Physically turning through part whole turns, including right angles, and establishing how many similar-sized jumps make a whole turn.
b. Experience of part whole turns when the starting orientation is not north, e.g. west, south, east, progressing to north east, south east, south west, north west.
c. Repeating the process but including clockwise and anti-clockwise rotation to clarify that the turn size is still the same.
d. Manipulating objects such as pencils, toy cars and broomsticks to provide multiple rep-resentations and experiences.
e. Applying the key learning to instructions as well as their own physical representation.

It is worth noting the fluency required at this point. The understanding may well be there but without the factual knowledge that there are 90° in a right angle, the answer is difficult to secure.

Q6

Amina posts three large letters. The postage costs the same for each letter. She pays with a £20 note. Her change is £14.96. How much did each letter cost to send?

To answer this question, a bar model could be used (Figure 10.8).

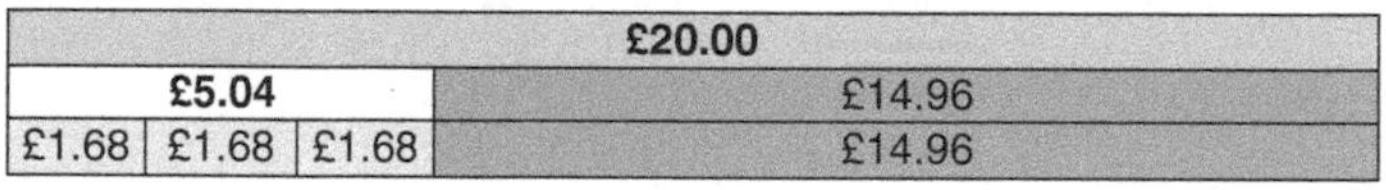

£20.00				
£5.04			£14.96	
£1.68	£1.68	£1.68	£14.96	

Figure 10.8 Example of a bar model to answer the question

If you buy stamps for three letters, then you need to divide what you have spent by three to find the cost of one stamp. In order to do that, we would have to find out what £20.00 subtract £14.96 is (£5.04). The cost of three stamps is £5.04.

504 ÷ 3 = 168

This will mean that one stamp costs £1.68.

This is a multi-part question that builds on the need to represent the problem through a part – part whole model, for example, bar modelling. The bar model itself demonstrates a lot of reasoning but the understanding shown would be deeper with a worded explanation. I worked out that the three stamps would cost whatever needed to be added to the change to get to the original £20 that Amina started with. That amount of £5.04 was the cost of three identically priced stamps and so needed to be divided into three equal parts. I converted £5.04 into 504p:

504(p) ÷ 3 = 168(p).

168(p) = £1.68

Q7

Adam says, '0.25 is *smaller* than ⅖'. Explain why he is correct.

If a whole is cut into fifths then each fifth has a value of 0.2 because ten tenths make a whole.

⅖ is equivalent to 2 × 0.2 which makes 0.4. This is bigger than 0.25 (Figure 10.9).

Figure 10.9 Demonstration of why Adam is correct

MASTERY AND GREATER DEPTH

Lucy Blewett, maths lead and organiser of the Primary Advantage Maths Conference in January 2018, defined the difference between mastery and greater depth. She argued that it was possible to 'master something without achieving greater depth'. She reasoned that 'all children should master all learning' and that 'some of them would be able to apply this knowledge at greater depth if and when we give them the chance' (Blewett, 2018).

The NCETM documents maintain that the understanding that we seek in children needs to be evidenced through explanation and multiple representation; apply the idea to your own work in making up further examples. Building on this, children need to be able to recognise new learning in new and different situations. This is not just some children; this is what we seek to do with all children. This is mastery; it is not necessarily working with a 'greater depth' of understanding. The NCETM identifies certain features that are characteristic of working with depth of understanding, including:

- Independence of work both in solving and investigating features.
- Communicating clearly and justifying reasoning are key.
- Questioning and responding to other theories and reasoning related to these responses.

Many writers including Tony Eaude reference the knowledge of a subject at a deeper level. Eaude (2014) references 10,000 hours as a guide to developing such a level of expertise and Skemp (1987) references relational understanding that analyses connections and sees links. Yeap Ban Har references Skemp in his descriptions about mastery and Singapore style CPA approaches through the 'Maths – No Problem!' scheme of work which he is closely associated with. Mike Askew, an experienced writer on primary maths teaching, writing in *Teach Primary* magazine (2016) distinguishes between a novice, an apprentice, mastery and mastery with depth.

Table 10.5 Distinguishing between novice, apprentice, mastery and mastery with depth (Askew, 2016)

	Fluency	Problem Solving	Reasoning
Novice	Evidence of limited knowledge and/ or incorrect understanding of the necessary mathematical concepts or procedures	No evidence of a productive method or strategy; the approach chosen will not lead to a solution Little or no evidence of engagement with the task	Reasons are put forward with no mathematical basis. No correct justification for answers is present
Apprentice	A correct, or partially correct, solution is reached, but naïve or inefficient methods are used	A partially correct strategy is chosen, or a correct strategy chosen that solves part of the task. Some previous knowledge is drawn on, demonstrating some appropriate engagement with the task	There is evidence of some correct reasoning, explaining or justifying, with trial and error, or unsystematic trying of several cases
Mastery	A correct solution is reached using appropriate prior knowledge and procedures	Correct strategies or methods are chosen basen on the mathematics of the task. Evidence of planning or monitoring approaches. Evidence of application of previous problem solving strategies	Reasons for explanations have a sound basis in mathematics. A systematic approach and/or justification of correct reasoning is present. There is some evidence of making connections
Mastery with depth	A correct solution is reached using effective and efficient prior knowledge and procedures	The problem solving method is efficient and effective. There is evidence of self-monitoring of progress and evaluating the solution. Adjustments to the method, if necessary, are made, and/ or alternative approaches are considered	Reasons are clearly communicated and well grounded in mathematics. Arguments are provided that justify and support decisions made and conclusions reached. There is evidence of connecting several aspects of mathematics

With mastery comes fluency and some confidence to reason and know why something is correct. There is quality and consistency in reasoning and justification as well as choices of communication. There are links with other aspects of maths. The metacognition (Flavell,

1976) qualities related to self-monitoring contribute to progress more consistently. This includes being able to detect errors and the need for adjustments to one's approach.

ASSESSMENT MATERIALS

The content domain exemplifies the minimum content pupils are required to evidence in order to show mastery of the curriculum. The cognitive domain aims to measure the complexity of application and depth of pupils' understanding. The questions, tasks and activities provided in these materials seek to reflect this requirement to master content in terms of both skills and depth of understanding.

(Askew et al., 2015a, b)

This is the key point. Mastery teaching involves teaching for understanding, not just answers. With that understanding comes the opportunity to begin to use it to develop deeper understanding. This involves starting to use reasoning and justification along with organisation of thinking. At the same conference as Lucy Blewett, speaker Sami Miller (2018), a consultant who works with Oxford University Press, built on this idea to reason that in order for children to become confident 'reasoners' and resourceful learners, they have to be given the chance to develop resilience, to question each other and to justify their thoughts.

I would agree with all of this, adding that we must actually strive to develop children as learners in maths, who are able to treat success and failure ('these two imposters' (Kipling, 1943)) in only one way, curiously. The only thing that matters is why it has happened. Thus, if they have not succeeded, then the important question is why. Likewise, if success has been achieved, the reason for it is all that matters. For too long, it has been the praise from the teacher that has underpinned what a child thought success was; that should not be the case. The teacher has to help children to develop resilience in their attitude to work. It is the struggle that we learn most through. Much of this thinking would be supported through Carol Dweck's work on 'mindset' (2017). With these thoughts in our mind, the NCETM resources support us well.

EXAMPLES OF MASTERY AND GREATER DEPTH

What we need are examples to demonstrate clearly the knowledge and understanding we are seeking for virtually all children and how we can keep providing extended work that takes this understanding to a deeper level. The initial example is the kind of thing some teachers already feel comfortable leading but many will be seeking to become confident to do so over time. Remember there will be texts with clear content and teacher notes as well as colleagues to co-plan and discuss with.

There is not more content covered but there is more time spent covering the same content. This might mean that if we spend more time covering the same content, we will get through less content in the time available, which is correct. There is already debate about whether the content in the curriculum is too extensive; certainly in Shanghai and Singapore some aspects of maths are covered later than we currently teach them; for example, the teaching of fractions. This allows the operations that underpin the mathematical nature of fractions, particularly division, to be understood more fully.

This initial example emerges from some extended work Jack Corson at Byron Court was doing with his class about fractions in Year 5. Let us look at this question:

- 'If we increase the numerator and denominator by one will we increase the value of the fraction? Always, sometimes or never?'

In order to answer this question, it is necessary to understand the meaning of numerator and denominator. That is achieved through focus on such terminology, repeated use of it by the teacher and children until it is accepted classroom vocabulary. Therefore, the vast majority of children will learn to solve the question by representing it, investigating it and coming to a conclusion (Figure 10.10).

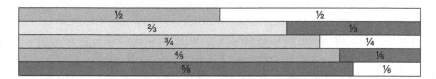

Figure 10.10 Representation of increasing the numerator and denominator by one

This fairly straightforward investigation can allow a child to conclude that there is a pattern whereby the remaining part of the whole is getting smaller.

Will the children be able to say why? Some will explain that because the numerator is increasing by one each time, the size of the remaining part of the whole is getting smaller, so the fraction size is increasing. In proper fractions, there will be the same number of missing parts of a whole if the numerator and denominator are increased. Some may conclude that the fraction will always increase in value.

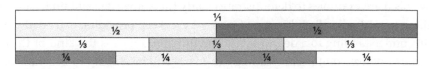

Figure 10.11 Representation of fractions with the same value

From Figure 10.11, we can see that the illustrated fractions have the same value even though numerator and denominator have increased by one:

$\frac{1}{1} = \frac{2}{2} = \frac{3}{3} = \frac{4}{4}$

There is no change in the value of the fraction when the numerator and denominator are the same. Increasing each simply maintains one whole. It is merely the number of denominations that is different. As the fractional value becomes greater than one the pattern shifts again:

- $\frac{2}{1}$ becomes $\frac{3}{2}$
- $\frac{3}{2}$ becomes $\frac{4}{3}$
- $\frac{4}{3}$ becomes $\frac{5}{4}$
- $\frac{5}{4}$ becomes $\frac{6}{5}$

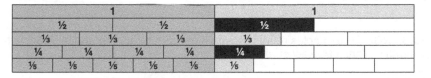

Figure 10.12 Representation of decreasing the value of the fraction

Now the addition of one to the numerator and denominator decreases the value of the fraction. The numerator is always one more than the denominator. However, now the single denomination above the whole gradually decreases in its value as the size of the denominator increases (Figure 10.12).

A teacher generating this activity and the accompanying thought to go with it, might ask children to record what is the effect of adding one to each value, both numerator and denominator. The children might be asked to record and reason using a stem sentence. Some teachers, as we have seen, will guide children to use denominator and numerator in their explanation so that learning can become explicit.

Possible answers to this might include:

- 'The value will stay the same because numerator and denominator have both been increased by the same amount.'

This is incorrect unless the numerator and denominator are the same to start with. If other children cannot disprove the claim, then the teacher might ask children to try to add one to the numerator and denominator in the fractions, $\frac{2}{2}$ or $\frac{5}{4}$, to draw, represent them and conclude; namely that this answer is only sometimes true.

- 'The value of the fraction will increase because the numerator is becoming a larger (greater) amount of the whole. Two thirds has a third missing. Three quarters has a quarter missing. A quarter is smaller than a third because the greater the denominator the smaller the value of each piece (denomination).' Although this is well-reasoned, it is only accurate for proper fractions but indicative of greater depth.

The teacher might prompt children to investigate fractions equivalent to one (a whole) and greater than a whole (improper fractions). What if the fraction had a value greater than one? What then?

NCETM EXAMPLES RELATING TO MASTERY UNDERSTANDING AND MASTERY WITH GREATER DEPTH

Table 10.6 shows examples relating to mastery and mastery with greater depth for Year 1 on number and place.

Table 10.6 NCETM examples relating to mastery understanding and mastery with greater depth in Year 1 (Askew et al., 2015a)

Selected National Curriculum Programme of Study Statements	Pupils should be taught to: count to and across 100, forwards and backwards, beginning with zero or one, or from any given number count, read and write numbers to 100 in numerals, count in multiples of twos, fives and tens given a number, identify one more and one less
The big ideas	The position a digit is placed in a number determines its value.
	The language used to name numbers does not always expose the place value, for example the word 'twelve' does not make it transparent that the value of this number is ten and two.
	It is important that children develop secure understanding of the value of each digit.
	Place value is based on unitising: treating a group of things as one 'unit'.
	In mathematics, units can be any size, for example, units of one, two, five and ten.
	In place value units of one, ten and 100 are used
Mastery	Compare amounts.
	What's the same? What's different?
	Children compare the bead strings and notice:
	One has nine beads and the other has six beads.
	Nine is three more than six.
	Six is three less than nine.
	Pupils should be able to successfully respond to questions such as:
	• Count forwards from 36, etc.
	• Point to the third object in the line.
	• Show me eight cubes.
	Pupils should demonstrate one-to-one correspondence, cardinality and conservation of number

Mastery with greater depth	I am going to count on from 20. Will I say the number 19? Convince me.
	I am going to count on in twos from three. Will I say an even number? Convince me.
	I am going to count backwards from 20. How many steps will it take to reach zero? Convince me.
	I am going to count backwards in twos from 20. How many steps will it take to reach zero? Convince me

The big ideas section in Table 10.6 helps to contextualise what the teacher is trying to achieve. It can be a starting point. Teachers and trainees may want to use a core textbook, such as Haylock (2019). The point is to ground yourself in overall goals related to understanding.

The mastery section references skills and thinking related to fluency and multiple representation. We see that the extended variation to develop wider understanding and the reasoning about why is what underpins greater depth of mastery.

Let us now look at one of the questions mentioned in Table 10.6:

I am going to count on in twos from three. Will I say an even number? Convince me.

Possible answers to this question include:

- I know we won't say an even number if we are on three and keep jumping in twos.
- Jumping in twos will keep me on whatever kind of number I start with because the pattern goes odd even odd even odd even. I will keep missing out the even numbers and land on odds.

It is the richness of the question that makes the child think about why something is so. Some children spot patterns and reason spontaneously. This approach, based on extensive reasoning and justification, ensures that more of the thinking that used to be spontaneous actually happens. We are seeking to prod firmly to get children to discover and articulate things that only happened now and again in enlightened moments.

The NCETM uses and identifies four key features as their basis for mastery teaching:

- Development of fluency.
- Multiple representation.
- Procedural and conceptual variation.
- Reasoning and articulation.

Whichever broad definition of mastery we use, we can follow the listed features. The mastery achievements outlined let us see the promotion of fluency in counting. These activities would be varied to include different objects (pegs, fruit, children, wheels) and orientations (rows, columns, spirals, diagonals). The greater depth would relate, as we see, to the variation in both the questioning and the need to reason as well as solve. The questions exploring depth require more fluency, they are cognitively more challenging requiring application of knowledge, and they need articulation to justify how the answer has been achieved and why this makes it correct.

The key thing is to be sure to internalise how the depth is achieved; it is through amending what is currently being done to provide a little more challenge. The variation is crafted to take the thinking around the same theme a little further.

Let us now see how this plays out in Year 3 (Table 10.7).

Table 10.7 NCETM examples relating to mastery understanding and mastery with greater depth in Year 3 (Christie et al., 2015)

Selected National Curriculum Programme of Study Statements	Pupils should be taught to: count from zero in multiples of four, eight, 50 and 100, work out if a given number is greater or less than ten or 100, recognise the place value of each digit in a three-digit number (hundreds, tens, and ones), solve number problems and practical problems involving these ideas
The big ideas	The value of a digit is determined by its position in a number. Place value is based on unitising, treating a group of things as one 'unit'. This generalises to 3 units + 2 units = 5 units (where the units are the same size)
Mastery	What number is represented in each set? (Picture of base ten Dienes – hundreds, tens and ones showing the numbers 231, 352, 423)
Mastery with greater depth	What is the value of the number represented by the counters in the place value grid? Hundreds, tens, ones? Using all of the counters, how many different numbers can you make? Have you made all the possible numbers? Explain how you know (see Figure 10.13)

Mastery-level activities explore different ways children can show understanding of represented amounts using powers of ten, e.g. ones, tens, hundreds (and later thousands and above). These will be explored through Dienes, place value counters and other pictorial representations of such groups (packs of books, pencils, etc.).

The greater depth questions explore the ability to reason and articulate that will show the ability to calculate, adapt learnt procedures and the application of knowledge moving towards justifying their choices.

The NCETM examples here explore the following kinds of question:

- If I rearrange the ten counters into hundreds, tens and ones, what is the highest total I can make.

Figure 10.13 Illustration of rearranging the ten counters into hundreds, tens and ones

Using the character 'Captain Conjecture', children have to decide whether Captain Conjecture is right to say the arrangement of counters in Figure 10.13 creates the highest three-digit number possible with these ten counters. They have to explain their choice. This takes the tasks to a new level. It is not just about understanding the procedure and answering the questions, although this is necessary. In this example, children have to reason, articulate and justify their decision. Clearly, discussion is a good thing, although teachers will want to ensure that a child can reason and to what standard.

Possible answers here would include:

- 'I think it wouldn't be right because all the counters could go in the hundreds column.' This is thoughtful but wrong; there are ten counters and they could not all go in the hundreds column as there would then be ten hundreds (1,000). This would be a four-digit number.
- 'I think it would be right because you have to have something in each column so eight hundreds and one in the other two columns is the best you can do.' There is logic shown in this answer, but it is inaccurate because we can of course have a placeholder. Therefore 910 and 901 are both higher in value than the 811 shown. Thus, in fact, 910 would be the highest three-digit number.

In terms of developing children's reasoning and articulation, working in pairs and then a whole class discussion could and would move a lot of thinking forward. Periodically a teacher would want to give children opportunities to work independently. The chance to reason independently emerges, I would argue, from refined reasoning from paired, group and whole class discussions, benefiting from guided tasks; periodically the reasoning needs to take place alone. Some teachers work from a model of thinking alone, discussing in pairs and small groups, and then as a class. The Year 1 and Year 3 examples shown in Tables 10.6 and 10.7 both allow for greater depth of understanding to emerge.

IS THIS KIND OF REASONING DIFFICULT TO DEVELOP?

I don't believe so. The issue for me is that in the past we have not ensured this kind of thinking happened regularly and with a wide range of children. It is a case of taking further what we gave the chance to be understood in the past. Children will, I believe, show us they can reason effectively, if given a regular and sustained opportunity to do so. Perhaps it is about ensuring the reasoning questions are such that they need to reach for the convincing language. Also, that they need to question and evaluate the comments of other children to agree or contest.

However, we can also see that the development is one we can and could plan for ourselves (see Chapter 8). Through this model, we see that we can and could develop skills and knowledge in all children. The chance to extend those skills and knowledge, through variation and opportunities to reason, gives us the chance to develop and evaluate how well children can explain, reason and justify. This is what demonstrates greater depth of understanding, and its progression can be described as follows:

- **Describing:** simply tells what they did.
- **Explaining:** offers some reasons for what they did. These may or may not be correct. The argument may not yet hang together coherently. This is the beginning of inductive reasoning.
- **Convincing:** confident that their chain of reasoning is right, and may use words such as 'I reckon' or 'without doubt'. The underlying mathematical arguments may or may not be accurate, yet are likely to have more coherence and completeness than the explaining stage. This is called inductive reasoning.
- **Justifying:** a correct logical argument that has a complete chain of reasoning to it and uses words such as 'because', 'therefore', 'and so', 'that leads to' ...
- **Proving:** a watertight argument that is mathematically sound, often based on generalisations and underlying structure. This is also called deductive reasoning.

(NRICH Primary Team, 2014)

Many have discussed reasoning in terms of progression. However, this outlined progression is one reference point to use to ensure increasing rigour in reasoning emerges. Of course it links to the teacher's ability to generate discussion and suspend resolution until the differing views have been aired. Not having an opinion is not an option.

Some exercises were used in the classroom to encourage reasoning and justification by children. For example, looking at Figure 10.14, in which shape has there been a greater proportion shaded? Explain your answer.

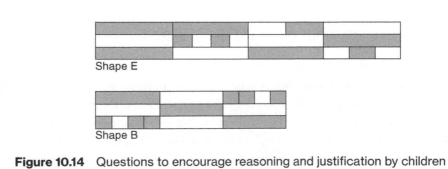

Shape E

Shape B

Figure 10.14 Questions to encourage reasoning and justification by children

Another exercise was used to further this reasoning and justification. Looking at Figure 10.15, how many of the four shapes have had half of the shapes shaded? Explain how you know.

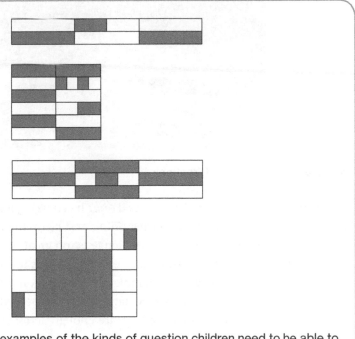

Figure 10.15 Further examples of the kinds of question children need to be able to reason about as well as answer

A number of schools are now collecting and analysing evidence of progression in children's work. This can be a rich idea in many ways, including:

- The progression from describing to explaining can be emphasised and evaluated. With the passing of time, this can be extended to develop deeper reasoning, justifying and articulation.
- It establishes a culture of learning that is extremely empowering for children. Gradually, they are taking on the idea that they can prove to themselves whether their claims and reasoning are valid.
- The use of peer learning becomes incredibly important. Rich problems are those that are not easily solved by just one person. The skill amongst peers becomes one of establishing who is saying something that is relevant and why.
- There is a new challenge for the teacher: evaluating the merits of children's claims demands that they know not just answers but the degree to which claims being made are justified. In turn, this emphasises the need to respond and question to clarify children's understanding and test the rigour of what they are saying. This can appear daunting at times, initially at least. Yet, the only real crime a teacher can commit is in *not* challenging themselves to lead these discussions and provide opportunities, regularly, for them to take place.

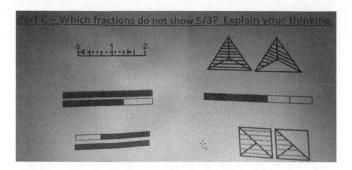

Figure 10.16 Examples of fractions

Why is the question in Figure 10.16 a good one? It can be argued that it is a good question because the focus is going to be on reasoning and clarifying beyond doubt why something is correct or not correct. If the challenge is too great, it can be scaffolded through peer support, teacher-led discussion and resources. If it is too easy, then it can be varied to create additional challenge, for example, by adding more complex denominators. We know there will be reasoning and articulation. The teacher will need to be clear how to evaluate whether the understanding is secure enough across the whole class or whether further scaffolding is needed for some.

IMPLICATIONS FOR ASSESSMENT WITHIN A MASTERY APPROACH

In the short term, there are one or two problems, already discussed. In the long term, the future looks potentially bright. We have seen how many of the current Key Stage 2 SATs questions can be accomplished well as a result of mastery teaching with an emphasis on reasoning and explanation. This is currently required only some of the time in the tests.

Given the wide-ranging attainment levels in primary maths lessons for our current Upper Key Stage 2 children, it is hard to implement effectively a complete mastery approach. As we have seen, our teachers are adaptive. They apply some of the mastery philosophy input, but only some because the conditions, involving wide-ranging current attainment and unfamiliarity with reasoning and explaining, make this a challenge. That will change in coming years if mastery approaches are embedded further down the school.

What we are now seeking is for the methods of assessing progress at the end of key stages to come in line with the philosophy behind a mastery approach. We are seeking multiple representation, fluency, reasoning and articulation. We need questions where greater depth gradually becomes the focus. We need good day-to-day teaching pedagogy in the majority of lessons taught, with crafted variation in the way children are exposed to areas of primary maths. I believe the process to achieve this is clearly underway. Sessions supporting the reasoning of teachers can really drive confidence forward.

CONCLUSION

What are the issues to have at the forefront of our minds as we teach? Well, certainly the four key concepts related to mastery and highlighted by the NCETM need to be present. Some would argue they all need to be centre stage in every lesson and others might suggest they should all be on your radar as a teacher even if they aren't always all emphasised in every lesson. Why wouldn't we develop fluency within a lesson? Why would we try to teach and learn without visual representation to support discussion about reasoning or to assist our explanations? As teachers, we need to develop our ability to structure learning so that we vary and adjust the focus, extend and deepen the reasoning and understanding needed.

We can expect to see more standardised tests drawing on reasoning and justification expressed in words and perhaps numbers, bar models and rules that capture key learning.

For instance, consider the articulation in the multiplication problem below.

Looking at the calculation 83×50, I know the answer has to be between 4,000 and 5,000 because of the following knowledge:

- $8 \times 5 = 40$
- $8 \times 50 = 400$
- $80 \times 50 = 4,000$

I also know that 100×50 is 5,000 by using the same process. The number 83 is between 80 and 100 and so the answer will be between those two points. I can also predict the answer will be closer to 4,000 because 83 is much closer to 80 than 100.

Such reasoning is being developed in our children in some of our classrooms currently.

At stake within this pedagogy is the belief that the power to control one's destiny and assurance of understanding is slowly but surely being passed from the teacher to the children. Related to this is another key point, that all teachers have to strive to develop their own ability to reason, justify and prove so that they can hand this key skill gradually over to the children. To this end, they deserve to be supported by decent-quality resources and methodical progressions in carefully thought through material. They also deserve to be supported through mentors and working partners, whose confidence lies a little ahead of their own. This is a necessity. Finally, we need to regulate, a little more, our established trend that uses old exam questions as the means to prepare children for tests. The committed approach of many schools to class teach (not set by attainment) and follow a mastery curriculum from Year 1 (if not before) can, will and does support these goals. This may not bear full fruit for a few more years. It is hard to whole class teach when children have had mixed early experiences in primary school. Maths teaching has the chance to become more consistent in ensuring basic understanding for virtually all children, and deeper understanding being pursued for many.

CHAPTER 11:

EARLY YEARS MASTERY

What you will learn from this chapter:

- How a mastery approach involving progression from concrete through pictorial begins naturally in the early years
- That deeper understanding of fundamental maths Is more important and necessary than progressing to larger numbers without secure understanding
- Planning mastery in early years is about ensuring multiple representations and variations are used constantly to ensure conservation of number
- That understanding, articulating and reasoning, and symbol recognition are at least as important as recording number in early years
- Young children can reason and articulate effectively if they are given the opportunity to do so

There is considerable debate about whether there is such a thing as mastery in early years. Some of the arguments relate to the fact that children are making their own sense of the world and we need to listen to their interests and be more flexible than, for example, some of the thinking, planning and teaching related to work with primary children in Key Stage 1 and Key Stage 2. However, there are also early learning goals. These are pieces of mathematical knowledge and skills that we should try and help children achieve at this age phase. The debate might be about how many of the four key mastery features apply readily at this age (3–5): fluency, multiple representation, variation, and thinking and reasoning.

One way to measure this is to take a definition of mastery teaching and examine how it could be applied to the early years. Let us take the NCETM document, *The Essence of Maths Teaching for Mastery* (NCETM, 2016) and look at the nine headings from this document as a basis for discussion.

1. **Maths teaching for mastery rejects the idea that a large proportion of people 'just can't do maths.'**

Effective early years teaching has always been about developing and responding to curiosity, about taking ideas further and about a rich concrete world of experience and discovery. In many respects, it is the perfect environment to promote learning that focuses on taking children's initial thoughts, responses and actions a little further through questioning, wondering and explaining as a means to continuing learning. As we shall see, an approach based on problem solving and reasoning can do this very well.

2. **'All pupils are encouraged by the belief that by working hard at maths they can succeed.'**

Fear of mathematics or a dislike of it has to be a learnt disposition and teaching in early years can ensure this doesn't develop in young children. This should involve three main things. Firstly, early years teachers should seek to engage children through relevant, meaningful experiences that relate both to number development and mathematical thinking and reasoning. Many early years teachers do this naturally. Secondly, they will require support to develop teacher pedagogy and depth of subject knowledge in maths. This is true across the primary age range. Some teachers are very sound and confident and others less so. Finally, schools need to target the whole primary age range, including early years, as a way of working with parents. This is to emphasise the belief and strategies related to how we are trying to teach. It is also to support parents' own understanding; that is to say their actual understanding of mathematical concepts. This is linked to their belief system about how mathematical development comes through effective questioning, experience, reasoning and rigour, not just by memorising as has been the norm for so long.

3. **'Pupils are taught through whole class interactive teaching, where the focus is on *all* pupils working together on the same lesson content at the same time, as happens in Shanghai and several other regions that teach maths successfully. This ensures that all can master concepts before moving to the next part of the curriculum sequence, allowing no pupil to be left behind.'**

There would be whole class experiences that are shared and discussed. In the main, these would have visual resources, concrete or pictorial, to support learning and understanding. There is the need to develop factual memory recall around the numbers, the sequence and symbols recognition. Much work is best done in meaningful contexts, for example, three what? This could be three pigs, pens, apples or children. The discussion around the counting principles identified by Gelman and Gallistel (1978), in the next section of this chapter, reveals how closely linked this goal is to early years philosophy. The whole class understanding is harder to ensure although assessment and revisiting key ideas does help.

4. **'If a pupil fails to grasp a concept or procedure, this is identified quickly and early intervention ensures the pupil is ready to move forward with the whole class in the next lesson.'**

We will consider this as we look at practice in a number of early years settings in school. However, good early years practice involves evaluating all children's understanding against key learning goals in maths. Thus, additional work would naturally be provided for children who don't seem to be making the progress needed to achieve these goals. This would be likely to involve familiar contexts such as songs, rhymes, match-up games with recognition, encouraging strategies in everyday life with parents and children in home life, laying the table and enough cakes for everyone.

Linked to this point is that the identification of learning difficulties is a feature of the teacher and school role at this stage. To some degree, this affects the child's readiness for developing deeper mastery understanding.

5. **'Lesson design identifies the new mathematics that is to be taught, the key points, the difficult points and a carefully sequenced journey through the learning. In a typical lesson pupils sit facing the teacher and the teacher leads back and forth interaction, including questioning, short tasks, explanation, demonstration, and discussion.'**

In most settings, as we shall see, there may be some of this style of work. Logistically, and pedagogically, it may well be that teachers and adults in early years work with smaller groups in a carousel of experiences, although parts of lesson time may begin to be spent in the way outlined here.

6. **'Procedural fluency and conceptual understanding are developed in tandem because each supports the development of the other.'**

It can be acknowledged that early years is certainly the place that the early journey towards fluency in both number and other aspects of maths truly gets underway, if it hasn't already started. In the examples about extending thinking through reframing problems and questioning, teachers can provide young children with good experiences related to mathematical thinking. Therefore, the variations related to mathematical problems are able to be covered at this age. For example, working with Numicon or Cuisenaire to establish that three and two make five it becomes clear that the same thing is true for both resources. Following the idea of different possible conversations, one teacher might ask children to find two other pieces (numbers) that match the five piece (using either manipulative (four and one or one and four)). Another teacher might ask 'how else might we make something the same size as five', e.g. three and one and one, or two and one and two. The mathematical thinking is being extended within a certain framework. There is variation and fluency is being developed.

7. **'It is recognised that practice is a vital part of learning, but the practice used is *intelligent practice* that both reinforces pupils' procedural fluency and develops their conceptual understanding.'**

Clearly, practice to develop fluency will take place, initially more to do with names, matching amounts with names, securing the sequence, reversing it and starting at different points. This will often start to match the numerical amounts with understanding in problems. Curiosity and focus are crucial. Children do enjoy number sequences and pattern through rhythm; they will also need to retrieve information.

What is the number before seven? Or what is one less than seven? Sometimes the number line or square assists the child, and some have begun to memorise and make connections and deductions.

8. **'Significant time is spent developing deep knowledge of the key ideas that are needed to underpin future learning. The structure and connections within the mathematics are emphasised, so that pupils develop deep learning that can be sustained.'**

Deep knowledge is not necessarily guaranteed. What can be guaranteed is that the teacher will plan to take thinking and learning far enough to allow evidence of deep thinking to emerge. Deep thinking is more likely where there is already secure understanding, although not always. Inspiration and making connections do not always emerge in a measured way. Progression can be linear but is more likely to ebb and flow, to slow down or leap forward rapidly.

9. **'Key facts such as multiplication tables and addition facts within ten are learnt to automaticity to avoid cognitive overload in the working memory and enable pupils to focus on new concepts.'**

As Jerome Bruner et al. (1976) would tell us, we can provide relevant early step learning to almost all children about any given theme. Some of these themes are more linked to Key Stage 1 but their early roots come before this. Canny early years teachers provide grouping tasks and discussion with questions to deepen understanding. For example:

- 'I can see you are putting the shoes next to each doll. So how many shoes are there for one doll? Two dolls? Three dolls?'
- 'Ah ... two, four, six. Very good.'
- 'How is it that the total never stops on five or three?'

Clearly, it is about the right question at the right time; the right concrete experiences and exploration need to precede such discussions. However, the timing of the questions to move learning forward and to deepen understanding is key. It is just as important in early years as anywhere. In fact, the lack of such questioning is in some ways more damaging in early years because young minds applying knowledge and reasoning create a positivity about learning in maths which means switching off or experiencing negativity become less likely.

THE COUNTING PRINCIPLES OF GELMAN AND GALLISTEL (1978)

The legendary articulation by these two researchers at Berkeley, California is still highly relevant 40 years on because nothing has really changed in our understanding of what is actually involved in counting. The key word here is understanding. Many children have been exposed to counting without well-structured experience and discussion to allow them to secure this knowledge effectively.

Some of the principles of how to count include:

- One-to-one correspondence. We tag one number onto each object that we count.
- Stable-order principle. Whilst tagging 1:1, we use a repeatable and known order to count.
- Cardinal principle. Principles about what to count.

Not only do we stop when we reach the final object, we know and understand that this final number is actually the total number in the group. It defines the total as well as being part of the count. For example, one, two, three, four. The total is *four* because we tagged four (see Figure 11.1).

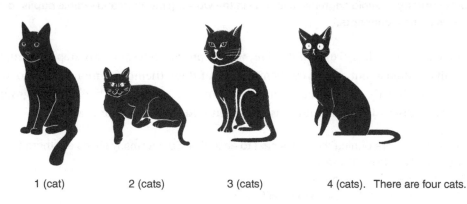

1 (cat)   2 (cats)   3 (cats)   4 (cats). There are four cats.

Figure 11.1 Four cats

This is a key point, indeed. Not only is it the fourth cat we come to but also the word that tells us how many there are in total. In fact, all the counting to achieve this total has been to ascertain how many cats we have so far. This concept is not always emphasised to children and can be a source of initial confusion for some of them. For example, in a classroom context, the following could happen:

- Teacher: 'How many cats?'
- Child: 'one, two, three, four.'
- Teacher: 'Good, so how many cats?'
- Child: (Gives a blank look.)

The child has used the first two principles (1:1 and stable-order) but not realised the cardinal principle of the final number denoting the group size.

There are some possible alternative conversations using the cats as examples (Figure 11.2):

1 (cat)   2   3   4

Figure 11.2   Three black cats and one white

Teacher: 'Is the white cat really called number two? Is that what his mum would call him if she could talk?'
Children: 'No.'
Teacher: 'So why do we call him two?'
Child: 'Because it helps us to count.'
Teacher: 'Oh. That's interesting.'

Now let us look at a different example (Figure 11.3):

Figure 11.3   Two black cats and one white

Teacher: 'Is the white cat the number two cat now?'
Children : 'No.'
Teacher : 'Why not?'
Child : 'Because he is now number three.'
Teacher: 'So he can have a different number if he comes in a different place when we count?'

It can then be said that 'the numbers help us to count' or that 'the numbers are not the names of the cats', and we would just need to change the 'cat' to any other thing that we would be counting.

We are now dealing with the final two principles, namely that the process applies to whatever we are counting, for example, children, cakes, dolls, bears, pens, or indeed a mixture of things. This is called the abstraction principle. This also touches on the order irrelevance principle. It wouldn't matter which end or point we started, the total would be the same if we tag counted each object once.

MULTIPLE REPRESENTATIONS

The NCETM guidance to mastery captures a pictorial table form of the mastery components including multiple representations, structure, mathematical thinking, fluency and variation (NCETM, 2017).

With very young children it is essential that this dialogue about counting is represented and experienced in many different ways in order to establish the permanence of the concept in both a real (world) sense and as an early basis for abstraction. The number after two in the count is three. It doesn't matter whether we are counting sheep, children, sweets, cars or sleeps until my birthday, the order we use is the same.

Beyond this early approach to 'fluency' and the crucial experiences of different representations of the same thing come the 'variations' and the opportunity to develop thinking and reasoning skills.

Let us now look at two examples of putting cats in boxes.

1.   'Are there enough boxes for the cats to have one each?' (Figure 11.4)

Figure 11.4   Three cats and two boxes.

2. 'What about now? Are there enough boxes for the cats to have one each?' (Figure 11.5)

Figure 11.5 Four cats and four boxes

When asking the children how they know the answers to these two questions, there are some possible answers that you could get, including:

- 'I know because there is a box for each cat' or 'I know because the number of boxes and the number of cats are the same.'
- 'There won't be a box for each cat if there are more cats than boxes.'
- 'It doesn't matter if there are more boxes because each cat can choose a box.'

These are now reasoning opportunities for developing deeper understanding. They have emerged from real world situations familiar to the children.

Let us now look at another example using objects from the real world, in this case, pencils and pencil holders.

Take three pencils and take four pencil holders (Multilink). Will there be enough pots for each pencil? How do you know?

Can you make your own question using pencils and pencil holders (Multilink) and say whether it will work and why? This provides the opportunity for greater depth. Firstly the child has to apply the knowledge to deal with the variation. Then, crucially, the reasoning and articulation.

Some of the answers to this questions would include:

- 'It *will* work when there are *more pots* than *pencils*.'
- 'It *won't* work when there are *more pencils* than *pots*.'
- 'It *will* work when there are *fewer pencils* than *pots*.'

(Continued)

(Continued)

- 'It won't work when there are *fewer pots* than *pencils.*'

Other similar representations to pencils and pencil holders would be plates for the pizza, hats for the bears, chairs for the dolls, leads for the dogs or bowls for the cats.

Older children will record stems or full sentences to demonstrate understanding. Younger children may need to verbalise something and an adult record. Or they could be taped and recorded. Either way it is the actual process of reaching for the explanation that is crucial. The use of language to explain understanding is part of the pedagogy of developing reasoning and being able to conjecture, and this starts in the early years. This taps into Vygotskian and Piagetian ideas about being active as you learn and in order to learn. The use of words can assist thinking.

Many early years settings have numerous references to number, pattern, data and shape. Often these will use information and visual connections related to children's interests, for example:

- Two children playing with a wheelbarrow.
- Three girls sitting on a bench.
- Four tricycles being ridden.
- Two shoes outside the door.

The class routines will show video footage of number representations and changes. Children will sing songs and say rhymes that both increase and decrease the count by one or two.

Table 11.1 Songs and rhymes to increase and decrease the count

Number focus	Songs and rhymes
Up in ones	• One man went to mow • One, two, three, four, five, once I caught a fish alive • One potato, two potato
Up in twos	• Two, four, six, eight, Mary at the cottage gate
Down in ones	• Five little ducks went swimming one day • Five little men in a flying saucer • Five little speckled frogs • Five sticky buns in a baker shop • Nine hairy monsters
Down in twos	• Ten fat sausages sizzling in a pan

The physicality of children acting the rhymes and songs out has potential in several ways. Subliminally, the order of the count is being secured or reinforced; this happens within known, visual contexts. Prediction and visualisation allow an early bridging of the gap between the visual, concrete world and that of the abstract.

For instance, a teacher could use this example in the classroom:

- 'Close your eyes now. We have just sung that we have "three little men in their flying saucers", but now Jack is going home. Sit down, Jack. Well done. So how many little men are there now? Hold your fingers up. Open your eyes. Were you right? There are two left. Let's sing again.'

This experience is very powerful for early years children when it is within a very-well-known context. This is the journey to abstraction; multiple experiences with powerful, different contexts allow connected knowledge about the permanence of number knowledge to be internalised. Piaget (1972) cites the value of the physical world for children's learning. Hughes (1986) articulates how young children can visualise and make sense of the world they cannot see but have recently and previously experienced. Let us look now at another example that a teacher could use in the classroom:

- 'So you agree that I have put five sweets in the tin. Now I take one out and put it over here. You can't see in the tin but talk to your partner about how many are still in the tin.'

This might lead to the articulation that 'I know there are four sweets left because one less than five is four'. Or an extended version of the same thinking, 'Here is the sweet I took out of the tin. There are three still in here so how many were there to start with'.

Visualisation is extremely useful for children; it has to draw on previous experience. It starts to bridge the real world with the abstract one where they don't physically have to carry out the actions to know that specific outcomes are true. Taking two from five leaves three regardless of the context. It is preparation for looking closely at how numbers are made up and what properties they have.

THINKING ABOUT VARIATION: SAME AND DIFFERENT

Let us now look at four patterns to decide if they are the same or different.

1. Jinath and Irina each have a pattern (Figure 11.6). What is the same about their two patterns? What is different? Could you carry each one on? Is there a rule?

Jinath's pattern

Irina's pattern

Figure 11.6 Jinath's and Irina's patterns

2. Ali and Bhavna each have a pattern (Figure 11.7). What is the same and different about Ali's pattern and Bhavna's (their) patterns?

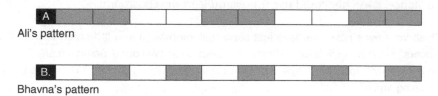

Ali's pattern

Bhavna's pattern

Figure 11.7 Ali's and Bhavna's patterns

The rich potential these kinds of activities provide is very closely linked to mastery-style teaching; more than this in fact. The ability to spot a pattern is related to early learning goal 12: shape and space: 'They recognise, create and describe patterns'.

Young children have quite egocentric approaches to patterns. They tend to branch out from what they intended, to seeing possible alternative solutions. In other words a multiple perspective world involves developing neural pathways for them.

Figure 11.8 A different pattern

The pattern in Figure 11.8 could be continued in many ways. As experience shows it can take children some time to accept different, valid solutions to their own intended one. One way to make a pattern is to be able to explain in words how it works, for example:

- Light, dark, white, light, then repeat.
- Light, dark, white, light, dark, white.

Another example of this would be using squares or triangles (Figure 11.9):

Figure 11.9 Different squares and a triangle

Young children can make choices and justify them in ways that might surprise us, if we give them a chance. For example:

Adam: 'I will put another small white triangle and then two large grey squares.'
Barbara: 'No. It now needs to do that again. Large grey, large grey and then small white.'

Young children naturally seek to try out ideas. Listening and accepting multiple perspectives can be a little harder when you're only four.

CASE STUDY 1: A FOCUS ON NUMBER

Kim Clark is the Deputy Head at Fairlawn Primary South East London and she currently spends a day a week in early years. She has a good working relationship with the early years lead and she has been keen to raise the profile of early years with the rest of the school. Year 1 and early years already understand more about each other's practice. Kim is keen that maths mastery is seen as a continuation of good practice that begins immediately after the children join the school.

As in many effective early years settings, the counting principles (Gelman and Gallistel, 1978) outlined earlier are valued highly. The belief is that children learn to think mathematically through real world, concrete experiences. Along with good, effective discussion and questioning by staff, this makes them think and explain. In addition to this, they need to become fluent in the early counting principles and to learn number bonds and then tables. Equally as important is being able to see and understand how these facts are derived.

INTEGRATED LEARNING THROUGH FAMILIAR EXPERIENCES

Kim and Kyla, the early years lead, are clear about the way in which they want to secure children's understanding. On the morning I visited the school, I was shown a daily ritual that reception children experienced, involving money. Snack time involved a piece of fruit or vegetable. The pre-preparation for this process involved a whole class discussion on the carpet about the price of fruit today at the shop: 10p had been selected on this occasion.

Kyla modelled one way of paying the 10p involving the interactive whiteboard coins. It was emphasised that the children would have to select coins that made exactly 10p and they were not allowed to use the 10p coin as this would reduce the task to coin recognition. The suggestions from two children in front of the class included a mixture of 2p and 1p coins. When all the children were then given the chance to select and pay for the fruit, it was made clear they would receive the fruit when the coins did actually total 10p and not before. Kyla and the teaching assistant acted as shopkeeper(s).

There were some issues related to this activity, including:

- **Coin values that extend beyond 1:1 matching:** Clearly, a number of children (more than half of the class) were comfortable with a single coin having a value of more than 1p.

A few children were tapping the 2p coin twice to show that they knew this and could use that knowledge. Some were only able to make the total with 1p coins. A few used 5p, 2p and 1p coins in a combination.

- **Cognitive load:** Careful consideration was given to the size of the number used as the price for the day, in this case ten (pence). For three or four children, this was a long journey. However, the pitch for the class was good; clearly smaller numbers had been used earlier in the term or year when there had been a weekly focus on particular numbers, but the children had become more secure about what underpinned the value of each number up to ten. Had this not been the case, Kyla would have chosen a smaller number.
- **Pre-preparation:** The initial interactive whiteboard-based class discussion allowed mental and physical rehearsal for the children of the task that they were about to undertake. Less-secure learners received valuable scaffolding here.
- **Assessment opportunities:** Kyla and the teaching assistant had prior knowledge of children's learning and understanding. The daily challenge gave them a valuable opportunity to evaluate all children. This included issues that affect most of the class. This might include questions such as, 'Do you think you can make 10p with 2ps and just one 1p? Why not?' The very nature of this dipping into reasoning, in this case related to odd and even, is instructive.

The depth of understanding related to pattern and reasoning in this way is more easily explored with small numbers up to, for example, five or six. Beyond this, the lack of familiarity with how larger numbers are made (conservation) means that the cognitive load is much greater and there is less space for young children to reason, in the main.

- The pitch makes for effective and manageable interaction with a decent number of children.

Kim points out the use of 'White Rose' resources through the school. We discuss that it doesn't yet include early years resources in number. Thus, NRICH is a valuable resource; there are sound articles and thoughts on that website too, related to maths in early years.

Kim identifies that there had been a tendency earlier in her time in the school for the move towards abstract learning to happen too quickly. Now, teachers in early years and across the rest of the school are beginning to realise this very important point: depth of understanding is achieved through deeper conversations alongside concrete and visual representations. The progression, from the beginning to understanding a concept, doesn't include the swift removal of the supporting resources too quickly. They form part of the thinking and the extended journey we have to take children on.

Kim emphasises the previous point, also pointing out that teacher subject knowledge needs to be accompanied by an understanding of how children learn. This is true throughout primary school learning and it is crucial to early years. It is part of what a number of people, including Jenny Back, term number sense.

The term 'number sense' is a relatively new one in mathematics education. It is diffi-cult to define precisely, but broadly speaking, it refers to 'a well organised conceptual framework of number information that enables a person to understand numbers and number relationships and to solve mathematical problems that are not bound by tradi-tional algorithms.

(Back, 2014)

As illustrated by Back, we were aware of the need to develop mathematical thinking in young children long before the journey to mastery began in the UK. However, it does give us a chance to emphasise key features of work with young children: deeper understand-ing through developing fluency, using variation and reasoning, supported by multiple representations.

Kim references a time in reception when she asked the children to explain how they knew which representations weren't of 100. One boy, who didn't often elaborate, started to compare the symbol 1 to 100 by counting. He carried on past 10 quickly, followed by the bulk of the class. Gathering momentum as they passed 30 and (with a prompt from Kim, 40, 50, 60) all the way up to 100. At this point, the loud roar confirmed, if confir-mation were needed, that a goal had been reached and a spontaneous, child-led, piece of learning had not been missed. The children had been allowed to show their number sense. Kim would have got an insight into how their current understanding could be supported.

'Part of me nearly stopped him.' she said. 'It has to be really helpful; with an eye for good mathematical development along the lines stated. It's about taking the opportunity when it arises,' she adds.

Other slides (Figure 11.10) support this development in understanding through multi-ple representations and discussions.

The beauty of multiple representations and reasoning is that they are the very basis of good discussion. For example, Figure 11.10 leads to questions with mathematical replies, such as:

- 'I did two and two and I know that makes four but not five.'
- 'There are five circles and the squares make the same height so aren't there the same number of them?' Young children can struggle with this. If we are not careful, they learn, falsely, that longer means more. It may do or it may not. It depends on other factors. Piaget was interested in this concept of conservation and planned a number of experi-ments to analyse children's development relative to age (1952).

Since Piaget's studies, other people, including Margaret Donaldson and Martin Hughes, have produced further studies that would disprove Piaget's focus on age-related develop-ment. Instead, many of us now believe that it is the nature of the activities, the discussion and the questions that we ask that can be the triggers to helping children to reason and make sense of the maths in our world.

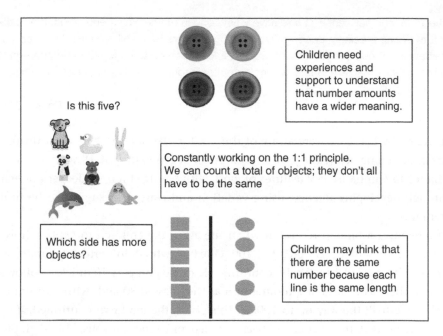

Figure 11.10 Multiple representations

Let us now look at an example of vessels. A young child may well think that a taller, slimmer vessel will hold more than a shorter, wider one. However, their reasoning will be interesting to hear. When the one they felt had less in it is seen to hold more of their favourite drink because it takes three smaller vessels to fill it rather than two, they may think otherwise. At least, an interesting discussion would be underway, feeding off the cognitive dissonance (Festinger, 1957) now present, as their original idea and belief comes under pressure from new information. Piaget's ideas about child curiosity would see them change their thinking as they encountered new things that were contrary to what they had expected or understood. His terms, assimilation and accommodation, relate to how much altering of their previous thinking is necessary (1952). Jerome Bruner's idea of scaffolding was part of his belief that children of any age could and can be supported to engage with challenging ideas if they are dealt with in a suitable way (Bruner et al., 1976).

FLUENCY IN THE EARLY YEARS

Reception children at Fairlawn work in the concrete with references to pictorial representations. They learn to recognise symbols; they can reason about their value. They are developing fluency well. Not until the summer term do they start to record symbols themselves (in a formal sense). In some cases, it is Year 1. This is mentioned to clarify that this is definitely a mastery-based curriculum. Fluency can be developed without formal recording in the early years. Almost all children were fluent in counting small groups of objects accurately (Figures 11.11 and 11.12).

Figure 11.11 Conservation of seven   **Figure 11.12** Conservation of eight

The multiple representations of seven emerge from young children's known world: cakes, animals and plastic toys. The mixture of dogs with a duck generates an interesting conversation drawing on the abstraction principle (Gelman and Gallistel, 1978). Our counting system works for any collection of things. Some answers that could emerge from this exercise include:

- 'I knew it wasn't eight ducks because the front duck doesn't have a partner.'
- 'It is four ducks and four ducks but the front duck gets counted twice'.

This is developing fluency but it is also developing reasoning too.

SUBITISING

We believe that we can count up to four or maybe five objects by simply seeing, knowing and taking all we see in at once (Figure 11.13). Beyond this, we need a counting system that is refined from our early ability to 1:1 match objects with a number.

Figure 11.13 Small amounts of objects up to five

People argue that they can recognise higher numbers than four, such as dots on a dice. The general thinking is that the dice patterns are quite standardised. They become a learnt association. Subitising (Piaget, 1952) is the amount we can take in from a visual stimulus in an unfamiliar arrangement.

Back (2014) identifies several named strategies for developing this early number sense that makes the 1:1 basis for counting more efficient, as the sense of number emerges with increasingly effective strategies used. These include creating two (or more) smaller groups (sub-groups). For example, five can be changed into:

- three and two;
- four and one;
- two, two and one;
- three, one and one.

CASE STUDY 2: FARZANA AT ELMHURST PRIMARY SCHOOL

Farzana is an experienced early years teacher with previous significant experience in Year 1. She feels that in some ways little has changed as a result of mastery initiatives. The children learn best when they are interested in the content, when they can physically see and touch the content being studied and when it links to their own personal experiences in life with things that are familiar to them.

In other ways, Farzana feels that the mastery approach is significantly different. As we speak, it is clear that a key theme for her is that 'less is more'. It is much more important to understand less at a much deeper level than a lot superficially. The theme of understanding early number comes up repeatedly. She too has a key number focus of a week related to the numbers one to ten. Then a lot of work is spent around varying the experiences related to these numbers: counting on, adding on, counting back and exploring different arrangements to make similar totals. In addition, different resources and content are explored in depth to create interconnected understanding, such as tens frames, Numicon, Numicon with stones to fill the holes and egg cartons.

She values the 'Maths – No Problem!' approach that identifies key learning closely. She uses that style as a basis for learning in early years. Children are not moved on to explore bigger numbers beyond ten until their understanding here is secure.

Farzana says that fundamental to learning has been 'getting children to use resources to explain answers and to reason. This has turned things around. Understanding comes from what the children are familiar with'.

In the past, practical maths was engaging but it stood alone – a week on addition, numbers, subtraction and there was little linking. In the past, differentiation occurred very quickly in Year 1 and in early years even – different numbers, different progression, different learning trajectories. The emphasis is now on allowing children to reason and explore further around the same areas.

Let us now have a look at the following example (Figure 11.14):

- 'Show me a different way to make six. How do you know it makes six? Is there another way to make it? Do any of your ways include the same numbers, e.g. four and two? Do you think it will make the same total if we switch the one and the five around?'

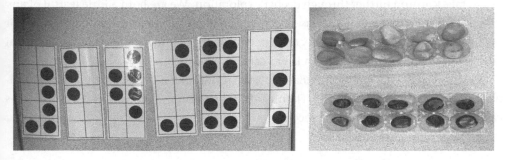

Figure 11.14   Laminated tens frames and also real bases to fill to help understand in a literal sense

Farzana emphasised that some of the children in reception were already noticing the effect of reversing operations using physical resources. This was, in part, because Farzana was creating conversations, and shared learning experiences gave the chance for this to happen. For example:

- 'So we put the four with the three and it has made a total of seven. If we take the three away again, how many do you think will be left?'

This threshold between the visual representation and the visualised representation is a deeply rich scaffold for beginning the process to seeing links and connected operations such as subtraction and addition. No need to be ratcheting up the size of the numbers, there is plenty of depth to explore here with the smaller ones.

A key part of Farzana's early years philosophy is creating experiences that reinforce ideas that have already been exposed around, for example, number. The number three is explored through siblings, pets, apples in a box, tricycle wheels, Numicon two and one, or one, one and one, etc. The ideas are revisited in the same and different forms to secure and develop understanding and make links with new learning.

- Three is like four because you can split them both up.
- Three is different to four because you can't split it evenly.
- Three and four can both be used as the wheels on a car.
- Four can be split to make two pairs but three has an odd one.
- Four has more ways of making it.
- Three straws make a triangle but four straws make a different shape (unless you use two straws for one side).

All of these ideas form part of discussions that deepen understanding. Fluency, variation and multiple representation all assist and underpin reasoning.

We agree that the mastery emphasis has meant more good conversations with young children, with emphasis on reasoning alongside physical representation of resources. In addition to this, it is possible, essential really, to question and facilitate lots of opportunities to take learning further through deeper exploration. We are both a little fearful of any proposed change that would increase the coverage of learning in the foundation stage. It would not appear to fit a philosophy of achieving depth of understanding of fundamental knowledge that is then extended in later years.

Fluency is achieved through regular exposure to number and discussion around number properties through reasoning. Flash cards, tens frames, Numicon and dice patterns can also be used to support this process.

CONCLUSION

Mastery in early years is a concept we are embracing, and we need to as it fits so naturally into early years practice. Active concrete situations with real world resources allow pattern and problem solving to develop along with articulation.

- How do you know these four apples will divide equally?
- How do you know these three sweets cannot be shared equally between the two of you?

Multiple representation, developing fluency, variation and reasoning with articulation all begin in early years, if not before. The early road towards abstraction begins through many good conversations around physical resources along with some pictorial ones.

REFERENCES

Askew, M. (2015) *Transforming Primary Mathematics*. Abingdon: Routledge.

Askew, M. (2016) 'Better maths tests', *Teach Primary*, Issue 9.8, p.47.

Askew, M., Brown, M., Rhodes, V., Wiliam, D. and Johnson, D. (1997) *Effective Teachers of Numeracy: Report of a Study Carried out for the Teacher Training Agency*. London: King's College, University of London.

Askew, M., Bishop, S., Christie, C., Eaton, S., Griffin, P., Morgan, D. and Wilne, R. (2015a) *Teaching for Mastery, Questions, Tasks and Activities to Support Assessment, Year 1*. Oxford: Oxford University Press.

Askew, M., Bishop, S., Christie, C., Eaton, S., Griffin, P., Morgan, D. and Wilne, R. (2015b) *Teaching for Mastery, Questions, Tasks and Activities to Support Assessment, Year 6*. Oxford: Oxford University Press.

Back, J. (2014) *Early Number Sense*, NRICH, available at: https://nrich.maths.org/10737 (accessed 28 September 2018).

Ball, D., Hill, H. and Schilling, S. (2004) 'Developing measures of teachers' mathematics knowledge for teaching', *Elementary School Journal*, 105(1): 11–30.

Blatchford, P., Webster, R. and Russell, A. (2012) 'Challenging and changing how schools use teaching assistants: Findings from the Effective Deployment of Teaching Assistants project', *School Leadership & Management*, 33(1): 78–96.

Blewett, L. (2018) Primary Advantage Maths Conference, 31 January 2018.

Boaler, J. (2009) *The Elephant in the Classroom*. London: Souvenir Press.

Boaler, J. (2013) 'Ability and mathematics: The mindset revolution that is reshaping education', *Forum*, 55(1): 143–52.

Bruner, J.S. (1960) *The Process of Education*, 2nd revised edition. Cambridge, MA: Harvard University Press.

Bruner, J. (1966) *Toward a Theory of Instruction*. Cambridge, MA: Harvard University Press.

Bruner, J., Wood, D. and Ross, G. (1976) 'The role of tutoring in problem solving', *Journal of Child Psychology and Psychiatry and Allied Disciplines*, 17: 89–100.

CDIS (Curriculum Development Institute of Singapore) (1982) *Primary Mathematics Text Book Series, Years 1–6*. Marshall Cavendish, Times Publishing Group.

Christie, C., Eaton, S., Griffin, P. and Morgan, D. (2015) *Teaching for Mastery, Questions, Tasks and Activities to Support Assessment, Year 3*. Oxford: Oxford University Press.

Cockcroft, W.H. (1982) *Mathematics Counts – Report of the Committee of Inquiry into the Teaching of Mathematics in Schools*. London: HMSO.

Collins Primary Dictionaries (n.d) *Collins Maths Dictionary*, available at: https://collins.co.uk/products (accessed 19 December 2018).

Cotton, T. (2016) *Understanding and Teaching Primary Mathematics*, 2nd edition. Abingdon: Routledge.

Crossley, M. and Watson, K. (2009) 'Comparative and international education: Policy transfer, context sensitivity and professional development', *Oxford Review of Education*, *35*(5): 633–49.

DfE (Department for Education) (2013) *The National Curriculum in England: Key Stages 1 and 2 Framework*, available at: www.gov.uk/government/publications/national-curriculum-in-england-primary-curriculum (accessed 19 December 2018).

DfEE (Department for Education and Employment) (1999) *National Numeracy Strategy*. London: DfEE.

Doig, B. and Groves, S. (2011) 'Japanese lesson study: Teacher professional development through communities of inquiry', *Mathematics Teacher Education and Development*, *13*(1): 77–93.

Donaldson, M. (1978) *Children's Minds*, London: Fontana/Croom Helm.

Drury, H. (2014) *Mastering Mathematics: Teaching to Transform Achievement*. Oxford: Oxford University Press.

Dweck, C.S. (2006) *Mindset, the New Psychology of Success*. New York: Ballantine Books.

Dweck, C.S. (2007) *Mindset: The New Psychology of Success*. New York: Ballantine Books.

Dweck, C.S. (2012) *Mindset: How You Can Fulfill Your Potential*. New York: Ballantine Books.

Eastaway, R. (2008) *How Many Socks Make a Pair? Surprisingly Interesting Everyday Maths*. London: JR Books.

Eastaway, R. (2016) Lecture at Harris Federation Maths Conference at Chobham Academy, East Village, E20, London, 'What can the Chinese learn from us?'. July 9th 2016.

Eaude, T. (2014) 'What makes primary classteachers special? Exploring the features of expertise in the primary classroom', *Teachers and Teaching*, *20*(1): 4–18.

Ferrari, P.L. (2003) 'Abstraction in mathematics', *Philosophical Transactions of the Royal Society of London B: Biological Sciences*, *358*(1435): 1225–30.

Festinger, L. (1957) *A Theory of Cognitive Dissonance*. Stanford, CA: Stanford University Press.

Festinger, L. (1962) *A Theory of Cognitive Dissonance* (Vol. 2). Stanford, CA: Stanford University Press.

Flavell, J.H. (1976) 'Metacognitive aspects of problem solving'. In L.B. Resnick (ed.), *The Nature of Intelligence* (pp. 231–5). Hillsdale, NJ: Lawrence Erlbaum.

Gelman, R. and Gallistel, C. (1978) *Young Children's Understanding of Numbers*. Cambridge, MA: Harvard University Press.

Gibb, N. (2016) 'Building a renaissance in mathematics teaching', Schools minister address to delegates at the Advisory Committee on Mathematics Education (ACME) conference, available at: www.gov.uk/government/speeches/nick-gibb-building-a-renaissance-in-mathematics-teaching (accessed 28 September 2018).

Gifford, S. (2005) *Teaching Mathematics 3–5: Developing Learning in the Foundation Stage*. Maidenhead: Open University Press.

Gu, L., Huang, R. and Marton, F. (2004) 'Teaching with variation: A Chinese way of promoting effective mathematics learning'. In L. Fan, N.Y. Wong, J. Cai and S. Li (eds), *How Chinese Learn Mathematics: Perspectives from Insiders* (pp. 309–47). Singapore: World Scientific Publishing Pte Ltd.

Gudmundsdottir, S. and Shulman, L. (1987) 'Pedagogical content knowledge in social studies', *Scandinavian Journal of Educational Research*, *31*(2): 59–70.

Hansen, A. (2014) *Children's Errors in Mathematics*, 3rd edition. London: SAGE.

Haylock, D. (2019) *Mathematics Explained for Primary Teachers*, 6th edition. London: SAGE.

Hughes, M. (1986) *Children and Number (Difficulties in Learning Mathematics)*. Oxford: Blackwell Publishing.

'Inspire Maths' scheme (2015) Foreword by Fong Ho Kheong in *Teacher's Guides*, Oxford: Oxford University Press.

Ireson, J. and Hallam, S. (2001) *Ability Grouping in Education*. London: SAGE.

Jerrim, J. and Vignoles, A. (2016) 'The link between East Asian "mastery" teaching methods and English children's mathematics skills', *Economics of Education Review*, *50*: 29–44.

Kipling, R. (1943) 'If'. In *A Choice of Kipling's Verse*. New York: Scribner's Sons.

Kullberg, A., Kempe, U. and Marton, F. (2017) 'What is made possible to learn when using the variation theory of learning in teaching mathematics?', *ZDM*, *49*(4): 559–69.

Lave, J. and Wenger, E. (1998) *Communities of Practice: Learning, Meaning and Identity*. Cambridge: Cambridge University Press.

Lewis, C. (2002) *Lesson Study: A Handbook of Teacher-led Instructional Change*. Philadelphia, PA: Research for Better Schools.

Lewis, C. and Tsuchida, I. (1999) 'A lesson is like a swiftly flowing river: How research lessons improve Japanese education', *Improving Schools*, *2*(1): 48–56.

Ma, L. (1999) *Knowing and Teaching Elementary Mathematics: Teachers' Understanding of Fundamental Mathematics in China and the United States*. London: Routledge.

Mascolo, M.F. and Fischer, K.W. (2005) 'Constructivist theories'. In B. Hopkins, R.G. Barr, G. Michel, and P. Rochat (eds), *Cambridge Encyclopedia of Child Development* (pp. 49–63). Cambridge: Cambridge University Press.

Mason, J., Stephens, M. and Watson, A. (2009) 'Appreciating mathematical structure for all', *Mathematics Education Research Journal*, *21*(2): 10–32.

McClure, L. (2013) 'What's the difference between rich tasks and low threshold high ceiling ones?' NRICH, available at: https://nrich.maths.org/10345 (accessed 28 September 2018).

Miller, S. (2018) Presentation 'Mastery Mathematics', at Primary Advantage Conference at Holy Trinity School, 31st January 2018, Hackney, London.

Ministry of Education of Singapore (2006) *Mathematics Syllabus (Primary)*. Singapore: Curriculum Planning and Development Division.

Morgan, D. (2016) Lincolnshire Teachers Conference on Mastery, 'What is mastery, why does it matter, and what are teachers doing where it's working well?' December.

Moyer, P.S. and Jones, M.G. (2004) 'Controlling choice: Teachers, students, and manipulatives in mathematics classrooms', *School Science and Mathematics, 104*(1): 16–31.

NAMA (National Association of Mathematical Advisers) (2015) *Five Myths about Mastery*, available at: www.nama.org.uk/Downloads/Five%20Myths%20about%20Mathematics%20Mastery.pdf (accessed 28 September 2018).

National Council of Teachers of Mathematics (2014b) *Procedural Fluency in Mathematics: A Position of the National Council of Teachers of Mathematics*, available at: www.nctm.org/Standards-and-Positions/Position-Statements/Procedural-Fluency-in-Mathematics (accessed 13 November 2018).

NCETM (2016) *The Essence of Maths Teaching for Mastery*, available at www.ncetm.org.uk/files/37086535/The+Essence+of+Maths+Teaching+for+Mastery+june+2016.pdf (accessed 13 November 2018)

NCETM (2017) *Five Big Ideas in Teaching for Mastery*, available at: www.ncetm.org.uk/resources/50042 (accessed 13 November 2018).

NCETM Mastery Teaching Videos (2016) *Clare Christie Teaching Place Value in Year 4*, available at www.ncetm.org.uk/resources/49420 (accessed 13 November 2018)

Newell, R. (2017) *Big Ideas in Primary Mathematics*. London: SAGE.

NRICH Primary Team (2014) *Reasoning: The Journey from Novice to Expert*, available at https://nrich.maths.org/11348 (accessed 21 December 2018).

Piaget, J. (1936) *Origins of Intelligence in the Child*. London: Routledge & Kegan Paul.

Piaget, J. (1952) *The Child's Concept of Number*. New York: Norton.

Piaget, J. (1972) *The Psychology of the Child*. Abingdon: Routledge.

PISA (2012) *Results: What Students Know and Can Do: Student Performance in Mathematics, Reading and Science* (Volume I), (revised edition February 2014). PISA: OECD.

Posamentier, A.S. and Krulik, S. (2015) *Problem-Solving Strategies in Mathematics: From Common Approaches to Exemplary Strategies*. Singapore: World Scientific Publishing.

Rowland, T., Turner, F., Thwaites, A. and Huckstep, P. (2009) *Developing Primary Mathematics Teaching: Reflecting on Practice with the Knowledge Quartet*. London: SAGE.

Ryan, J. and Williams, J. (2007) *Children's Mathematics 4–15: Learning from Errors and Misconception*. Maidenhead: Open University Press.

Shulman, L. (1986) 'Those who understand: Knowledge growth in teaching', *Educational Researcher, 15*(2): 4–14.

Skemp, R.R. (1978) 'Relational understanding and instrumental understanding', *Arithmetic Teacher, 26*(3): 9–15.

Skemp, R. (1987) *The Psychology of Learning Mathematics*. Mahwah, NJ: Lawrence Erlbaum Associates.

Stripp, C. (2014) *Charlie's Angles: Shanghai Surprise!* NCETM, available at: www.ncetm.org. uk/resources/44150 (accessed 28 September 2018).

Stripp, C. (2015) 'How can we meet the needs of all pupils without differentiation of lesson content? How can we record progress without levels?', NCETM Director's Blog, Charlie Stripp, April 2015.

Sweller, J. (1988) 'Cognitive load during problem solving: Effects on learning', *Cognitive Science*, *12*(2): 257–85.

Sweller, J. (2011) 'Cognitive load theory', *Psychology of Learning and Motivation*, *55*: 37–76.

Thompson, I. (2008) *Teaching and Learning Early Number*, 2nd edition. Maidenhead: Open University Press.

TIMSS (Trends in International Mathematics and Science Study) (2015) *International Results in Mathematics*. Newton, MA: International Study Center, Lynch School of Education, Boston College.

Vignoles, A., Jerrim, J. and Cowan, R. (2015) *EEF Mathematics Mastery Primary Evaluation Report*. London: UCL Institute of Education.

Vygotsky, L.S. (1978) *Mind in Society*. Cambridge, MA: Harvard University Press.

Wiliam, D. (2015) 'Why students make silly mistakes in class (and what can be done)', *The Conversation, UK*, available at: http://theconversation.com/why-students-make-silly-mistakes-in-class-and-what-can-be-done-48826 (accessed 28 September 2018).

Wiliam, D. (2017) Podcast, available at www.tes.com/news/school-news/breaking-views/listen-growth-mindset-cognitive-load-and-role-research (accessed 28 September 2018).

Williams, P. (2008) *Independent Review of Mathematics Teaching in Early Years Settings and Primary Schools – Final Report*. London: DCSF.

Yeap Ban Har (2011) *Teaching to Mastery Mathematics Bar Modeling: A Problem-solving Tool*. Singapore: Marshall Cavendish.

INDEX